LIFE AND DEATH WITH AUST

SUMMIT
8000

ANDREW LOCK

MELBOURNE
UNIVERSITY
PRESS

MELBOURNE UNIVERSITY PRESS
An imprint of Melbourne University Publishing Limited
715 Swanston Street, Carlton, Victoria 3053, Australia
mup-info@unimelb.edu.au
www.mup.com.au

First published 2014
This edition published in 2016
Text © Andrew Lock, 2014
Design and typography © Melbourne University Publishing Limited, 2016

Cover design by Phil Campbell
Typeset in Bembo 12/15.5pt by Cannon Typesetting
Printed in Australia by McPherson's Printing Group

National Library of Australia Cataloguing-in-Publication entry

Lock, Andrew, author.

Summit 8000: life and death with Australia's master of thin air / Andrew Lock.
9780522871050 (pbk)
9780522871067 (ebook)

Includes index.

Lock, Andrew.
Mountaineers—Australia—Biography.
Mountaineering.

796.522092

To my mother, who for over twenty years stoically waved me goodbye, then acted as my personal assistant, answering my mail and paying my bills, all the time waiting for the dreaded phone call that said there was no point paying them any more.

To those genuinely passionate climbers who followed their dreams purely for the spirit of the adventure but did not survive to tell their own stories and whose losses in great numbers have gone largely unnoticed.

To three specific individuals, and all those like them in Scouts and other volunteer organisations, who give their time to inspire and develop the youth of this country: Adrian Cooper OAM, who introduced me to the thrill of outdoor adventuring; Bob King, who nurtured my outdoor passion through leadership and guidance; and Geoff Chapman, whose altruism and unceasing belief in me enabled and motivated me to keep going.

Thank you, all.

CONTENTS

The 8000ers

There are fourteen peaks in the world whose tops reach above 8000 metres, and it is these that mountaineers refer to as the '8000ers'. The altitude into which they tower is so extreme that it is known as the 'death zone', where climbers must reach their goal and descend in a matter of hours before their bodies shut down and they literally die from 'thin air'.

The 8000ers are not to be confused with the 'Seven Summits', which are the highest peaks on each of earth's seven continents. Everest is one of those seven summits—it is the highest mountain on the continent of Asia—but the rest of the seven summits are lower than 7000 metres and as low as 2200 metres, in the case of Mt Kosciusko in Australia. The 8000ers are all to be found in the Himalayan and Karakorum mountain ranges of South Asia—India, Nepal, Tibet, China and Pakistan. The most westerly 8000er, Nanga Parbat, stands just above Pakistan's Indus valley and the most easterly, Kanchenjunga, sits 2400 kilometres to the southeast, just above Darjeeling on Nepal's eastern border with India.

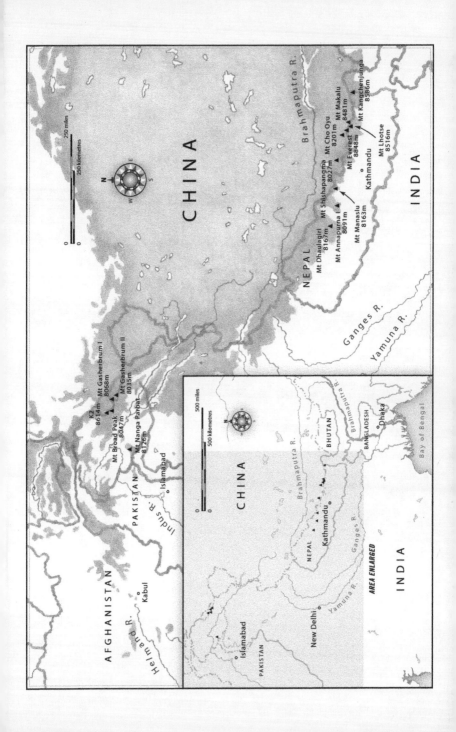

FOREWORD

MOUNTAINEERING IS AN apex sport and as Hemingway apparently put it, 'all the others are merely games'. So where do mountaineers go to reach the pinnacle of their sport? The incomparable Himalayas.

The world's fourteen highest mountains all exceed the 8000-metre mark (or just over 26 000 feet) and they are all in the Himalayan and Karakoram ranges of Pakistan, China and Nepal. They are by far the tallest mountains on the planet. Shards of stone pushed higher than all the rest by extraordinary tectonic forces. Everest leads the pack by a commanding 250 metres over K2. (By comparison North America's highest mountain, Mount McKinley, is 6194 metres and 2600 metres lower than Everest.) For mountaineers these huge Himalayan peaks—Kanchenjunga, Nanga Parbat, K2, Annapurna—are the stage where much dramatic history is acted out; they are the battle grounds of the 'conquistadors of the useless', as Lionel Terray aptly described his chosen pursuit.

By a strange quirk these great peaks that penetrate into the jetstream also coincide with the maximum physiological altitude that we humans can attain. In 1953 when my father and Tenzing first climbed Everest, the physiologists of the day debated whether it was even possible for humans to reach 8800 metres. So why take the risk? George Mallory put it most simply—and perhaps most memorably—when asked in 1924 during a press conference and a succession of mind-numbing questions about his motivations for why he would attempt to climb Mount Everest. 'Because it is there,' he said. And while climbing it may be a human contrivance, its presence is as genuine and beckoning as the Atlantic was to Columbus. And now we all know we can achieve these goals and this knowledge opens the doors to individual possibility. You can go there too! If you have the grit and the blinkered focus.

Mountaineering in the modern era tackled issues to do with style and philosophy. 'Alpine style' changed the mode of ascent more than anything before. Bold and purist teams of unsupported climbers pushed elegant lines up the great mountains without oxygen and logistical support. The great exponents of this development were people like Hermann Buhl, Reinhold Messner, Jerzy Kukuczka, Jean Troillet and Doug Scott, who made numerous astonishing climbs that changed the way mountaineers saw what was possible.

Interestingly, the current era in mountaineering has transformed substantially into everything from media stunts, commercially guided groups enabling ambitious CEOs to tag the top, speed ascents up prepared routes strung with rope, capsule style climbing, alpine style and bold solos by outstanding practitioners of Himalayan alpinism. You shouldn't judge the media reports from Mount Everest today as being typical of Himalayan climbing, as they are not and Andrew's story illustrates this well. Today all these expeditions are equipped with satellite telephones and internet connections. These distractions have made Himalayan mountaineering more complex and less focused; more summit-driven and less interested in climbing excellence. There is nothing wrong with it but the media soap operas are not the leading edge of the sport.

The popular 'seven summits' (the highest peak on each continent) campaigns are, with the exception of Everest, more of an exciting adventure travelogue than a climbing-fest (and I completed the seven as a consolation prize when I couldn't complete all the 8000ers I wanted to climb). By comparison the small number of mountaineers who have climbed all the fourteen 8000-metre peaks are the 'real thing.' The leaders in this quest climbed their mountains by establishing new routes and pushed frontiers like no one had before. They were armed with superb technical skills, extensive alpine experience and an astonishing determination—Reinhold Messner of Italy, Jerzy Kukuczka of Poland and Erhard Loretan of Switzerland. They showed us, on their separate expeditions, what could be accomplished. They are to mountaineers what the 8000-metre peaks are to the Appalachian Mountains or the hills of Ben Nevis. They are giants.

You never conquer an 8000-metre mountain giant. At best, you thread a line through its hazards to the summit where you simply turn around, for this is half way. The technicalities of descent are bedeviled by fatigue and wandering concentration. Gravity prowls the flanks of the peak; it neither holds dear nor respects innocence or reputation. But this is why we come, to tread the line of jeopardy and to assume responsibility for our own actions.

This game is about commitment. Once in, you must go the distance. As Rob Hall told me once: 'To summit an 8000-metre peak you must be pushy. Even on a good day. But if you are too pushy you won't come home.'

Andrew's ambitions have been as steeply inclined as the peaks themselves. Because when you are out there—tired, frightened, thirsty—the only real companion you have is you. 'You are all you have!' That's a very fundamental realisation and not many of us want to go there.

When you see this man's eyes ... you know he has.

Peter Hillary
May 2014
www.peterhillary.com

*Peter has climbed Mount Everest twice and his father Edmund Hillary
made the first ascent with Tenzing Norgay in 1953.
Peter is on the board of the Australian Himalayan Foundation.*

PROLOGUE: 30 JULY 1993

FALLING! A nearly vertical ramp. I flail desperately with my ice axe, but it bounces off impenetrable rock and the abyss below rushes at me like a black hole that sucks everything into its void.

I thrash desperately, clawing at the thin covering of soft, wet snow—my only hope of stopping the fall. The bottom of the rock ramp is just metres away, and below that is a vertical drop of over a thousand metres. Still sliding, I kick my feet out wide, using my legs to catch more of the snow beneath me. It's a risk—if I build up too much snow underneath me, I'll topple over backwards and lose all control. But it's a risk worth taking—if I don't stop right now, I am dead anyway.

Nothing. Still sliding. A thought flashes through my mind: *Christ, it's all over ...*

Then I sense the slightest slowing, almost unnoticeable. The snow beneath me forms a small wedge between my legs. The build-up between my arms gives me enough balance so I don't topple backwards. Slowing, slowing ... stopped.

Temporarily safe, my body remains in overdrive. I gasp so fast that I literally scream for breath. Sucking in great frozen lungfuls, I cough violently as the cold, dry air tears at my throat. My heart pounds so hard my chest hurts.

I latch on to the mountain like a drowning man clutches a plank. *Get yourself together. Get control.* Ever so gradually the tension eases—my heart slows, my reeling head steadies, my gasping reverts to simple panting. I cough again and spit thick, bloody sputum into the ice in front of me. My face drops into the mess, but I don't care. Breathing is all that matters.

I am still alive. *Still.* For this has not been an isolated slip that nearly ended badly, it's been my descent for the last hour. A frantic, desperate series of uncontrolled leaps of faith. No, not faith, but hope. Hope that I will stop in time. Hope that I will slow before I pick up so much speed that I cannot. It is a hope born of hopelessness, as there is no other way down. I can stay up here and die in the thin air, or take my chances.

I am unprepared for this. I've spent too long at high altitude. I'm tired and dehydrated, exhausted from what has already been eighteen hours of climbing above 8000 metres without supplementary oxygen. I'm way too inexperienced to have any right to be here. This has been my first successful 8000-metre summit, and it is on the majestic but notorious K2, which sits on the border between Pakistan and China. I can already hear the veterans laugh: 'You climbed K2 for your first 8000-metre summit? Are you crazy?' Maybe.

All that's on my mind right now, though, is survival. I've already seen the results of a K2 expedition gone wrong. He's lying frozen and lifeless at our Camp 4, and I'm struggling simply to get down to the relative safety of that high-altitude cemetery. The mountain has turned nasty, and the slope we'd climbed earlier in the day is now virtually unable to be down-climbed, because the softening snow gives no purchase and the smooth rock underneath it is as hard as steel. There is simply nothing to hold on to.

Just to my right is the end of the rope that we'd anchored to the face earlier this morning on our way up. We'd only been carrying 40 metres and had placed it on the most dangerous part of the climb, a traverse under a giant cliff of ice. My hand is shaking, more from adrenaline than from the piercing cold, as I reach out, ever so carefully, to clip a sling to it, fearful that even the slightest movement will dislodge me. I slump gratefully to let it take my weight, the security like a mother's comforting embrace.

My desire to sleep is almost overwhelming and I must snap my mind back to consciousness. With the safety of the rope I traverse across to another steep chute known as the Bottleneck, which leads down to a broad ice face below. Unclipping from the rope, I carefully kick each step and place the ice pick as though my life depends on it, which it most certainly does. I find that I am talking myself through every movement: 'Focus ... Look for a good handhold. Don't relax now. Focus. Check that rock—is it loose? Get rid of it. Okay, step down. Easy ... Easy. Okay, get the pick in.'

This isn't a sign of madness but a habit that I've kept up throughout my climbing career. It is when you are descending from a summit, exhausted beyond comprehension, that you must think the most clearly. Having put every bit of energy into the ascent, many climbers have nothing left in reserve when they turn to go down again. So they relax, take shortcuts, make mistakes. And die.

I tell myself I will not relax, take shortcuts or make mistakes, and with every downward step, the angle of the slope lessens, until at last I am able to face out and walk the rest of the way back down to Camp 4. It is surreal descending these slopes in the dark of night, alone on the massive mountain face, having just survived the most dangerous experience of my life. The summit was good, but survival is even better, and I luxuriate in the feel of every breath, the warmth of my down suit, the energy of life.

I am in good spirits as I approach the tent. It is 11.30 p.m. and I've been on the go for almost twenty hours. Two of my teammates, Anatoli and Peter, descended from the summit ahead of me, and as I reach the tent I hope that they've melted enough snow on the stove to give me the drink I desperately need.

There is rustling in the tent and I hear Anatoli's voice: 'Peter, is that you?'

'No, it's Andrew,' I reply, a little confused.

Anatoli's shocked face immediately appears through the tent door. I stop moving, a sense of dread suddenly upon me.

Peter had left the summit with Anatoli. You can't get lost on this route. If he'd stopped to rest, I'd have seen him in the bright moonlight. If I haven't passed him, then he is no longer on the mountain. We scan the slopes above us, but there is no sign of another human life.

So exhausted that it takes me twenty minutes just to remove my crampons, I crawl into the tent, hoping that I'd somehow passed Peter as he rested. But I know deep within me that the worst has happened.

I am wrong, however. The worst is just beginning.

1

BEGINNINGS

But risks must be taken because the greatest hazard in life is to risk nothing.

'To Risk', William Arthur Ward

I WASN'T BORN to mountaineering—far from it. With my two brothers, Dave (two years older) and Stew (six years younger), I grew up in the Sydney suburb of Killara. Our parents, Don and Margaret, sent us to the prestigious private school Sydney Grammar.

Dad was keen for his sons to get into careers that earned big money. As an only child who had grown up during the Depression, he had experienced genuine poverty after his own father had died when Dad was only five. Dad left school early and gained a trade as a fitter and turner. Desperate to build a better life, however, he put himself through night school, emerging as a manager and moving quickly into a career as a management consultant. Ultimately, he became a founding member of the Australian Institute of Management Consultants—a 'poor boy done good'. Apart from his work, Dad also loved real estate. He excelled at identifying outstanding real-estate opportunities, buying beautiful but dilapidated houses

I

on Sydney's north shore and renovating them. In this way he provided our family with comfortable homes, as well as substantial profits on each purchase.

I was different. I could never quite embrace a perspective that focused primarily on money and image. Indeed, throughout my life I have struggled to desire anything more than basic financial security. Life was what could be experienced after school and after work, away from career, family and society's expectations. This was the cause of lifelong tension between Dad and me, and I never bonded with him in the way my brothers did.

A teacher and then a publisher's assistant editor, Mum was the emotional rock of our family and kept us going through all the turbulence of life. It was left to her to raise the family as Dad spent considerable periods away from home on work projects. A strict disciplinarian, she was quick to reach for the strap any time it was needed. With three wild young men to manage, that strap had quite a workout! But Mum also saw that life was about much more than work alone and encouraged us to engage in the outdoors, the beach and sport. I think my outlook was much more similar to hers than Dad's, and I also believe I inherited her physical stamina.

At school, I just didn't fit in. Although I was athletic and had good physical endurance, I wasn't a big kid and was no good at the usual sports. Nor could I get interested in my studies. I dreamed constantly of escape, which I found in the Endeavour Club, an outdoor-adventure group headed by one of the teachers, Adrian 'Ace' Cooper. I'd already spent some years in the Scouts, which I'd really loved, but the activities had mostly been daytrips. With the Endeavour Club, I did my first multi-day bushwalk over the Easter break of 1974, through the Budawang Range on the south coast of New South Wales.

For four days I lugged a heavy backpack that contained a ludicrous amount of gear and food, while legions of leeches drained my puny body of much-needed blood. It rained most of the time, my tent leaked, my food was sodden and the mud was up to our knees—and I loved every single minute of it. Soaked to the skin and freezing, knowing that we had kilometres more to walk in the same conditions, I thrilled at the challenge. It gave me an inner sense of achievement that I hadn't felt in any sport or other activity. I felt a glow within me—I was hooked on 'the bush'.

For several years I threw myself at the outdoors every time there was a camping trip with the club. We bushwalked throughout the Blue Mountains near Sydney, and also took on more challenging activities, such as abseiling, caving, canyoning and cross-country skiing. The harder or more adventurous it was, the more I loved it—partly for the thrill of the adventure but also for the satisfaction of coping with the hardships it posed.

Adrian provided the opportunity for kids to experience the outdoors, but there wasn't much sympathy for those who found it tough. Generally the adventures were long and hard and pushed us to our limits. Adrian was famous for underestimating the length of any walk. If he told us we had an hour to get to the campsite, it would invariably be two, three or more. After a while, we'd stop asking how far and just push on until we arrived. This might have developed our mental toughness, but it also prompted me to learn to read maps so I could make my own judgements.

My first alpine experience—a cross-country skiing trip to the Australian Alps—was an epiphany. Led by Adrian, a few of us from the club started out from a place called Munyang, on the famous Snowy River in Kosciuszko National Park. My equipment consisted of woollen, army-surplus clothing, an oiled Japara jacket and a wafer-thin sleeping bag rated to plus 5 degrees Celsius, but I felt ready to face whatever the mountains could throw at me.

Wrong. Even Australia's low, scrubby mountains can be harsh environments. On the first night I probably should have frozen in my woefully unsuitable sleeping bag, particularly since the cotton tent I slept in had no floor. During the night, as the temperature

dropped to minus 15 degrees Celsius, which was way below anything I'd previously experienced, I kept telling myself to think
warm, to stop shivering and to imagine I was feeling as comfortable as I really wanted to be. The shivering stopped and I slept.

At some point that night, the plastic sheet under my thin
sleeping mat became a toboggan and, still asleep, I slid slowly under
the door of my tent. When I awoke the next morning, covered in
frost, I was about 10 metres down the hill.

A couple of days later the other boys and I set out for an alpine
hut about 6 kilometres further into the mountains. We followed
a track marked with orange 'blizzard poles' and therefore didn't
bother with our maps and compasses. Within an hour, the weather
deteriorated and we were caught in a howling blizzard. Visibility
was down to 40 metres, then 30, then 20. We lost sight of the poles
and then the track. Unable to find our way back, we pressed on as
the wind increased and the temperature dropped.

I tried to recall what the map had shown of the lay of the
land and its key features, and I thought I knew where we were.
But after another hour, by which time we should have reached
the hut, we were still inching our way forward. We were all highly
inexperienced, but in the freezing temperature we knew we had to
escape the storm, so we agreed to look for a snow bank and dig a
survival shelter. We turned off the track and moved down the slope
and after 30 metres we skied straight into the side of the missing
hut. We had been lucky. It was a valuable lesson about not taking
anything for granted in the mountains, especially navigation.

Of course, it wasn't all freezing nights and getting lost in
blizzards. That first foray into an alpine wilderness exposed me to
the extraordinary beauty of the mountains: the pure silence, the
freshness of a clear mountain sky, the sparkle of new snow, and
the pristine emptiness, which invited exploration of this magical white wonderland. I thrilled at the exhilaration of striding for
hours, every muscle working hard, to achieve a rhythm that tired

but didn't exhaust the body. Discovering the Alps had added a new dimension to the outdoors for me.

While these activities fulfilled my needs in the outdoors, they did nothing to help my education, or to win any favour with Dad, who quite rightly felt I wasn't focusing on my studies. Trapped behind an old wooden desk for hours each day, the endless monotone of my teachers unable to hold my attention, every muscle in my body ached to be marching hard through the bush. Outdoor adventure was such a magnet for me that I could think of nothing else. The more time I spent in the outdoors, the less I liked the indoors, and the more I wanted a career that would keep me outside.

When I was about fourteen, my parents divorced. Dave and I stayed living with Dad, while Stew went to live with Mum in her apartment. My relationship with Dad only deteriorated in these circumstances, and I sought any opportunity to escape the friction. I pursued adventure whenever possible, regardless of the cost. The odd broken bone or wound needing stitches were just battle scars, and rather than scaring me away from risky activities, they convinced me that the human body could absorb a lot of punishment and would usually bounce back. Anyway, I wanted more of it.

*

At fifteen, I joined the 1st Killara Venturers (Senior Scouts) Unit in Sydney. Dave was already a member and, it seemed to me, he was having even wilder escapades than I was. The unit was incredibly active and as the youngest member of the group I had to learn fast to keep up with the older guys. More caving, abseiling, bushwalking, cross-country skiing, sailing, whitewater canoeing and general adventuring followed over the next few years.

As the older members left, they were replaced by guys and girls my own age. Some came and went but a core group developed, many of whom are still my closest friends today: Mike, Warwick, Steve, Mark, Paul and me—or, as we still know each other, 'French', 'Wazza', 'Bergy', 'Duds', 'Leeky' and 'Droid'. The three regular girls, Meg, Kate and Julie, were spared such ignominy. We took on bolder and bolder adventures and, luckily for us, gained a leader named Bob King, who gave us great guidance. In fact, with his selfless patience, he probably stopped us from killing ourselves.

By the time I finished school I was convinced I needed a career that would keep me outdoors in the wild environments I'd come to love. I'd jackarooed on friends' farms a few times during my school holidays, so I decided on a career as a beef-cattle grazier and enrolled in Yanco Agricultural College near Leeton in country New South Wales. The classes about agronomy and laser land-scaping didn't match my dream of a simple life mustering livestock, but I did enjoy the lessons about explosives and the mechanical sessions on old Land Rover engines.

Like most students I was always broke, so on weekends I worked at nearby farms, walking across paddocks and picking up sticks or piling rocks into heaps for the farmer to collect, so that he could plough his fields more easily. At two dollars per hour in 40 degrees Celsius heat, the work was debilitating and, at the end of each interminable day, I'd crawl into the nearby hotel with a measly twenty dollars in my pocket, only to drink thirty dollars' worth of beer.

Things were not working out as I had hoped. By the end of my first year I was searching for something else. About that time, I saw an advertisement to join the New South Wales Police Force. I'd never thought of being a cop but was already in uniform part-time, having joined the Australian Army Reserve the year before. It seemed like a good stopgap measure while I figured out what I wanted to do with my life.

At my interview I was sent off for a physical examination and was promptly rejected—too skinny. Not to be defeated, I engaged in a solid program of beer, steaks and weightlifting, and two months later scraped through the physical with barely a gram to spare. I was the skinniest bloke in my class at the police academy.

In January 1982, after just three months of training, I graduated from the academy with a badge, a gun and a vision of saving the world. Reality was quickly thrust upon me when I was assigned to the police station in Redfern, which at the time was a troubled, inner-city Sydney suburb with a low socioeconomic status, significant unemployment and a high crime rate. Like any other suburb, though, the majority of its residents were good people trying to do their best in difficult circumstances, and I enjoyed the worthy pursuit of trying to protect them and improve their lives.

At first I found the work itself stimulating as every day brought some new excitement. On one occasion my partner and I chased a stolen car at breakneck speed through back alleys so narrow that our big paddy wagon had only centimetres to spare on either side. When the driver dumped his car, I was out and chasing him on foot before we had even stopped. After finally running him to ground, we opened his bag to find a large amount of drugs and a pistol.

Another day, my partner and I drove to the nearby railway station to arrest a young man who'd assaulted a woman and tried to steal her handbag. As we pulled up, a second young bloke stepped out of the shadows across the street and hurled a bottle against the side of our police truck. He ran off but I was instantly in pursuit. I chased him around the dark and narrow streets, finally tackling him to the ground. As we fought and rolled in the street, I struggled to get the handcuffs on him while he yelled out for help.

When at last I had him pinned him to the ground, I looked up to see a circle of twenty or more local residents around me. Most were holding lengths of timber, steel pipes or bricks. I was in deep trouble and had nowhere to go, but I had no intention of releasing my prisoner.

There was no point panicking but it was likely I was about to be killed, so I pulled out my revolver, pointed it at the crowd and shouted at them to back off. They stopped advancing but waited menacingly for an opportunity to get me. I desperately hoped that my partner would appear with the police truck, but I suddenly realised that I still had the keys to the vehicle in my pocket.

To my relief, I heard a vehicle racing around the nearby streets, gradually getting closer, until it charged into my street. Out jumped my partner from a truck that he'd commandeered from a passing motorist. In an instant we'd tossed the prisoner in and were racing back out of that street, all the time being pelted with bricks, bottles and stones. Needless to say, my partner counselled me about running off on my own, but it turned out that the guy I'd caught was an escaped prisoner with years still outstanding on his sentence—probably why he'd fought me so hard!

Not every shift brought that kind of excitement, but policing the streets meant that we never knew what to expect when we came to work. On a good day we might find a lost child, locate some stolen property or capture a wanted felon, but a bad day could see us fighting drunken mobs, notifying distraught and uncomprehending family members of the death of a loved one or handling the rotten corpse of a lonely pensioner who'd passed away, unnoticed by their closest neighbours until the odour caused someone to complain. Drug overdoses, violent assaults and drunken accidents kept us busy. Death was a constant reality in that area, probably due to the high-density government and rental housing that contained mostly elderly pensioners or people at the bottom of the socioeconomic ladder.

The most dangerous and least pleasant jobs of all, though, were the domestic arguments, when emotions were at their peak and former lovers vented their frustration at the loss of their relationships through brutality towards each other. Until the police arrived. All too frequently, they would see us as the common enemy, a focal point for that anger. Tears could turn to attack in an instant, and 'domestics' had one of the worst statistics for injuries to police officers.

Policing is an incredibly challenging profession and I don't for a minute regret having signed up. The men and women with whom I worked were generally of the highest moral calibre and were dedicated to their task. I was proud to do a job that sought to improve the lives of others. I believe very strongly in fairness, and crime, in my eyes, was unfair. Being a cop enabled me to help correct that. I'd certainly had my share of mischief as a youth—perhaps even a little more than my share—but with maturity came a desire to 'do the right thing' in life, and an expectation that others should also be fair-minded. A breach of that standard is a betrayal and I can be very slow to forgive.

Despite my enjoyment of the work, I became increasingly frustrated with the impact the job was having on my life. I was city-bound, for one thing, and I had to do shifts, which often meant working on weekends and missing out on my re-energising fix of outdoor adventuring. After two years, I needed to get out of the city, and so in 1983 I transferred to the New South Wales country town of Wagga Wagga. The more relaxed country lifestyle—and crimes of a generally less serious nature—was much more to my liking, although life's traumas were just expressed in a different way, most often through horrific high-speed car crashes on the country highways.

In Wagga Wagga I was able to throw myself back into the outdoors, taking on more and more activities, including rafting, paragliding, motorcycling and four-wheel driving. Multi-day bush-walking was a real passion at the time, and I was always keen for something new. I managed to get a last-minute permit to walk the world-renowned Milford Track in New Zealand, and realised that I could link that walk with another one called the Routeburn Track. After four incredible days on the stunning Milford Track,

I wandered into the village of Milford, hoping to replenish my supplies from a supermarket. To my chagrin, I found only a milk bar and a guesthouse.

I wasn't about to give up on the Routeburn Track, so I bought out the milk bar's supply of chocolate and sultanas. At the guesthouse, which had a bar, I bought out their supply of peanuts, then mixed the lot into an oversized bag of scroggin, a staple snack for Australian bushwalkers. This wasn't to be a snack, though, as it was breakfast, lunch and dinner for the next four days. In truth I love scroggin and it didn't diminish the experience at all—the Routeburn track is an extraordinary alpine trek—although I was certainly ready for a steak by the time I reached civilisation.

Back in Australia, I continued my outdoor activities but I knew I hadn't yet found my niche. I took on harder challenges, undertaking solo bushwalking journeys through some of Australia's toughest wilderness, like the Western Arthurs in Tasmania. I rafted our wildest river, the Franklin, also in Tasmania, in a one-man rubber raft for ten days, and went on extended solo cross-country skiing trips in the Snowy Mountain ranges of New South Wales and Victoria.

On one of my ski trips, I set out alone on a 115-kilometre traverse of the 'main range' in New South Wales, going from a point known as Kiandra to the ski resort of Thredbo. The beautiful sunny conditions as I started out, on what should have been four days of pleasant skiing, quickly deteriorated into a blinding blizzard. For eight days I pushed into the storm, navigating as precisely as I could to find key locations along the route, points that I couldn't see until I hit them. It was very slow work, but I was on a high for the entire journey, finding the critical saddles to connect ridgelines, the correct gullies to access valley systems, and watercourses that confirmed my position. When I finally skied to the top of the mountain that overlooked the ski resort, still in whiteout, I felt that I'd tested my navigation skills to the limit and passed.

The boost that that journey brought to my confidence in the outdoors was significant, because on numerous occasions in the years since I've trusted my navigational skills in the most dire of circumstances, when a mistake could have been disastrous. And so far, I've been right. Additionally, and I've learned more about this aspect over the many years of expeditioning, I seemed to be good at 'feeling' whether I'm going the right direction or not. I don't see this as anything paranormal but more to do with a heightened perception of key features around me. Perhaps it is a subconscious noting of those features, so that, when the actual navigation doesn't accord with my subconscious interpretation of where I should be going, alarm bells sound and I check my navigation again. In the big hills of the Himalaya, that inner voice matured further and played a significant part in my survival.

Still these adventures weren't enough. I was searching for something, but I didn't know what. Women told me I needed a wife, and religious friends suggested a god, although neither appealed at the time.

*

In 1985 a door opened to a path that would dictate my life's journey. I had recently discovered a new outdoor magazine, *Australian Wild*, which had reported on several Australian expeditions to the Himalaya. Then Tim Macartney-Snape and Greg Mortimer, the two successful summiteers of the 1984 Australian expedition to Mount Everest, came to Wagga Wagga to present a slide show about their climb, the first successful Australian expedition to the world's tallest peak. The venue was the back room of Romano's Hotel, a local watering hole. Only about twenty people turned up, but I was one of them.

It was as if an act of destiny had brought me there—I was spellbound. Their stories of great derring-do, danger, camaraderie, sacrifice and ultimate success were totally captivating. Those images of massive exposure, bitter cold, objective dangers—of human fortitude against the elements in the toughest environment conceivable—drew me in like a magnet and I decided on the spot that I must experience all that myself. I would climb Mount Everest. It was one of the most powerful experiences of my life.

This was what I'd been looking for, and I was now on a mission. Of course, there was one small problem with the concept. Despite my broad range of other outdoor activities at the time, I'd never actually done any serious climbing. I decided the best approach was to break the main objective of climbing Mount Everest into shorter-term, more achievable goals. First I would learn to rock climb, then alpine climb, then enhance my planning, logistics and organisational skills, before experiencing medium altitude and then the high altitude of the Himalaya.

It didn't occur to me to pay someone to guide me up Everest, as many people do today. I'd always experienced adventure on my own terms, and I wanted to learn to be a climber and to climb the mountain under my own steam. Letting someone else take the responsibility and leadership away from me would be anathema. I would climb Everest completely under my own ability and resources, or not at all. I felt strongly that if I were to succeed in testing myself on the world's highest peak, I would prepare thoroughly, and be fully capable of surviving in the harshest environment on Earth. No problem.

Within a few months I'd arranged a transfer in the police force to a plain clothes investigations squad back in Sydney and joined both the Sydney Rock Climbing Club and the Army Alpine Association, better known as the AAA. I immediately threw myself into the rock climbing, and loved it. I climbed on every possible weekend or day off from work. The Blue Mountains, two hours west of Sydney, became my regular destination and I left many a piece of skin and more than a little blood on its raw sandstone bluffs over the ensuing years.

With my rock-climbing skills coming along well, I needed to learn how to apply them to the alpine environment. As Australia lacks any serious mountains, I booked a mountaineering course in the Mount Cook National Park in New Zealand. The New Zealand alps are probably the most underrated alpine training ground in the world. Set on the west coast of the south island, they rise very steeply from the coast to the highest summit of Mount Cook at 3750 metres. Not significant in altitude—although certainly enough to give you a headache—they're still substantial mountains, given that their base is almost at sea level.

The course was everything I'd hoped for. The instructors taught us to apply rock-climbing techniques to ice and snow, to assess avalanche risk, to survive blizzards and to rescue one another from crevasses. It was exhausting and at times intimidating but totally exhilarating. I was hooked on this new sport, and I regularly returned to the New Zealand alps over the next few years, developing my skills for bigger mountains and more serious climbs.

Invariably I wanted to push harder and longer than my climbing partners and I soon ran out of willing victims at home. I found myself just turning up at Mount Cook village and climbing with whomever I could find in the campground or bar at the village. Mount Cook was a climbers' hub and it was pretty much guaranteed that I'd find someone with good skills to team up with.

On one of those trips, I joined a highly accomplished rock climber from Australia, Lucas Trihey, for a climb up a couloir—a steep, narrow gully—on a peak called Mount Darwin. We set out at midnight, the usual 'alpine start' in New Zealand, to give ourselves enough time to climb to the top and back down the peak before the heat of the afternoon made avalanche conditions too risky.

After crossing a glacier below the mountain, we started up the long and sustained couloir, using a 'running belay'—a technique where both climbers are tied together and move in unison up the mountain. The lead climber places protection along the way, which the second climber retrieves when he reaches it in order for it to be used again higher on the mountain. While the safety benefit is less than that afforded by belays from fixed stances, a running belay allows for significantly faster climbing. Hour after hour passed as we forced our way up the never-ending steep snow and rock gully and, by the time we finally reached the top, it was right on dusk.

A storm was forming and we couldn't see the way down, so we elected to bivouac on the summit. There wasn't enough snow to dig a shelter and we had only lightweight fleece jackets. Although we had no down clothing or sleeping bags, we were carrying survival bivouac sacks for shelter. After building a low wall of rock and snow to block some of the wind, we climbed into our respective sacks for what we knew would be a chilly night.

Chilly? It was bloody freezing! We lay head to foot because the summit was so small. At one point I was shivering so violently I thought I'd lose control, but then Lucas started rubbing his feet up and down my back. That little bit of friction made quite a difference and I regained composure and persevered through the night.

By the next morning the storm had cleared, and we emerged chilled and appreciative of the sun's warmth. I thanked Lucas for rubbing his feet on my back in the middle of the night as it had really helped me. To my surprise, he responded, 'I didn't do it to help you. I was just so cold that I lost control and my legs started shaking!'

We were both pleased to learn later that we'd opened a new route on the mountain by completing that ascent.

*

My first opportunity to experience significant altitude came in 1987, when the AAA organised a seven-week expedition to climb Alaska's Mount McKinley, the highest mountain in North America. McKinley is a big hill, standing 6194 metres, with its base camp starting point on an ice runway at an altitude of just 2150 metres, making an ascent of 4 vertical kilometres, more than most Himalayan climbs. Our team was big, too, with eleven climbers and a huge amount of equipment. We had to comply with the army's requirement for a broad range of experience within the team, and to bring enough equipment to deal with every contingency.

After driving north from Anchorage to the frontier town of Talkeetna, we flew in a Cessna aircraft equipped with skis to the massive Kahiltna Glacier, and from there we launched the climb. For the first month, on skis and towing sleds laden heavily with two months' worth of tents, rope, food, fuel and all the extras, we ferried loads up a broad ridge on the mountain known as the West Buttress. This is the easiest route on the mountain and the majority of people going to McKinley attempt it. For us, though, it was only to be our acclimatisation phase, before we'd descend the mountain and traverse to the base of the more technical West Rib route, up which we intended to climb to the summit.

Although not an 8000er, McKinley is still a formidable challenge, with temperatures regularly dropping below minus 40 degrees Celsius, and wind speeds of 100 kilometres per hour or more. That sort of wind chill freezes exposed flesh instantly, and frostbite is one of the most common injuries on McKinley.

At the 4270-metre Camp 3, the team split, with four climbers electing to continue up the easier West Buttress route to the summit and forgo the West Rib challenge. The remaining seven of us, by then fully acclimatised, returned to our advance base camp on the Kahiltna Glacier and traversed around the mountain to the West Rib.

A massive ridge of rock, snow and ice, and steeper than the West Buttress, the West Rib is difficult to get to, with a major field of crevasses at its base. For reasons best known only to himself, the leader elected Matt Godbold and me, the least experienced mountaineer on the team, to tackle the main challenge of fixing rope up a 600-metre couloir at the base of the West Rib. It took us two days to carry the hundreds of metres of rope up the gully and anchor it to the snow and ice so the rest of the team could follow safely.

As it was my first experience of climbing with huge exposure below me on the steep face of a major mountain, it was an education. Like rock climbing, the focus required was almost meditative as we tentatively picked our way up the long, exposed gully, hyper-vigilant for loose snow or rock that could cause a fall or avalanche. At the top, we revelled in our accomplishment.

When the team joined us, we pushed further up, eagerly seeking the thinner air with every step. For us, this was an unknown world. Altitude headaches pounded, nausea was a constant companion, and the cold, the bitter cold, cut through every layer of clothing. When, after some days climbing higher and higher, we made our dash for the summit, I was literally drunk from the altitude as my brain struggled to cope with the lack of oxygen. It took all my focus to stay on my feet and not topple from the mountain. I would learn, however, that headaches are just the introduction to high altitude.

A short distance from the top, as I stopped to rest, I felt, or perhaps even heard, what seemed like the bursting of a blood vessel in my head. Instantly I felt a pinpoint pain and knew that something was seriously wrong. It was more than a little disconcerting, as I didn't know exactly what had happened or just how serious it might be, so I was quite pleased that I didn't simply drop dead. There was nothing I could do to treat the injury near the summit of the mountain, but I knew that I had to get out of the high altitude so I immediately started to descend. It would take several days for the headache to ease and I just hoped that it wouldn't kill me before I could get back to civilisation and see a doctor.

Tired and feeling quite poorly, I had little patience for the plastic sled on which I was towing a heavy load. As we skied down the mountain, the sled kept sliding past me and then rolling over and stopping dead, which acted like an anchor and brought me abruptly crashing to the ground. After a couple of days of this, I lost my temper at the top of a massive slope known as Heartbreak Hill. I undid the tow rope and kicked the sled down the hill, expecting it to run for 20 or 30 metres and then roll over and stop. No such luck—the bloody thing flew down the hill in a perfectly straight line, all the way to the bottom.

Before I could congratulate myself on a good decision, it suddenly veered sideways and shot out onto a broad crevasse-ridden basin about 50 metres off the track. It was my own fault, but inanimate objects that don't perform the way they're meant to bring me to a fit of rage. If I hadn't kicked it down the slope I would probably have hacked it to pieces with my ice axe.

From my position at the top of the hill I could see the faint lines under the snow that indicated major crevasses beneath. But I had to retrieve the sled as it had group gear as well as my own. At the bottom of the slope I skied ever so tenuously, heart in mouth, over to the sled, reattached it to my harness and gently picked my way back to the safety of the track. I vowed to keep control of my temper in future—at least on the mountains—as the odd malfunctioning computer has still been known to achieve free flight at my house.

The ski plane out from the mountain deposited us back in Talkeetna, where we installed ourselves in the town bar, the Fairview Inn. A character-filled establishment, it is the perennial watering hole for visiting mountaineers, resident daredevil mountain pilots and locals. In the mood to celebrate, the team made up for our long abstinence, and before long it wasn't just the locals who couldn't understand what we were slurring.

On the wall at one end of the bar hung a large, fairly kitsch painting of Denali National Park, with Mount McKinley in the distance and a brown bear standing proudly in the foreground.

Over the years, climbers from about ten different nationalities had stuck cocktail flags from their drinks into the summit of the mountain. Not surprisingly, the US flag was at the top of the cluster. With alcohol-fuelled enthusiasm, one of our number suddenly jumped onto the bar, pulled the US flag from the summit of the mountain and stuck it into the bear's bum. Not a good move, given the more than 2-metre stature of the lumberjack-like locals, whose pickup trucks sported enough bear-killing firepower to take on the entire Australian Army, let alone seven of its more inebriated representatives! We climbed over each other to replace the flag to its rightful place as quickly as possible, while throwing all the money we had into a pile to shout the bar. An international incident was avoided, although it would have been a very short-lived incident.

Back in Australia, a CAT scan indicated that all was okay in my brain, but the doctors weren't able to tell me what had occurred or whether it could happen again. However, I knew that I'd been very lucky to survive some kind of altitude-induced event. If I was to continue climbing at altitude I could not suffer another impact like that and I reflected on why it had happened to me and not other climbers in the team. The key point concerned the different speeds at which our team members had acclimatised on the expedition. I'd suffered altitude sickness and headaches more than most, despite following the same routine as the more experienced climbers. If I were to continue climbing these hills, I would need to ensure that I acclimatised at my own rate and not allow myself to be forced to follow others' agendas. Mountains demand flexibility, not rigid adherence to itineraries.

I had made some great friends on that trip, particularly Matt Godbold and Mike Pezet, and we continued to climb together for many years. Back home I threw myself into rock climbing with even greater gusto, attacking every route I could climb in the Blue Mountains. I also climbed further afield, including on the wildly exposed and unprotected slabs of Booroomba near Canberra, Frog Buttress in Queensland, and Australia's rock-climbing mecca, Mount Arapiles. In doing so I formed new friendships as I discovered a kinship with people from all walks of life who enjoyed this strange sport.

I loved the physicality of climbing—the careful execution of precise moves, balancing precariously on tiny edges, limbs stretched and every muscle tensed. And I revelled in applying the mechanical systems involved in climbing—placing protection that would jam in a crack and hold me if I fell; advanced techniques for belaying and, if necessary, rescuing my climbing partners if they fell; and self-rescue systems if my partner couldn't help me.

The real discovery for me, though, was within—finding the mental strength to push through personal fear and overcome the intimidation of leading climbs on vertical cliff faces, and forcing myself to commit to moves where any failure of my climbing equipment or a mistake by my belayer would be fatal for me. I came to relish that feeling of personal achievement. The greater the fear, the greater the victory when complete.

The skills I developed would save many lives, including mine, in the years ahead.

2

A TASTE OF THIN AIR

Those who travel to mountain-tops are half in love with themselves,
and half in love with oblivion.

Robert Macfarlane

IN 1988 I made my first visit to Nepal to attempt a peak called
Mount Pumori, which sits immediately adjacent to Mount
Everest. *Pumori* means 'beautiful daughter' and, despite being
completely dwarfed by the matriarch of the Himalaya, Pumori is
a significant mountain at 7161 metres. It is a striking peak with a
quintessential pyramid shape. I was twenty-six years old, and this
was my first trip to a non–Western country. I was in for a shock.

In the streets of Kathmandu I saw horribly disfigured beggars
sitting metres from the opulent hotels where foreigners scurried,
trying in vain to avert their eyes. But at the same time there was no
better place to experience the hectic, bustling madness of an Asian
city, with overloaded rickshaws, their horns constantly blaring,
racing wildly through market streets packed with pedestrians,

somehow avoiding dogs, children, chickens, cows and monks. I was quickly won over by the peaceful, friendly nature of the people and their acceptance of life, whatever their status, in this richly cultural but financially stricken country.

There was one aspect of Asia, though, for which I was completely unprepared: the hygiene, or rather the lack of it. I picked up a succession of stomach ailments that stayed with me for the whole two months we were in Nepal and for some time afterwards. I have never been so sick. Course after course of antibiotics treated first one affliction, then another. By the time we started climbing, I'd lost more weight than I'd expected to lose over the course of the entire expedition. I spent most of my time at base camp, throwing up or bent double with stomach cramps.

Another new experience for me was the expedition puja ceremony, where a Tibetan Buddhist monk is engaged, either at base camp or at a monastery en route, to seek from the gods safe passage for the climbers during their expedition. This was my first real experience of another culture's beliefs. Food and drink were offered to the gods, and our ice axes and crampons, which would come into contact with the mountain, were blessed. For almost an hour the monk recited chants from an ancient handwritten prayer book, enclosed in slim, timber slats tied with string. I felt powerfully linked to the spirituality of the ceremony and that feeling has increased over the many puja ceremonies I've attended since.

The south ridge of Pumori is very steep and provides few locations for campsites. Our first camp, at 6000 metres, was a tiny ledge hacked out of an ice ridge at the top of a near-vertical ice face. It was so narrow that the edges of the tent hung over each side, with a 600-metre drop to the glacier below. It was exciting stuff, although we were careful not to toss and turn too much in our sleeping bags in *that* tent.

To progress beyond the tents, we climbed along the ridge, but the way was soon blocked by 3-metre cornices—great mushrooms of wind-blown ice that accumulate on exposed ridges and dislodge easily—and we were forced to drop over the edge, onto the steep face below. Within a short distance, that way was also blocked and we had to dig a tunnel for several metres straight through the ridge to the face on the other side. The ice wasn't too hard here and it only took a few hours to hack through the ridge. But it was hugely exposed on each side and very intimidating to gaze down to the glaciers below. This was real alpine climbing and I thrilled at the adventure.

A couple of weeks after we'd started climbing, we were joined at our Base Camp by a small Norwegian–English team, whose four members were hoping to climb the same route as us. There were so few locations for tents on our ridge that we told them they'd have to wait until we were finished—potentially a month or more—or else climb another route. They chose the latter and found a steep and very challenging line on Pumori's south-west face.

For a while it was fun to look across and watch them, mere specks on a massive expanse of rock and ice as they worked their way up the mountain. Then one day we couldn't see them. A few days later we learned that the leading pair of climbers had disappeared. Their teammates organised a Nepalese army helicopter to search the mountain face and the glacier below, but no sign of the two was ever found.

Somewhat sobered, my team continued, and a bold dash to the top saw four of our seven members reach the summit. Their descent was successful but not without cost. One teammate, Armando Corvini, had suffered from cold feet during the climb and had added extra layers of socks to compensate. This complicated the issue, compressing his feet inside his already tight boots. The restricted blood flow and the freezing temperatures caused both frostbite and trench foot. As we peeled off his blood-soaked socks back at base camp, the entire soles of his feet fell away. He had to be carried back to civilisation by yak.

Matt Godbold and I made our own summit attempt a few days after the others, but I was again struck down by a gastro attack at Camp 1. I lay curled up in the foetal position for hours as waves of cramps swept over me. The next day I had neither the mental nor the physical strength to continue, so we descended to Base Camp, our expedition over.

While my first Himalayan summit attempt was unsuccessful, I had learned much about climbing at high altitude and on steep ground, and my enthusiasm for the mountains was undimmed. Being so close to Everest had brought home to me the intimidating reality of an 8000-metre mountain. I had climbed to around 6000 metres and been defeated. I knew that to achieve my goal of climbing to the highest place on Earth, I would have to be better prepared, both physically and psychologically.

I had seen the potential cost of high altitude, too—death and serious injury. Despite this, and despite my illness, I had felt the thrill of the high mountains. I was captivated by the spirituality and majesty of the Himalaya and I knew I would return.

*

The next year, 1989, I set out to climb Pik (Mount) Korzhenevskaya in the Pamir ranges of Tajikistan with a friend from the Sydney Rockclimbing Club, Ian Collins, and a couple of other guys. The climbing was technically easy and we soon made our first summit attempt, which turned out to be another lesson in the dangerous effects of altitude.

Ian, who was suffering from altitude headaches on the summit day, waited in the tent at our highest camp while I made a bid for the top. After making him a cup of tea and leaving another pot full of snow on the stove to melt, I set off.

'Good luck,' Ian said as I left the tent. 'I'll have a cuppa waiting when you get back.'

Twelve hours later, after being defeated by a blizzard a short distance from the summit, I returned to camp, looking forward to that cup of tea. Instead, the door of the tent was wide open and Ian was buried under half a metre of snow inside the tent.

God—he's dead! I immediately thought. *I guess that means no cup of tea, then.* But to my great relief, Ian sat up, the snow falling off him in a wave. It turned out that after I'd left the tent, he'd fallen straight back to sleep. With the door open when the blizzard hit, the tent had soon filled up with snow and buried him in his sleeping bag—all without disturbing him, such was the coma-like state of his altitude-induced stupor.

While Ian was okay, there would still be no tea because our stove had been ruined and it was a tough descent over the next few days as we struggled to melt enough snow to drink. Undeterred, we re-equipped at base camp and ascended again, reaching the summit a few days later. At 7105 metres, it was my highest peak to date.

In December that year I joined another AAA expedition, this time to Aconcagua, the highest mountain in South America, and in fact the highest mountain in the southern and western hemispheres. As one of the so-called Seven Summits—the highest peaks on each of the world's seven continents—Aconcagua is very popular, but it's quite easy and so the normal route can be crowded. We chose instead to climb the Polish Glacier route, which was less visited and more challenging.

From Base Camp, we made speedy progress as far as Camp 2, where we were disconcerted to find the body of a climber wrapped in plastic—the man's corpse was slowly mummifying in the cold, dry air. We later learned that he'd been injured high on the mountain several years earlier, but when a rescue helicopter had attempted to extract him it crashed, killing the crew. A second helicopter crew had apparently retrieved the bodies of the first helicopter crew but were so angered by the death of their comrades that they abandoned the climber to his fate. He died there and has been enjoying the view ever since.

Several weeks into the expedition, we were ready to make our summit attempt. The slope above the high camp looked bare of snow, exposing steep and treacherous ice. Our team was not highly experienced on that terrain, so rather than follow the true Polish Glacier route to the top, we decided to traverse around the mountain to the normal route and finish the climb that way. As I picked my way carefully across the slope, I found an old ice axe with a wooden shaft. The pick at the top was almost dead straight, indicating that the axe was quite old. Its owner clearly didn't need it any more, so I put it into my backpack and continued the climb. I still have that axe at home today.

After reaching the summit, I started my descent to Base Camp. I wanted to get down quickly, but en route I passed a Japanese team on its way up. It was immediately obvious that one of its members, a young woman, was seriously attitude sick—she was lurching and falling and could barely speak. I wasn't overly experienced at high altitude at the time, but I certainly knew that she needed to descend, and quickly. I advised the leader to take her down straightaway, offering to accompany her.

He refused and said, 'Some will summit; some will die.'

'Are you serious?' I asked. He grunted and pushed past, so I spoke to the young woman directly.

'You must go down or you will die.'

'No, no. Summit,' she mumbled as she lurched onwards.

Interesting approach. I'm all for pushing oneself to the limit of one's ability but climbing is about identifying and working within the limits of acceptable risk. The girl had long since passed that limit. At that point she was just competing for a Darwin award. And her leader was encouraging it! It was the first of numerous examples of bizarre leadership that I would see on the high mountains. I don't know if any of that team summitted, but I suspect the leader was right about the second part of his comment.

From Base Camp I made my way to the nearest major town, Mendoza, where I met up with the rest of my team and celebrated the summit in good style. After that, I split from the group and headed off for eight months of backpacking around South America. I'd taken the whole year off from the police, so I had plenty of time to engage with the South American culture. I also wanted to explore some of the continent's wilderness areas and mountain ranges.

I had been in a serious relationship for several months before I'd departed and Joanne and I had agreed to keep our relationship going while I was away. We missed each other a lot, though, so after a couple of months Joanne took leave and flew across to join me. Together we travelled, trekked and backpacked through Argentina, Chile, Peru, Bolivia and parts of Brazil. We were on a shoestring budget—by the end of it, we could only afford one meal per day—but it was fabulous fun to be young, together and without a care. It was one of the most enjoyable holidays I've ever had. Actually, it was one of the only non-climbing holidays I've ever had.

*

Joanne and I returned to Australia in August 1990, and she went back to work. I still had several months of leave, though, so in September I took a job leading a trekking group to the Karakorum Mountains of Pakistan, in which stands K2, the world's second-highest mountain. It was at once hugely intimidating with its steep, black, rocky faces and its massive cliffs of ice—known as seracs—but it was also powerfully magnetic. By the end of the trip I knew I would one day return to climb it. First, though, I had to develop my technical climbing ability and gain more high-altitude experience.

In April 1991, I returned to Mount McKinley to attempt the difficult and very challenging Cassin Ridge. My climbing partner was Piotr Pustelnik, a Polish climber I'd met in Tajikistan in 1989. On McKinley, we first set out on a very fast ascent of the West Buttress route for acclimatisation, successfully reaching the summit just eight days after arriving at the mountain. I'd left my warmest clothing at Base Camp to save weight, with the intention of picking it up before we moved around the mountain to climb the Cassin Ridge to the summit, so when we decided to go for the summit on the West Buttress route I had only a lightweight down jacket and gloves. I had to line my jacket with a garbage bag and put plastic shopping bags over my gloves to help block the wind. It worked, although I was more than a little chilly on the top, given that the temperature was about minus 30 degrees Celsius with a strong wind blowing.

This time, thankfully, I didn't suffer any brain explosions, but reaching the summit during our acclimatisation phase actually worked against us, as it robbed Piotr of his motivation to complete the Cassin Ridge. He didn't say outright that he wouldn't continue but I could tell he was having second thoughts.

After returning to Base Camp and collecting our equipment, we trekked up the north-east fork of the Kahiltna Glacier. We marched for several hours under massive ice cliffs that threatened to release from thousands of metres above and crash down upon us. We made it through unscathed and set up camp in a bergschrund—a crevasse that separates the mountain face from the glacier it feeds—at the base of the Japanese Couloir—the start of the Cassin Ridge route. By then it was late in the afternoon, so we decided to start our ascent of the couloir the following morning.

We settled into our tent and melted snow for tea. Sitting in our lofty lookout, we marvelled at the immense ice faces all around us. Then we spied another two climbers following in our tracks way below. They looked absolutely insignificant compared with the massive blocks of ice above them.

Suddenly the ice cliffs broke free and tumbled down the face of the slope. As they fell and bounced, they broke into smaller but still enormous chunks, some the size of fridges, others as big as houses. The two tiny figures made a vain attempt to escape the path of the avalanche, but within seconds they had disappeared from our view as the blocks of ice crashed in front, behind and over them.

Piotr and I, some 500 metres away, could do nothing but retreat into our tent, hurriedly zipping closed the door. A massive blast of wind hit us moments later. Our tent poles flattened and the shelter was crushed by the force of the air for about thirty seconds. Once it passed our tent sprang back into something resembling its original shape and we peered down into the valley, waiting for the snow cloud to clear. Incredibly, we spotted the two little figures still running for their lives. How they survived I have no idea, but someone or something was looking after them that day. Half an hour later they reached our camp, still so high from adrenaline that they could barely speak.

That night passed slowly, as avalanches reverberated around the mountain. The next morning Piotr declared that he didn't want to continue the climb. The two climbers—who were British, it turned out—didn't want a third person on their team, and the Japanese Couloir was too technical for me to solo. My expedition was over. *Great!* I thought. *That was time and money well spent.* Our frosty trek back to base camp, had nothing to do with the temperature, and I collected my gear and walked out of the mountains alone.

*

In mid 1991, having returned frustrated after the lost opportunity on McKinley, I was invited by my friend Ian Collins to join him on an expedition to the big one, Mount Everest. This was it! After six years of climbing around the world I now had the opportunity to realise my dream.

At that time, the normal process if you wanted to climb Everest was to apply to Nepal's Ministry of Tourism two or three years in advance. But a Russian team had cancelled their permit at the last minute and Ian had managed to secure it. In a short time we'd formed a team comprising Ian, me, Michael Groom and expat New Zealander Mark Squires.

I'd rock climbed with Ian and Mark for several years but hadn't met Groom, who lived in Queensland. He was the only one on the team with 8000-metre experience, having twice climbed on the world's third-highest peak, Kanchenjunga. He'd also made two unsuccessful attempts on Everest. He was best known for his second attempt on Kanchenjunga, when he suffered severe frostbite on his descent from the summit and subsequently had to have the front portions of both his feet amputated, including all ten toes.

Everest's history is well known. It was identified as the highest point on Earth during the Great Trigonometric Survey of India in the nineteenth century and received its western name from the Royal Geographical Society in 1865, in honour of Sir George Everest, a surveyor-general of India during the survey. The locals, of course, had known it by a quite different name, and for quite some time. To them it was, and is, Chomolungma, meaning 'Mother Goddess of the Earth'.

As with several other 8000ers, the border of Tibet and Nepal runs up and over its summit. During the 1920s and 1930s, the British launched six attempts to its north side, several of which came within just a few hundred metres of the summit, despite the climbers' rudimentary clothing and oxygen systems. The disappearance of George Mallory and Sandy Irvine close to the summit in 1924 left an as yet unsolved mystery as to whether they may have reached the top twenty-nine years earlier than the first official success.

The Second World War interrupted proceedings, as did the Chinese invasion of Tibet in 1947, and the subsequent closing of Tibet's borders to foreign expeditions for many years. Attention switched to Nepal, which until that time had kept its own borders locked but had relaxed its restrictions with the coming of democracy to the kingdom in the early 1950s. Some preliminary exploration identified that a route might be climbed through the Khumbu Icefall, and up the mountain's south-east ridge to the summit. Success finally came to the British on 29 May 1953, but not before the Swiss almost stole the crown in 1952 when they reached the south summit, just 100 metres from the top.

Mallory and Irvine weren't the only climbers to make Chomolungma their last resting place. Around 250 have now perished in pursuit of summit 'glory'. The two worst incidents were in 1996, when fifteen climbers died on the mountain (eight in a single storm), and 2014, when a single avalanche crushed sixteen High Altitude Porters in the Khumbu icefall.

Everest has two main climbing seasons: pre-monsoon, which runs from late March to the end of May, at which time the monsoon starts, and post-monsoon, which is officially defined as September to November. Pre-monsoon presents a mountain that has largely been swept clear of excess snow by the winter jet-stream winds that pound the mountain at over 300 kilometres per hour. It becomes warmer as the season progresses towards the beginning of summer in June, so the risk of frostbite is reduced. In the post-monsoon season, the mountain is covered in snow, which actually makes the climbing easier. But the avalanche danger is much greater and the temperatures become colder as the season progresses. Most expeditions prefer to climb in the safer, pre-monsoon, season.

Our Everest expedition, however, was scheduled for the post-monsoon season because that was what the Russians' permit had dictated. In early September, Ian and Mark travelled to Kathmandu to start the preparations, while I stayed for a few more days to marry Joanne in the Blue Mountains west of Sydney. Jo was a real homebody and desperately wanted to be married, but I confess that it wasn't high on my list of priorities. The pull of the mountains was getting stronger and stronger, and I was about to have my first real taste of thin air. I knew that, ultimately, trying to satisfy both commitments would cause conflict. Fittingly, it snowed on our wedding day, so I was well acclimatised to the cold when I arrived in Kathmandu, sans wife, a few days later.

*

I knew from my experience on Pumori that Nepalese customs officials would inspect my bags and find some 'technical issue' with the amount or type of equipment that I was bringing into the country. They would either delay me extensively or confiscate something, which would disappear into the great black hole of their impounded-goods warehouse, never to be seen again. It was all a scam, of course, as the inspectors were simply seeking some minor bribe to complement their lowly wages. But I wasn't prepared to give up any of my essential equipment, nor did I know what the appropriate financial 'incentive' was. To overcome this, I purchased a bottle of duty-free spirits at the airport and put it into my luggage while waiting to be inspected. When my bags were opened, the expected topic was raised.

'Actually, sir, you have too much equipment here. It is not possible to take all this equipment into Nepal.'

'I see,' I said. 'Well, you know, I really don't need that bottle of alcohol at the top of my bag. Could you help by disposing of that for me? And would that bring my equipment back to an acceptable amount?'

'Oh, yes, sir,' came the very pleased reply. I was soon out of the airport with all my equipment, and back in the hustle and bustle of Kathmandu.

It was with a certain trepidation that I was returning to Nepal—the memory of that disastrous intestinal experience during my expedition there in 1988 was still agonisingly strong—I was desperate to get into the mountains healthy so I could take on Everest. Accordingly, I took great care that every bite and every sip of liquid I consumed was as hygienic as it could be. At least one restaurant owner was well aware of the needs of tourists like me, cleverly displaying a sign that read, 'We soak all our vegetables in 2% iodine solution'. His restaurant was packed solid every night.

We spent several days purchasing what we needed for our climb—food, rope, propane/butane gas canisters for our stoves, a couple of bottles of oxygen (we would be climbing without oxygen but still wanted a bottle or two for emergencies), snow pickets and other necessary expedition paraphernalia. We had engaged a local trekking agent, who liaised with the authorities on our behalf, and employed a cook and a *sirdar* (much like a foreman). The *sirdar* then hired and managed the porters who'd carry our equipment to base camp. The agent also provided us with a kitchen tent and cooking equipment. We would fend for ourselves while up high on the mountain, but while we were resting at base camp and recovering from our climbing sorties, it would be wonderful to have someone else do the chores.

Prior to departing for the mountain, we had to undergo the arduous briefing process required by the Nepal Ministry of Tourism, which involved hours in a musty office filling out numerous documents in triplicate, all of which needed laborious and rather snooty consideration by the responsible official—and extended tedium while we waited for his benign consent. After a full day spent battling our way through bureaucracy of which any civil servant would be proud, we finally received his approving decree and were free to start our journey to base camp.

The first leg was a thirty-minute flight from Kathmandu to a remote mountain airstrip at a village called Lukla in an ancient twenty-seater Twin Otter aircraft. Lukla's airstrip is one of Sir Edmund Hillary's many extraordinary achievements. It is literally perched halfway up a mountain—its runway has a fifteen-degree slope. Our little aircraft clawed its way over successively higher mountain passes until we skimmed over the highest gap just above the treetops, then dropped steeply towards the dirt runway. As we plunged through the clouds, I saw through our plane's windscreen, on either side of the landing strip, the wreckage of aircraft that had previously landed poorly. Now, that makes you fasten your seatbelt!

Thankfully, our pilot was better than those from the various wreckages and, after a siren had sounded at the airstrip, motivating the locals to usher their grazing cattle out of the way, we landed with a thud before going to full revs to drive uphill to the top of the strip. We quickly disembarked and our luggage was tossed out after us, then the little plane roared back down the hill, dropping out of sight into the valley until it gained sufficient airspeed to start the climb back to the high pass, en route to Kathmandu. That flight is surely one of the world's classics. Since my first visit, they have tarred the runway, cleared away some of the wreckage and built a fence around the airstrip, if only to keep the cattle safe.

From this high mountain village (altitude 3300 metres), deep within the Sherpa region of Nepal, we commenced our trek to Everest. Over ten days we moved through progressively smaller and more remote villages, until we left the last shacks behind and crossed the Khumbu Glacier to reach Everest base camp.

The camp was pitched somewhat haphazardly on the rock and ice moraine of the Khumbu Glacier. Many hours of labour were required to hack relatively flat spots for our tents and to build our home for the next two months. As necessary as it was to focus on the work at hand, I could barely concentrate. In front loomed the world's highest mountain, its cloud-enshrouded summit an overwhelming 3.5 vertical kilometres above us. It was absolutely monstrous. The years of training and climbing around the world I'd done to prepare for this very moment seemed worthless. I felt very small indeed.

We decided that the best way to succeed, and survive, would be to tackle the challenge in the traditional way of climbing at high altitude, known as siege style. This meant that we'd acclimatise as we climbed, rather than acclimatising elsewhere and then trying to ascend the mountain in a single push. At 8848 metres, Everest reaches well into the 'death zone', where a human body can spend only a limited amount of time before its internal mechanisms start to shut down, leading devastatingly quickly to death. The death zone is what makes Everest—and indeed all the 8000-metre peaks—so dangerous.

The world's atmosphere, the air, has weight. At sea level, all that atmosphere weighing down on you creates pressure. Measured in millibars, it is around 970 to 1030 millibars, depending on the weather systems. The higher into the atmosphere you climb, the less of it there is above you, and therefore the less weight, or pressure, there is bearing down on you. Atmospheric pressure impacts on your ability to absorb oxygen from the air. At 8000 metres, the pressure is around 250 millibars, just a quarter of the pressure at sea level, so from each breath the body gets only a quarter of the oxygen that it needs. That's why we call it 'thin air'.

The human body is, to a certain extent, adaptable. Over time it can adjust to lower pressure. That's what acclimatisation is. One thing the body does is develop more red blood cells (haemoglobin) in order to better absorb the oxygen. Up to around 3000 metres, there is little need to acclimatise, but above that the general guide is that you should ascend not more than 300 metres per day to allow your body to adjust. The base camps of the 8000-metre peaks are at altitudes of between 4000 and 5100 metres, which means the journey in requires a minimum of four to five days, and up to two weeks, to achieve the appropriate acclimatisation en route. For that reason, we'd deliberately taken ten days for our trek to Everest base camp.

Acclimatising to the base camp altitude simply means you have adjusted enough not to drop dead right then and there. Of course, as you proceed up the mountain you must continue to acclimatise, and even that will allow you only the briefest moment on the summit. It is a long, slow process, taking about a month at

4000 metres or higher to be sufficiently acclimatised to make an attempt on an 8000-metre summit.

Nobody, including the Sherpas, can acclimatise enough to live at high altitude permanently. Above about 4000 metres, you are on borrowed time—and that time reduces exponentially as you go higher. So acclimatisation is about spending the appropriate amount of time up high for your body to adapt to the altitude, but not too long, because your body starts to shut down from the moment you reach base camp.

With that understanding, we spent a couple of days setting up our Base Camp and acclimatising to its altitude, then started the assault by climbing each day for about six hours up the 800 metres from Base Camp to Camp 1, through the infamous Khumbu Icefall. This is a jumble of massive ice blocks, some as big as multi-storey buildings, which have broken away from the face of the glacier above and tumbled partway down the steep slope towards Base Camp. They balance precariously on top of each other, threatening to collapse without warning. It is the most objectively dangerous part of the entire climb.

The route winds its way beside, between and over these ice blocks, and we frequently felt the entire icefall rumble and shunt as a block collapsed somewhere, dropping hundreds of tonnes of ice onto the path. On one occasion I saw a massive ripple sweep from one side of the icefall to the other, around 500 metres in width, as the glacier below settled. It made for nervous climbing and we stopped only when desperate to catch our breath, and even then only for the shortest time necessary.

At the top of the icefall, we found a suitable site for our Camp 1. On a level patch of ice surrounded by crevasses we erected two tents, to store all the provisions and equipment, then, given we'd climbed more than the recommended 300 metres per day, descended to base camp that afternoon. A typical load was around 15 to 20 kilograms, and consisted of a tent, four days' worth of food and gas, a sleeping bag and also our everyday items—a couple of different jackets, water, a couple of snack bars, mittens, gloves, glasses, goggles, pen knife, balaclava, sun hat, radio, sunscreen, camera, climbing equipment for the route, ice axe and crampons. For several days, we repeated the process until we had sufficient supplies stored at Camp 1 to enable us to occupy that camp and commence carrying loads to Camp 2.

Simultaneously we were enhancing our acclimatisation by climbing up to the higher altitude of Camp 1 each day but returning to sleep in the thicker air of Base Camp each night. The high-altitude acclimatisation mantra is 'climb high, sleep low', which is precisely what we were doing. By the time we'd fully stocked Camp 1, we'd also enhanced our acclimatisation sufficiently to be able to stay at that camp without serious ill effects. This is siege-style climbing.

The route to Camp 2 was much less intimidating than the Khumbu Icefall but had its own challenges. Rising from 6100 to 6500 metres, we trudged our way up a long glacier known as the Western Cwm (pronounced Coom). The cwm is littered with giant crevasses, some as wide as 10 metres. To cross them, we tiptoed carefully over aluminium ladders lashed together and laid across the black voids below. That glacier is several hundred metres in depth—not the place to lose your balance.

From Camp 2 the route rises steeply up an ice slope known as the Lhotse Face. This is absolutely enormous. It stretches from around 6500 metres to the very summit of Lhotse, almost 2 vertical kilometres above. It is a huge concave expanse of ice, wider than it is high. From a distance, climbers look like fly specks against its vastness. This is the part of the mountain that sorts the pretenders from those with the motivation for the summit.

Hour upon hour, climbers must haul themselves up this slope with their loads balanced on their backs, the steep angle stressing their ankles, calves and thigh muscles to exhaustion, every step into ever-thinning air. At 7300 metres, about halfway up the face, ledges are hacked from the ice for Camp 3, and tents are positioned among small, stable cliffs of ice that, at best, provide scant protection from the threat of avalanches. This camp is so high that you look down at the summit of Pumori. And Camp 3 is barely halfway up Everest.

Above Camp 3, climbers ascend steepening ground, before traversing leftwards up and across the entire Lhotse Face towards Everest. En route, they must overcome a cliff of slippery limestone rock known as the Yellow Band, and a final steep and shattered cliff called the Geneva Spur before staggering onto the South Col to place Camp 4 at 7950 metres. A saddle between Lhotse and Everest, the South Col is enormous and would accommodate several football fields. It is relatively flat and provides a great point from which expeditions can launch their summit attempts. But it is fearfully cold and almost constantly windy, as it provides a convenient passage for weather systems to move between the mountains.

We followed the same process of ferrying loads to higher camps, acclimatising as we did so, until all four camps were in place. It was exhausting work and we frequently returned to Base Camp to rest for a couple of days, as physical recovery is much better there than at higher altitudes.

While chilling out at base camp, I met the Kazakhstani mountaineer Anatoli Bukreev, who was climbing with a French expedition. Ethnically a Russian, Anatoli was powerfully built, and he soon proved that his reputation as a very strong climber at high altitude was no myth. He had been a member of the 1989 Russian expedition that had completed the first traverse of the four peaks of Kanchenjunga. Technically, a mountain may have only one summit, but Kanchenjunga has four distinct peaks, all above 8000 metres. Traversing all four was a superb mountaineering achievement. Before coming to Everest in 1991, he had just completed a new route on the West Wall of Dhaulagiri, another 8000er.

A few weeks into our expedition, I had the opportunity to observe him in his element. While I was climbing from Camp 2 to Camp 3, at around 7000 metres' altitude, I was stunned to be overtaken by Anatoli, who was carrying twice my load. Even more amazingly, though, he was wearing only a pair of sneakers on his feet, while I was clumping my way up in a pair of heavily insulated mountain boots.

Clearly unflappable by nature, Anatoli had a quiet temperament and a ready smile. Most evenings at Base Camp he'd play his guitar and sing mournful Russian folk songs in the French team's dining tent. I didn't understand the words but loved the melodies. One night I asked him what he was singing about. In heavily accented English, he said, 'I sing that the winter is cold, the snow is deep, the cattle is dead, the crops is failed, my wife is leave me and my children is in the war, but … life is okay.'

I soon discovered that the expedition cooks were also doing their best to amuse us, mainly through their interpretation of westerners' diets. They developed the idea, probably after we showed them how to cook a pizza, that we liked cheese melted over the top of everything. On more than one occasion our cook served us a chocolate cake or apple pie with melted yak's cheese on top. The quality food in Base Camp, though, was a far cry from our diet on the mountain.

I'd been on several expeditions to mountains with summits that rose above 6000 or 7000 metres. On those trips I'd found it easy to eat most things, because the altitude of our camps had not been too extreme. But Everest introduced me to the harsh realities of *living* at the altitudes of those summits as we struggled towards a far higher peak. Eating above Base Camp was almost impossible, as was sleeping. Cooking food and melting snow to drink meant using precious canisters of gas. The human body can't digest protein at altitude, and does a pretty poor job of absorbing nutrients generally, so we ate mostly biscuits and saved the gas for tea. The recommended fluid intake at these altitudes is 8 litres per day, due to the extremely dry air and constant exertion of six to eight hours of climbing. At best we were able to melt around 3 litres each per day. We were constantly nauseous, with splitting headaches from the altitude and dehydration. On the odd occasion that we did eat, more often than not we threw it straight back up. We could literally see our bodies withering.

The other new experience for me was the intense cold of high altitude. Not having sufficient oxygen to survive meant that we couldn't generate adequate body heat to stay warm. To compensate, we wore numerous layers of clothing—long heavyweight thermal underwear, then a layer of fleece and then a down vest. At the lower altitudes we wore a windproof suit over the top of these layers, but above 7000 metres, substituted it with a massive, down-filled suit. It was like climbing in a sleeping bag. Yet still we were chilled to the core.

Despite all the obstacles though, we were focussed and loved the experience. We were on Everest!

We made steady progress up the mountain as we acclimatised. One day, however, Groom was working with the French team high on the Lhotse Face, fixing ropes from Camp 3 across the Yellow Band towards Camp 4, while Ian, Mark and I were at Camp 2, around a thousand metres below. With binoculars, we could just make out the tiny figures on the massive mountain face. Suddenly an avalanche let go from the slopes above them. We watched, fascinated but helpless, as a wave of snow rolled inexorably down to the climbers, who were frantically trying to run across the slope to avoid the onslaught.

Most of them made it to safety, but one climber did not. The river of white hit him with such force that his rope snapped like string, and he was swept the full 1000 metres down the face, to the glacier below. Down at Camp 2 we waited, hearts in our mouths, as the snow cloud slowly cleared, revealing two black dots amid the ice debris at the base of the Lhotse face. We didn't know who'd been avalanched, but it was a climber, or climbers, so we raced to help.

In the rarefied air it took us twenty minutes to get to the face. We shuffled and struggled as fast as we could, filled with dread at the thought of what we'd find. Incredibly, as we approached, one of the black dots started moving. We soon realised it was Groom. He was battered, bruised and concussed but okay. The other black dot turned out to be his backpack. Groom was able to walk, so we escorted him back to Camp 2, wrapped him in a sleeping bag and tended to his many grazes and bruises. After a couple of days' rest he descended to Base Camp, his expedition over.

Groom's survival was unprecedented. Everyone else who has fallen so far down that face has been killed, and usually ended up inside the massive bergschrund between the bottom of the Lhotse Face and the Western Cwm. He probably survived because we were climbing in the post-monsoon season, which meant that the Lhotse Face had a good covering of snow. He had a relatively soft ride. The bergschrund was filled in, so he tumbled right over the top of it. By rights, he should have been broken into little pieces but, miraculously, he had survived. Some Sherpas said that he'd left one life and begun a new one.

Groom's injuries were not even the worst from the incident. While he had been caught in the middle of the face, other climbers, who'd made it to the side of the slope and out of the path of the avalanche, had nonetheless been attached to the same rope that had snapped. The violent jarring of the rope caused them to lose their footing. One was knocked from his stance and fell several metres, landing on the leader of the French expedition. The twelve steel points of the falling climber's crampons, so effective at penetrating hard ice, sliced neatly through the Frenchman's skin and bone, badly injuring him. What followed was a long and difficult evacuation, as his team lowered him down the face.

Our much smaller team was soon reduced to two because Mark hadn't acclimatised well. This meant that only Ian and I would attempt the summit. We climbed to Camp 4, rested for a few hours, then set out at midnight, without oxygen. It was cold, dark and intimidating. At around 8200 metres Ian's headlamp failed. We continued by the light of my headlamp, but at around 8300 metres Ian complained that his hands were freezing and that he had to go down. Without a headlamp, he couldn't see the way.

I had no choice but to give up my own summit attempt and escort him down. We descended all the way to Base Camp over the next few days because, having climbed so high without auxiliary oxygen, I hadn't the strength to launch a second summit attempt without a rest. After a couple of days at Base Camp, I started out again by myself and climbed to about 7000 metres. But by then the mountain had sapped all my strength and I had to face the reality that my expedition was over too.

Still, I reflected, it wasn't a bad first attempt. Without the head-lamp issue we might actually have made it. I was disappointed but not put off, and I resolved to return and complete the challenge.

*

Soon after I returned to Australia, Tashi Tenzing, a Sherpa who was working for an Australian trekking agency, asked me to help him put together an expedition to Everest for 1993. I learned that Tashi had been approached by two expatriate Macedonians living in Australia, Trajce Aleksov (known as 'Alex') and Dimitar Todorovski, who wanted to go to Everest to recover the body of a friend who'd died high on the mountain a few years earlier. Both were very strong climbers but were unsure how to initiate an expedition from Australia. They'd approached Tashi because they'd seen his name in the media somewhere and assumed he was an experienced climber.

Tashi was a maternal grandson of Tenzing Norgay, who'd made the first ascent of Mount Everest with Edmund Hillary in 1953. Tashi wasn't an experienced climber, but he had worked for an Australian trekking company and had later married one of the

Australian trek leaders. He'd graduated to working as a trek leader and adopted his grandfather's Christian name as his surname.

As he had never actually participated in an Everest expedition, Tashi came to me for help. He proposed that we create a joint Australian–Macedonian expedition. The Macedonians would then be able to achieve their goal, and a few Australian climbers would be able to make their own bids for the summit. Fresh from my recent disappointment, I agreed. It turned out to be a big mistake. It would be the most dysfunctional expedition I would ever go on, and would deteriorate into a sordid episode that ultimately ended in tragedy.

We achieved some minor sponsorship, but the majority of the funding for the expedition came from the Macedonian community in Australia, whose members worked tirelessly to raise the money. While they were doing that, we learned that Tashi had independently approached the watchmaker Rolex and organised sponsorship for himself. I was our expedition treasurer, and after this I started to get a bad feeling about the whole enterprise.

The team comprised Tashi, a friend of his, Mike Wood, and me, together with the two Macedonian climbers and a friend of theirs, who would come to Base Camp. We agreed the Macedonians would recover their friend while the rest of us climbed to the summit, and we would share resources and logistics and work together to achieve both outcomes.

I agreed to Tashi being the expedition leader, on paper, as that was likely to attract more media attention and sponsorship. It turned out to be a disastrous move. Tashi, using the paper authority of his position, began making other arrangements without our knowledge. He invited Michael Groom to join our expedition for free, and then agreed to allow a very inexperienced climber, David Hume, to buy his way onto the expedition for about $15,000. Tashi also arranged for one of his uncles, Lobsang Bhotia, a Sherpa living in Darjeeling, to join the expedition as a team member.

I saw no reason to offer Michael a free trip when the rest of us were working hard to raise funds for the expedition. It was clear, though, that Tashi was hoping Michael would help get him to the summit. David was a different issue. Despite bringing some valuable income to the expedition, his inexperience meant that he would need careful supervision on the mountain. Only Tashi's uncle Lobsang brought any real benefit to the group, as he was a strong and experienced climber. He would climb as a team member, not as a support Sherpa.

The dramas didn't end there. We planned to use oxygen for the ascent, so I researched and found an American supplier of a new system called POISK. But before I made the purchase, Tashi advised me that an uncle of his in Nepal had a supply of the same oxygen, left over from another expedition, which we could get for a cheaper price. He guaranteed us that it was exactly the same system. When we arrived in Nepal, though, we found out that it wasn't the same system at all. The bottles were too small and too heavy, meaning that it would be impossible to carry enough of them to get us to the summit and back on a continuous flow.

Despite all these issues, the expedition went forward and we travelled to Base Camp in April 1993. But our group remained disjointed and there was constant acrimony between the team members, particularly between Tashi and me. The team split into factions: Tashi, his uncle Lobsang and Michael Groom in one; me, David Hume and the two Macedonians in the other. I found the whole thing extremely distasteful and not at all in the spirit of mountaineering.

As expected, David struggled on the mountain. One day, after we'd carried loads from Camp 2 to Camp 3, he returned six hours after the rest of us, stating he'd never been on such steep terrain. In reality, that face was only 30 to 40 degrees. This is not to speak ill of David; he was just inexperienced. But that inexperience meant that he needed constant supervision, which affected everyone else's climbing ambitions. Tashi and Michael weren't interested in watching over him, and so it was left to me and the Macedonians to keep him alive.

As with all things, though, there was good among the bad. The Macedonians were great guys and David, in particular, provided some rich entertainment at base camp. One day he decided to have a haircut. Several of us offered to do it for him but he insisted on doing it himself. What could go wrong? I found the first-aid kit and we sat down to await the inevitable, which came soon enough when he tried to cut through a particularly thick clump of hair, only to find out that it was his ear. Luckily, he hadn't cut it off, but he had snipped it in half.

At base camp I met Michael Rheinberger, a veteran Australian Everest expeditioner. Mike was considerably older than me, perhaps in his fifties, and had made seven Everest undertakings over the years without ever reaching the summit. He'd tried different sides and different routes, but there had always been something to prevent him from reaching the top. He could see that our expedition was a complete disaster, and he kindly shared a cup of tea with me every now and then. He was the wise old man of the mountain, and our chats gave me enough motivation to continue with the climb.

Despite the disharmony, or perhaps because of it, I became determined to ensure that the Macedonians were treated as equals. Since we had the wrong oxygen system, there wasn't enough of it for both teams. I located some spare tanks in a Russian expedition, which I bought for Alex and Dimitar, and it turned out to be a better system than the one we'd bought earlier.

I found myself climbing predominately with Alex and Dimitar. While Alex was strong at altitude, Dimitar struggled, and they reached a decision to abandon their attempt to locate their friend's body, as Alex couldn't manage it by himself. This was particularly disappointing for him, because Alex was a national mountaineering hero in Macedonia, and there was considerable expectation that he would recover his comrade's body. It was the right decision in the circumstances, though.

Rather than give up on the mountain, Alex was still keen to climb. I'd come to like and respect him more and more throughout the journey. He was the most generous person and enthusiastic climber I'd met. We agreed to climb together for the top.

For the summit push, the factions climbed independently. Groom, Lobsang and Tashi were in the first group, to be followed the next day by me, Alex and David. Lobsang and Tashi used the oxygen system sold to us by Tashi's uncle, but the bottles were so small and heavy that it was impossible to carry enough oxygen to complete the climb and return safely.

As the first group made its attempt on the summit from Camp 4 on the South Col, my team climbed from Camp 3 to Camp 4, so that we would be in a position to go for the top the next day. A couple of hundred metres above Camp 3, at around 7500 metres, we met Tashi coming down from the South Col, using oxygen. He told us that snow blindness had stopped him on his way to the summit in the middle of night. Somehow, it appeared, he was miraculously cured in the harsh light of day.

Tashi told us that he'd climbed with Lobsang to 8300 metres but that when he'd given up, Lobsang had continued for the summit, despite the inappropriate oxygen system.

Alex and I kept climbing and arrived at Camp 4 in the early afternoon, where we sheltered in our tent and spent hours melting snow to drink. Just as the pot was full of water, David arrived. We yelled at him not to enter but he didn't seem to understand, perhaps because of the bandage on his ear. He dived into the tent, knocking over 3 litres of water, which soaked our sleeping bags, down clothing and everything else before freezing almost instantly. Frozen clothing does not insulate at all well, and I might have taken an ice axe to David's head if Groom hadn't returned to camp at just that moment, having successfully reached the summit.

Too exhausted to speak at first, he needed assistance. Disconcertingly, Lobsang was still high on the mountain but Groom didn't know whether he was okay or not. As the day closed, a wind storm developed, which prevented us from going up to look for him.

The storm persisted into the next morning, so all the other teams, as well as Groom and Hume, descended to lower camps. Alex and I stayed at Camp 4, hoping for a break in the weather so we could search for Lobsang. We thought that he might have taken shelter in a tent on the Balcony, which was several hundred metres higher and hosted a rarely utilised Camp 5 that another expedition had installed.

It was now our second day above 8000 metres and we were feeling the effects of our long stay, but the storm eased a little and we took turns to go out and search. Late in the afternoon Alex found Lobsang's body at the bottom of the face above the South Col. His oxygen mask and regulator were in his backpack, meaning that, as we suspected, he had run out of oxygen. He would have saved the mask and regulator because of their value. Once out of oxygen, it seemed likely that he'd suffered severe hypoxia and made some kind of mistake that led to him falling down the face.

What a waste. Lobsang had made his own choice to continue when Tashi had given up, but he did so with an inappropriate oxygen system. I wonder if his family in Darjeeling were ever told why the expedition had been using the wrong oxygen equipment?

It was too late in the day for Alex and me to descend, so we were forced to spend another night on the South Col, despite the likelihood that the altitude would incapacitate us. By morning, we were so fatigued from our long stay at 8000 metres that we literally crawled down the mountain to a safer altitude. Lobsang's body was later recovered and cremated according to Sherpa custom.

After a few days' rest at base camp, I made ready for another attempt, but David insisted that if I went back up, he would also try again. While I respected his tenacity, I believed that it could only result in another accident, so I abandoned my plan. Thus ended, thankfully, the worst expedition I have ever taken part in. The only good to have come from it was the friendship I established with Alex. We went on to become the best of mates, and still are to this day.

I returned home angry and disenchanted. I'd joined a disparate group of individuals, not a unified, functioning team. I made a decision that, from then on, I would only climb big Himalayan peaks with friends or climbers with whom I'd already climbed elsewhere. This may have been idealistic—perhaps too much so—but the events I'd witnessed fired my resolve to never allow such a tragedy to occur again.

Postscript

Unfortunately, Mike Rheinberger failed to summit during his 1993 attempt on Everest. He returned yet again in 1994, this time with a professional guide, and together they made a documentary of their climb. Finally, after eight expeditions, Mike achieved his dream and stood on the summit of Mount Everest. On the descent, however, he succumbed to cerebral oedema and collapsed. He and his guide bivouacked high on the mountain, but by morning Mike was in a coma, and the guide had to be rescued. Tragically, Mike died and never had the chance to enjoy his summit.

In 1995, David Hume, against my strong advice, launched his own Himalayan expedition to climb another of the 8000ers, Mount Makalu. He reached the summit but made a basic mistake during the descent and was killed in a fall.

3

THE SAVAGE MOUNTAIN

Climb if you will, but remember that courage and strength are naught without prudence, and that a momentary negligence may destroy the happiness of a lifetime. Do nothing in haste, look well to each step, and from the beginning think what may be the end.

Edward Whymper

M Y NEWFOUND CLIMBING resolution would soon be tested. Before going to Everest, I'd applied for a permit to climb K2 during the Pakistan climbing season of June to August. Standing 8612 metres high, and second only to Everest in altitude, K2 is generally considered to be the hardest mountain to climb on Earth. Apart from its altitude and generally poor weather, it is extremely steep and requires excellent technical-climbing ability. I hoped that by coming straight from Everest I'd be well acclimatised and really fit, and would therefore have a pretty good chance of making it to the top.

A mighty and intimidating massif, K2, like so many of its peers, has a controversial history of skulduggery, triumph and tragedy. It received its unusual name in 1852 during the Great Trigonometric

Survey of India, when it was assigned the designation 'K' for the Karakoram Range and '2' since it was the second peak to be surveyed in that range. It is completely coincidental that it is also the second-highest peak in the world.

K2 was almost the first 8000er ever to be climbed, when an American team attempted the ascent in 1939. Expedition leader Fritz Wiessner, a German who lived in the United States, climbed to within 250 metres of the summit, at which point his climbing partner, a Nepalese Sherpa, begged him to stop as he was fearful of mountain spirits that might come with the onset of darkness. They agreed to continue climbing in the morning, but by then the weather had deteriorated and they'd missed their chance. On the descent, four members of the team were killed.

In 1953, just weeks after Edmund Hillary and Tenzing Norgay successfully summitted Everest, another American expedition launched a bid for the summit of K2. One of the members, Art Gilkey, developed blood clots and the team abandoned their climb to lower him down the mountain. During their descent, the able-bodied climbers left Gilkey anchored to the snow while they reconnoitred a safe route down. When the climbers returned to get Gilkey he had disappeared. It seems likely that he was swept away by an avalanche, although a theory exists that he threw himself from the mountain to allow the others to save themselves. Today, a memorial cairn at the base of the mountain is known as the Gilkey Memorial and, sadly, it is now adorned with many, many plaques in memory of climbers since lost on this killer mountain.

The mountain's summit was finally achieved by an Italian expedition in 1954, but the ascent was mired in controversy. One of the mountaineering legends of that era, Walter Bonatti, supported the summit pair in their push for the top by carrying oxygen up to the high camp for the summiteers to use. But the summiteers later claimed that Bonatti had either used or released some of the oxygen from the cylinders due to his jealousy of not being a member of the summit team, and that they would not have succeeded except for their own incredible fortitude. Bonatti denied this but was ostracised for decades. He was exonerated only when one of the summiteers, Lino Lacadelli, wrote his memoir fifty years after the event, admitting that Bonatti had done nothing wrong. Understandably, there was little forgiveness from Bonatti.

The mountain's most infamous season occurred in 1986. Thirteen climbers, including some of world's best alpinists at the time, perished as a result of falls, avalanches, crevasses and altitude sickness after being trapped by a storm high on the mountain; thus earning K2 the nickname 'Savage Mountain'.

*

Once I was back in Australia after the Everest climb, my intended climbing partner for K2 told me that he could no longer go. I was really disappointed. I had no one else to climb the mountain with and, given the mountain's fearsome reputation, I knew that I needed to climb with a skilled partner. It also meant that I would lose the $3000 I'd paid to the Pakistan government for the expedition permit—a hefty amount of money. I resigned myself to having to try again the following year. Just weeks before the climbing season began, however, my trekking agent in Pakistan told me of a German expedition that needed another member, because one of their team had dropped out.

I was dubious. I'd just sworn to myself that I would not climb with people I didn't know, but the agent then told me that the team actually comprised three Germans and the mighty Russian climber Anatoli Boukreev. This changed my mind and I accepted.

My flight to Islamabad in late June 1993 was uneventful, although I did have some new experiences. Despite sitting in a non-smoking row, I found it a little difficult to see whether the seatbelt sign was illuminated or not, due to the voluminous clouds of cigarette smoke that billowed across from the smoking rows in front and behind. I decided against making a comment when I saw that the passengers on either side of me, in the one non-smoking row on the entire plane, were also using the dying butts of their last cigarettes to light the next ones. In any case, it appeared the seatbelt sign didn't work.

I was enlightened as to my fellow passengers' general perspective on fate, however, when we started our descent from the skies. The stewardess announced, 'Ladies and gentlemen, *Insha'Allah*'— meaning 'God willing', or 'by the grace of God'—'we shall shortly be landing at Islamabad International Airport.' I hoped that the pilot would have something to do with it, but I was also thankful that God was both willing and graceful that day.

Stepping off the plane was an incredible shock. The temperature was well over 40 degrees Celsius, and the humidity in the high nineties. It was like being thrown into an overheated sauna and within seconds I was drenched in sweat.

I soon caught up with Anatoli and the Germans at our hotel. Reinmar Joswig and Peter Metzger, both aged fifty-one, were the joint leaders of the expedition, and their friend Ernst Erberhardt, fifty, was the other member. We also met a Pakistani Army officer, Captain Asif Rashid, who was to be our Liaison Officer throughout the expedition. He would accompany us on the trek to base camp and remain with us to assist in our negotiations with porters and the local mountain people. He would also ensure that we abided by the mountaineering regulations set by the Ministry of Tourism.

After receiving the usual briefings from the ministry, we travelled to the northern town of Skardu, the last significant settlement on our way to the mountain. While the rest of us trusted in God again and took a quick 30-minute flight, Peter drew the short straw and set off up the tortuous Karakorum Highway in a decrepit but garishly painted truck with all our expedition equipment.

This road, known to many as the KKH, was a joint project between Pakistan and China. It is the highest paved highway in the world, and the main thoroughfare from Islamabad to its northern neighbour. Around 1300 kilometres long and built over a period of nearly twenty years in the 1960s and 1970s—with 35,000 workers and more than 800 deaths—it winds its way through precipitous rock and dirt mountains that are all but bare of vegetation. The road clings to dangerously loose slopes, often unsuccessfully, and carries you above seemingly bottomless gorges that are lined with thundering torrents of water. Many trucks, buses and other vehicles have ended their days—and those of their passengers—in these gorges, as they clawed their way tortuously to a high point of 4700 metres on the Kunjerab Pass, the border between the two countries.

Despite the danger, or perhaps because of it, the KKH is an exciting ride through wild and remote villages, whose grubby streets are lined with even grubbier occupants. Many sport home-made versions of military weaponry, and offer none-too-friendly glances at passing westerners. Such is the frontier-like nature of the KKH that many vehicles travel in convoy to lessen the risk of being robbed by bandits en route. The imposing presence of Nanga Parbat—another of the 8000ers, which looms above the highway near Chilas, the most disreputable village of them all— seems positively sanctuary-like by comparison.

Our flight up to Skardu diverted around Nanga Parbat rather than going over it, such is the height of this Himalayan massif. With cameras clicking incessantly, we identified possible routes and began hatching plans to return and climb that beast. Such is the thrilling lure of these monoliths to mountaineers that, even before we'd faced the challenge of K2, we buzzed with excitement at the sight of another big mountain.

Although Skardu is relatively close to the Karakorum mountain range, it is baking hot in summer, so T-shirts, shorts and sandals are the dress code. After we had settled into our basic but comfortable hotel, the beat of a helicopter soon drew our attention to the nearby landing field. A short time later its passengers revealed themselves: two injured Slovenian climbers who'd been badly frostbitten in a storm on K2 a few days earlier and their expedition doctor. Another teammate had died and they'd had to leave him in a tent at Camp 4.

In truth, I was unsure just who had been less fortunate. The two young survivors were both terribly frostbitten and would later have all their fingers and toes amputated. It was gut-wrenching to see these two men, who'd no doubt come to the mountain with great aspirations and dreams of conquest, invalided for life. The younger lad, who was only about twenty, found it difficult to walk because his footwear did not fit over his heavily bandaged feet. When he looked dolefully at my sandals, I realised I had no option but to give them to him. I spent the rest of the expedition worrying about what I'd wear if I suffered the same fate.

Peter arrived a few days later, simultaneously wide-eyed from his experience on the KKH but also semi-comatose from lack of sleep. While he collapsed into a twenty-four hour stupor, the others and I finalised the arrangements for our departure the next morning. We'd spent the preceding days engaging a cook for our Base Camp, as well as support staff and a *sirdar*. We'd also purchased kerosene, food and kitchen equipment, and had organised jeeps to drive us to the remote village of Askole, the starting point for our trek to base camp.

The next morning we set off in three jeeps. We, the *sahibs*, were in one, and the other two vehicles were for the porters we would engage while passing through the desolate villages along the way. While our *sirdar* selected the more able-bodied applicants—about a hundred villagers would surround him and clamour until he agreed to employ the lot of them—I ducked into the local café. These usually comprised a mud hut, a rickety table with even more rickety stools out the front and, in the more salubrious establishments, a piece of rusty corrugated iron overhead to protect you from the debilitating sun. A cup of their finest was often a small glass of strong, hot, milky and very sweet tea, accompanied by a slab of naan bread that was steaming hot and straight from the tandoori oven. There is no better bread in the world—smoky, buttery, melt-in-your-mouth. The typical wood-fired oven in these parts creates a unique flavour that simply cannot be replicated by our high-tech western kitchen gadgets.

Unlike in Nepal, where the trek to a mountain base camp usually moves through villages that are dotted along the route, expeditions in the Karakorum start their long trek from the last village and must then be completely self-sufficient. As well as the porters we employed to carry our expedition equipment, we needed porters to carry provisions for them. Amazingly, for our seven-week expedition, which comprised just five climbers and two Base Camp staff, we needed 120 porters, each of whom would carry a 25-kilogram load. That meant a total of 3 tonnes of food and equipment.

We couldn't transport all the additional porters to Askole in the two spare jeeps we had, so we arranged additional vehicles. Thus, several more jeeps groaned into our camp one evening, bristling like porcupines with their laughing, singing cargo—there were twenty or more men in a single jeep. These people must be the toughest on the planet. Desperately poor, eking out an existence from land that's drier than the Australian outback, living in squalor with virtually no education or access to health services, yet quick to laugh and to share their last piece of naan, they are the most fiercely proud people I have ever met.

The next morning, after some heated debate about wages, the porters lined up to sign their employment contracts with a thumbprint from an inkpad, after which they queued for their loads. As well as a 25-kilogram plastic drum or cardboard box of equipment, they had to carry their own personal gear, but that generally consisted of a blanket and not much else. Pakistan's mountaineering regulations required that we supply specified rations and equipment to the porters, which consisted of meat, flour, salt, lentils, sugar, tea and tobacco. Shoes, socks, gloves and glacier glasses to protect our employees' eyes complemented these rations. While the basic food items were easy to obtain and preserve, meat was another issue, so we purchased three live goats and hired a goat herder to shepherd the animals until they hit the cooking pots.

*

The trek from Askole to K2 Base Camp takes about ten days. After moving through dry fields and rocky escarpments, we crossed several glacial torrents fed by the distant mountains towards which we were so hungrily marching. Despite the freezing water of the rivers, the air temperature in these lower valleys was absolutely searing, as the sun's rays blazed down from cloudless skies and then reflected off the polished rock slabs that extended for thousands of metres above and around us.

Three days into the trek, we camped in a wood called Paiju, just short of the mouth of the Baltoro Glacier. From that point on we could have no fires, so the porters took the opportunity to prepare their food for the rest of the trek. They'd have kerosene stoves on the glacier to heat water for their tea but preferred to cook the food here, so they could carry only the minimum amount of fuel. They cooked lentils and made *roti*, a round flatbread similar to damper, and transformed poor 'Billy' and his two brothers into piles of fresh meat. This was divided among the 120 porters by hand but with more accuracy than the best butcher's scales. Woe betide the poor fellow charged with sharing out the spoils if it was deemed that so much as goat's whisker more fell on someone else's pile!

The slaughtering of the goats and preparation of the other food was a cause for celebration among the porters, and all were in great spirits as the evening approached. At dusk I wandered down to the small rock enclosures in which the porters camped and was honoured when I was offered some of Billy's freshly cooked liver— a real delicacy. I ate only a little so as not to deprive the workers, but I appreciated the gesture.

As I moved among the men, chatting with them in my very basic Urdu, I heard a most incredible sound. One porter had moved away from the main camp and was singing the Islamic call to prayer. His was the singularly most soulful, lilting male voice I have ever heard in song. In the eerie dusk of the Karakorum wilderness it was immensely moving. The sound seemed to emanate from nature itself. It was a heartfelt invitation for his brothers to join him in devotion, and for the pious it would have been impossible to resist. Indeed, I wanted to join them just to observe, but thought it would not have been appropriate so I returned to camp.

Later that evening, the porters returned from prayer and resumed their celebrations. Soon a small group of them had circled one of the fires and started singing their local folk songs. Without instruments, they clapped their hands and used a plastic barrel as a drum while taking turns to sing the verses. More joined the circle and the volume of the singing increased. They took turns to dance in the middle, and this continued for many hours. Once more, I was impressed by the resilience of these people, and by their capacity to find joy even in the most inhospitable environments.

The following day we moved on to the Baltoro Glacier, a massive river of ice that runs for 62 kilometres from the very heart of the Karakorum Mountains. We would walk its full length over several days, before moving on to another glacier, the Godwin-Austen, for the final day's trek to Base Camp at K2. On the Baltoro, I found it hard not to trip and stumble, because my eyes were constantly drawn upwards to the incredible rock spires on either side of us. All had inspiring names—Trango Towers, Uli Biaho, Muztagh Tower, Mitre Peak and Masherbrum—and all towered thousands of metres above our heads.

We took a rest and acclimatisation day at the campsite of Urdukas, on the side of the glacier and gratefully replaced our walking boots with runners, as there were several large boulders that demanded to be climbed. We also took the opportunity to issue the sunglasses to our porters, as we anticipated trekking on snow the following day. The glasses were definitely not the latest styles from Ray-Ban, but you wouldn't have known it from the excitement our porters showed. They were men who had virtually no possessions, so this small gift was of immense value to them. They refused to take the stickers off the lenses, and even kept the sunglasses on at night.

After several more days trekking we reached Concordia, the confluence of the Baltoro and Godwin-Austen glaciers. Inconceivably, the vista at this point only got better, as Concordia is almost crushed beneath the overwhelming magnitude of four 8000-metre peaks—K2, Broad Peak, Gasherbrum 1 and Gasherbrum 2. There are also several other peaks that just fail to touch that magical altitude. Nowhere else on Earth will you find so many high peaks in such concentration.

We reached Base Camp on 6 July, only to learn that K2 had claimed another casualty just days before. An American–Canadian expedition had successfully reached the summit, but one of their team had fallen to his death during their descent. K2 was living up to her reputation as the Savage Mountain.

*

After depositing our loads on the glacier at Base Camp, our porters collected their pay and raced back down the glacier to their villages, either to toil in their fields or find work with other expeditions.

We wouldn't see them again until we sent a message at the end of the expedition to return and collect us.

I soon discovered that my teammates were on a mission to climb the mountain as quickly as possible. They were keen to commence immediately, which conflicted with my preferred style of taking a couple of rest and acclimatisation days upon arrival at Base Camp. Having joined the expedition in Pakistan, I'd missed the opportunity to contribute to the planning, so I was only just learning about their climbing style. Luckily, I still had some residual acclimatisation from the Everest expedition a few weeks earlier, so I adjusted to the altitude well.

Our route on the mountain was the Abruzzi Ridge, named after an Italian explorer who had made an aborted attempt on the mountain some eighty-four years earlier. The Abruzzi is a beautiful but dangerous route. Climbing over 3300 vertical metres from Base Camp to the summit, you are exposed to severe weather, rockfall, crevasses, avalanches, serac collapses and, of course, extreme altitude. What more could you want?

Our plan was to ascend the mountain in traditional siege style, placing well-stocked camps all the way up the mountain to safeguard both our summit attempt and our subsequent descent. Lots of gear was needed at various points up the mountain, and the only way to get it there was to carry it on our backs, as we had no high-altitude porters—the Pakistan equivalent of climbing Sherpas—to assist us.

Each day we rose around 4 a.m., had a quick cup of tea and a bowl of porridge and made the two-hour walk up the glacier to the start of the climb. We would climb for around six hours to reach Camp 1, then deposit our loads and return to Base Camp by about 5 p.m. each afternoon. Dinner, sleep and do it again. After a week we had stocked Camp 1 with everything we needed both for that camp and for the ones above it, so we moved up, occupied the camp and started the same process up to Camp 2.

While Camp 1 was on reasonably flat ground, being perched on a little knoll that jutted out from the mountain face, the climb to Camp 2 was steep and technical. The crux of this part of the mountain was 30 metres of climbing known as House's Chimney, named after an American climber from a 1938 attempt on K2. Once above that cliff—and by now at 6700 metres' altitude—we hacked out of the ice on the steep mountain face a site for Camp 2.

By the time we'd fully stocked this camp, we'd been on the go for almost two weeks without a break. I was in real need of a couple of rest days at Base Camp, but the Germans would have none of it. Although I thought we were at risk of burning out, we were making good progress up the mountain and were quickly passing the high points of the several other expeditions that were climbing K2 that year.

For the most part, the other teams waited at Base Camp for a spell of good weather. We'd been climbing in consistently foul weather, and had been hammered every day by freezing winds and driving snow. Our plan was to overcome the low-altitude difficulties during the bad weather, position ourselves high on the mountain by the time the good weather came, and thereby give ourselves the strongest chance of reaching the summit. It was a sound philosophy but exhausting.

K2 is infamous for having some of the worst weather in the Himalaya and Karakorum Mountains. Standing alone and so tall, it interrupts weather systems to generate wild windstorms and massive snow dumps. Typical weather for the region during the climbing season is to have several days of good weather followed by five or so of storms. There is no such pattern on K2, and weeks of bad weather are not at all uncommon. Years have passed without a single ascent of the mountain due to its tough conditions.

As it happened, the Germans' plan to push on without respite was thwarted unexpectedly, and very nearly tragically. Climbing from Camp 2 to Camp 3, we encountered the most technically difficult part of the Abruzzi Ridge, known as the Black Pyramid. This 400-metre face of evil-looking black rock requires steep, sustained rock and ice climbing at an altitude of 7000 metres. Yet again we climbed in a blizzard as we forced our way upward, clinging to loose, often vertical, rock. We scrabbled to find purchase on the wet, snow-covered ledges with our crampons. When we finally flopped onto the easier snow slope above, where we would later erect our Camp 3 tents, we stayed long enough only to bury our loads, to prevent them from being blown off the mountain, then marked the spot with a bamboo wand before descending back into the tempest.

It was dusk when we reached our nylon tents at Camp 2, which were barely withstanding the gale. We quickly fired up the stoves to heat some tea while waiting for Reinmar, who was still coming down the ropes. He was 30 metres above the rest of us when we entered the tents, but half an hour later he had still not arrived. I went out to check what the problem was and, to my surprise, he was nowhere to be seen on the slopes above.

Then I spotted him, 20 metres below, flailing groggily in the snow. I dropped down to find him bleeding severely from the head, concussed and unable to speak clearly. After getting him back up to the tent, we established that, just before entering the tent, he'd been struck by a falling stone, knocking him unconscious and causing him to fall. Incredibly, he'd landed in a tiny patch of snow. Had he been even a couple of metres to either side, he'd have hit steep rock and kept on bouncing down to Base Camp, 1.5 kilometres below.

Reinmar had actually been the only member of the team to refuse to wear a helmet as we climbed that day. While he would regret that decision, a part of me was somewhat grateful for it because the following day we had to help him down to Base Camp. He received a few stiches to his wound, administered by a friendly member of a British expedition, and was obliged to rest for several days. I was only too happy to assist, and I slept and ate solidly for the next three days.

The rest also gave us time to socialise with the other expeditions, and I found out that the leader of the British expedition, Roger Payne, and his wife, Julie Ann Clyma, were the two lucky avalanche survivors I'd seen outrun that massive serac collapse on Mount McKinley in 1991. This is one of the aspects of extreme mountaineering that I have always enjoyed. The community is reasonably small, so it's quite common to run into friends with whom you've shared great climbs or who have survived major catastrophes. There's a real sense of camaraderie. I suppose most friendships born of adversity have strong bonds.

The break at Base Camp allowed me to spend some more time with Anatoli, who for the majority of our climb so far had been sharing a tent with Reinmar, while I was sharing one with Peter and Ernst. Anatoli had a wicked sense of humour and was quick to bait anyone less easygoing than himself. As it turned out, that was Peter. It was Anatoli's habit to eat honey by the spoonful—the jarful, actually—but that meant double dipping his spoon, which was something Peter could not abide. All too frequently, Peter could be heard in the meal tent, saying, 'Anatoli, please don't put your dirty spoon back in the honey jar! *Ja*?'

Anatoli's response, after sucking his spoon clean, would be to ever so laconically reach out, with a slow but inevitable movement, and dip it back into the honey jar, with a deadpan face but a sparkle in his eyes.

I was less fussed by his manners, and I enjoyed learning about the highly regimented communist climbing bureaucracy through which Anatoli had persevered to satisfy his mountaineering passion. With the collapse of the Soviet Union in 1991, it had become much easier for him to travel, and he'd since spent considerable time in the United States. Over yet another miel *fest*, which he enhanced by chewing cloves of raw garlic ('Good for blood, Andre'), Anatoli told me of one his recent American experiences.

Although he was by nature fairly shy, Anatoli was an international mountaineering celebrity, so he had agreed to be interviewed by an American journalist. He arranged to meet the journalist at an all-you-can-eat restaurant, which suited Anatoli as he had little money and a big appetite. The journalist, an attractive young woman, waited patiently while Anatoli finished one serve of food and then another. She then began to speak, but he held up his hand and took his empty plate back to the buffet. This went on for quite some time. Finally, Anatoli indicated that the journalist could ask her first question, which was, innocently enough, 'What brings you out of the mountains to civilisation today?'

Anatoli leaned forward, a hungry look still in his eyes, and said, 'I come down for food … and woman.'

Having seen what he'd just done with the food, the journalist was up and out of the restaurant in seconds. She never contacted him again.

*

After three days of rest, our interpretation of the weather indicated that a good spell might finally be approaching K2, so we agreed to start our summit bid the next morning. Two days of climbing saw us arrive at Camp 2, only to find that it had been all but destroyed by gale-force winds. We had spare tents, but the real disaster was that Peter's sleeping bag had been blown away. His expedition appeared over, but then Ernst offered his sleeping bag to Peter, so he would be able to continue.

Ernst had been the weakest member of our team, because he had been struggling in the high altitude. We all knew that he had the least chance of reaching the summit, which was still several difficult days of climbing above us. Offering Peter his sleeping bag was the right thing to do, but it was still a hugely magnanimous gesture, and indicative of his very strong friendship with Peter.

Ernst descended to Base Camp while the rest of us settled into our new tents, but that night a howling gale blew in. The wind wailed throughout the night and the following day. Sleep was impossible, our nerves were on edge and boredom was at an all-time high.

On the morning of the second day, with the gale still raging, Reinmar shouted from his tent that he and Anatoli were going to continue climbing towards Camp 3. I could see little sense in that, because climbing in such a storm was fraught with frostbite danger. True, when the window of good weather arrived they'd be a day closer to the summit, but if the storm continued they'd be stuck at the higher camp, and getting weaker by the minute. Peter and I decided to stay put.

The wind blew throughout that second day and all we could do was keep warm in our sleeping bags. Finally, on the morning of our third day at Camp 2, the wind eased and the clouds parted to reveal blue skies. We were quickly out of our tent, eager to get on with our summit attempt.

Arriving at Camp 3 that afternoon, we expected to find that the other two had continued up to Camp 4, but they were still there. The climb up from Camp 2 and the subsequent need to dig a snow cave rather than put up a tent in the savage storm had exhausted them so much that they needed a day's rest. It was good to be back together as a team, and the view from our tent at 7300 metres was extraordinary. The Godwin-Austen Glacier was now more than 2 kilometres below us, and the nearby mountain giants of Broad Peak and Gasherbrum 4 seemed like they were almost within reach.

The next day, the four of us pushed up through deep snow across several crevasses, then climbed onto a flattening of the Abruzzi Ridge known as the Shoulder, at an altitude of 7900 metres. There we set up our Camp 4, a short distance from the wind-battered tent that had been abandoned by the badly frostbitten Slovenians some weeks earlier. Their dead friend was still inside. This ridge was incredibly beautiful, with majestic views of nearby mountains and the lofty summit of K2 looming overhead, yet it has been the scene of much tragedy. In 1986 seven climbers had also died here, trapped by a storm. Many others have perished in the same location since then.

In the evening glow, the route to the summit was laid out before us: a steepening slope of snow and ice to a narrow chimney called the Bottleneck, followed by an exposed traverse beneath a massive 100-metre-high serac to a steep snow gully that led up to the long, easier-angled slopes of the summit pyramid, and finally the summit itself. I was excited but also intimidated. I found myself wondering: *Do I actually have what it takes to summit this mountain of mountains?*

As we settled into our tents and started the stoves for an evening meal of soup and cheese with biscuits, a noise alerted us to the arrival of two more climbers. Unbeknownst to us, two members of a Swedish expedition, Daniel Bidner and Rafael Jensen, who was actually a Norwegian, had been following us up the mountain, apparently climbing a few hours behind us each day. Naturally, we were thrilled to have been able to provide the trail for them at our own physical expense!

We hunkered down for a few hours of rest, agreeing to make a start at 2 a.m. My experience on Everest told me that a midnight start would be better, because the extremely rarefied air in which we'd be climbing would slow our rate of ascent to as little as 50 metres an hour. A midnight start would give us twelve hours to climb the 700 vertical metres to K2's 8612-metre summit and still leave us enough time for a safe return to Camp 4 before nightfall. I tried to make this point to Reinmar but failed to convince him.

We rose at midnight to heat a last drink and don our frozen boots. When 2 a.m. finally came, Reinmar felt too cold to begin and demanded that we wait for dawn, which would be at 4 a.m. I was extremely frustrated, but the others agreed to wait. Since I was the outsider on the team, I felt it would only cause friction if I went off by myself, so I lay in my tent for the next two hours. All I could think about was how this delay could cost us the summit. In retrospect, I think Reinmar was still exhausted by the tough climb from Camp 2 to Camp 3 during the blizzard, and successive nights at progressively higher altitude had only sapped him of his strength.

As we waited for the sky to lighten, we divided up the equipment that our group would need on the climb. This included 40 metres of rope, divided into two lengths of 20 metres; two radios; a first-aid kit; spare gloves and goggles; and a small amount of food. Right on four o'clock we were out of the tent and strapping on our crampons. Peter, Reinmar, Anatoli and I were quickly away, the firm snow crunching noisily underfoot in the bitter cold. The Scandinavian pair set off some time after us—again—but as Reinmar's exhaustion slowed his progress, he dropped behind and joined them, effectively forming two groups of three climbers.

Peter, Anatoli and I climbed steadily on the steepening snow and ice for the next few hours, moving up and into the Bottleneck. This couloir extended for nearly 100 metres and steepened to an angle of 75 degrees or more, forcing us to climb delicately on the front points of our crampons. Not anticipating such steep ground, I'd only brought one ice axe, a decision I regretted greatly. If I made even the slightest slip while swinging my axe, I'd be unable to stop my fall down the mountain face.

As we emerged from the Bottleneck, we found perilously loose snow that clung to rock-hard ice. To safeguard our traverse to the left under the enormous ice cliff above us, we needed to fix both of our 20-metre lengths of rope to the ice, but Reinmar had one of the lengths in his backpack. After three hours of climbing, he was now nearly an hour behind us. We had no choice but to wait. We watched, freezing and hanging tenuously from our ice axes, as he made his way ever so slowly up to us.

As soon as Reinmar reached us, we grabbed his rope and attached it to ours, then belayed Anatoli from a safe anchor of ice screws as he led the way across the slope. At the far end he attached the rope to the ice with another ice screw, then Peter and I followed him across. Had there been just the three of us, we'd have retrieved the rope and carried it with us, so we could use it again further up the mountain, but Reinmar and the other two were resting at the lower end and showed no signs of getting a move on.

We couldn't waste any more time. Hoping that they'd bring the ropes with them, we pushed on. This was a mistake that would have devastating consequences.

*

Mountains are funny beasts. On K2 that morning the weather was incredible—windless and sunny. In fact, it was so warm that I took off my inner down vest, leaving just two layers inside my down suit, and clipped it to the last ice screw. To lighten my load by just a few more critical grams, I also left my headlamp and goggles there, since I knew that we'd have a full moon that night. If caught out by darkness, I would be able to climb down to that point by the bright moonlight alone. The downside of that lovely warm sun was that the snow had softened so much that it provided no support whatsoever.

As we moved onto the steep ramp that would take us up beside the ice cliff and towards the final summit ridge, we found ourselves flailing, virtually swimming, in unconsolidated wet muck. Worse, the slope was very steep, and beneath the wet snow was smooth rock into which our crampons could not penetrate a millimetre. For every two feet we clawed our way up, we'd slide back one, two or sometimes even three feet. If we slipped too heavily, we knew we'd fly straight down the slope and over the buttress, perhaps bouncing a couple of times before landing at Base Camp, which was now 3 vertical kilometres below. There would be plenty of time to think about it on the way down. If we'd been able to retrieve the rope that we'd fixed on the traverse underneath the big ice cliff, we could have fixed it here to protect both our ascent and descent. As it was, we just hoped that Reinmar would bring it with him and fix it here himself.

It took hours to force our way up this 100-metre ramp, and it was the most exhausting thing I'd ever done. We were now at an altitude of 8300 metres, and climbing more strenuously than I could have imagined. My lungs heaved to the point that I nearly blacked out, and my heart was pounding so hard that my chest hurt. I honestly expected to have a heart attack at any moment.

At some point I lost track of both time and reality. I forgot the view of the route that I'd seen from our Camp 4 tent and started to imagine that the top of this ramp was actually the summit. The thought that I was so close renewed my energy, and I fought insanely to paddle my way up the snow.

Finally, exhausted beyond words, I reached the top of the slope and fell to my knees. With my last vestiges of strength I could now hold aloft my Australian flag and slap the backs of my friends in celebration. And then I looked up ... and up. What I'd thought was the summit was just the start of yet another long slope that stretched into the sky—the true summit was still hours away. The realisation was soul-destroying. All my exhausted body wanted was to lie on the slope and sleep.

Exhaustion alone was not enough reason to stop. I wasn't on the mountain to nearly summit, I was there to actually summit. Wearily, I stood, faced my opponent and took the next step. I don't know exactly where that strength, that motivation, came from. It was almost painful in its own right. It was certainly tangible. There was never any question of stopping or going down; it didn't even occur to me. I accepted that the pain was going to last for a while longer, and that was that. *Might as well get on with it.*

The angle of the climb was a little kinder now, but the snow on the ridge was shin-deep below a fragile windblown crust. With each step, I'd balance precariously on its surface, praying that it would hold and allow me to take another, but as I'd move forward the crust would collapse and down I'd plunge for a couple of feet. Every step was the same, and my progress was agonisingly slow. I started counting my steps.

'Okay, ten steps and then a rest,' I said aloud. But I couldn't make it. 'Five steps, then. One.' Pant, cough, gag, spit. 'Two.' Pant, pant, wobble. 'Three.' God, I can't make five steps. Pant, pant, pant. 'Come on, get on with it! Four.' Gasping for breath, head reeling. 'C'mon! One more. Five!' I slumped forward over my ice axe, my head spinning and lungs bursting. Panting, constantly panting.

A minute passed, then another. Still panting. 'Okay, get on with it. One …'

At nearly 8600 metres, and without additional oxygen, Peter, Anatoli and I were all now seriously hypoxic. The climb seemed interminable, but at 5 p.m., thirteen long hours after we'd set out from Camp 4, and six hours after I'd mistakenly thought we were near the top, the ridge flattened and we finally stood on the summit. The real summit.

Too tired to cheer, we hugged each other carelessly. I looked around, taking in the row upon row of jagged, icy mountains in every direction, the highest of which was 600 metres lower than K2—just less than the height we'd climbed that day.

We each took photos of the others, one of which I shall always cherish. It is of Anatoli and me, together, on the top. I'd reached the summit of my first 8000-metre mountain, and it was the one generally accepted as the hardest in the world to climb. Not only that, I'd done it with perhaps the strongest high-altitude mountaineer in history. Not a bad way to start the game.

*

We spent twenty minutes on the summit, in beautifully calm conditions. The sun was settling low in the sky and we were certain to be caught by nightfall. I wasn't too fussed by that, knowing that the full moon would soon rise and that the weather was perfect. Peter and Anatoli started their descent back to Camp 4, but I decided to enjoy the view a little longer. My camera clicked away. It was so warm—perhaps only minus 15 degrees Celsius—that when my film ran out I was able to remove my mittens briefly and load a new roll.

As the sun set, the enormous shadow of K2 stretched out for hundreds of kilometres across the Karakorum Mountains and into China. It was the most amazing vista I'd ever experienced. I was aware it was a sight that few in the world would ever see. The astounding beauty made all the pain and hardship I'd put myself through worthwhile.

As I was preparing to begin my descent, the Norwegian, Jensen, arrived on the summit. I took some photos for him and he told me he'd wait for his friend Bidner to summit, as he was close behind. I asked whether his group had moved the rope up from the traverse and fixed it to the steep gully above but he told me no, they'd left it in place under the serac. *Damn.* I began making my way down. About 7 p.m., a little way above the top of the snow ramp that had caused me so much trouble on the way up, I came across Reinmar. He was clearly very tired. I asked him whether he should consider going down but he wasn't in the mood either for the question or for a debate about it.

It was a tough situation. I could see Reinmar would struggle to make it to the top and back to Camp 4, and by then the night was upon us. But I couldn't force him to go down. For a start, I'd probably kill him and me if I tried to fight him down but, more than that, it was obvious he hadn't lost the capacity to make a sound decision, so he had every right to decide to press on. I wished him the best, eased myself over the edge and started down that perilous snow ramp.

What a nightmare. What had been an exhausting, painful ascent now became a desperate fight not to fall to my death. The snow had only softened further since I'd left the ramp that afternoon. Every downward step became an uncontrolled slide towards oblivion. My crampons and ice axe were useless in the soft snow and bounced off the hard rock underneath like it was steel.

The only possible way I could stay on the mountain, I realised, was to face into the slope and wrap my arms around the snow in front of me, like I was hugging a giant toy. Then I'd take one tentative downward step. Immediately, I would start to slide, and I'd desperately try to clutch more snow to act as a brake. Despite my exhaustion, I was fully awake, my every sense attuned to the fact that I was a hair's breadth away from tumbling down the slope, over the buttress below and into the void. I was fully aware that my first 8000-metre summit could well be my last. It was terrifying, but there was no other way down.

Every step was the same: step down … slide, scrabble frantically, slide—'Fuck … fuck, stop!'—still sliding … a slight slowing, slowing, stop. My breathing was hysterical, my heart pounding. I was drenched in sweat despite the minus-20-degree temperature. Step down …

I kept on in this way, adrenaline pumping through my body with every barely controlled slide, until it seemed I was on the very precipice of the void. At last I spotted my down vest hanging from the ice screw, which marked the start of the traverse back to the Bottleneck.

I clipped a safety strap to the ice screw and hung from it, recovering, until I'd regained my breath. As I donned my vest and headlamp, I saw that the rope was still in place where we'd fixed it this morning, so I clipped to it for safety and traversed across the slope. The moonlight was as bright as I'd hoped it would be, and I could see where I was going very clearly. Once I made it through the nearly vertical chute at the top of the Bottleneck, I descended carefully but very enjoyably to Camp 4.

I'd done it—I'd climbed K2, the hardest mountain in the world. I'd achieved something that few people—few even of the world's best mountaineers—would ever experience. I was alive and uninjured. Life was good. What a great adventure!

My euphoria disappeared as I approached our tent and heard Anatoli's voice: 'Peter, is that you?' I knew immediately that Peter was dead. There could be no alternative.

Clutching at hope alone, Anatoli and I scanned the slopes above and below, but Peter was nowhere to be seen. We knew now that he never would be. The only part of the route that we couldn't see was near the summit, but Peter had been with Anatoli when they'd descended that part so he certainly wasn't still up there. At some point, as Anatoli went ahead, Peter had fallen. There was nothing to be done.

For the next few hours we tended the stove and rehydrated with sweet, milky tea. From time to time we'd scan the slopes above, looking for Reinmar and the Scandinavians. Around 2.30 a.m. we spotted two headlamps on the dangerous ramp. For their sakes, we hoped that the snow might have firmed up in the cold of night. We could do nothing to assist them, so we retreated into the warmth of our sleeping bags to wait.

At 3 a.m. I looked out again but could see only one headlamp, this time on the fixed rope traverse. I assumed that, in the bright moonlight, the other climber was saving his batteries. Finally, at 4 a.m., a figure in red staggered into camp. It was Rafael Jensen. He was distraught but could not speak. He lay on the snow for ten minutes drinking the hot water we passed him before he could finally muster the energy to talk.

'Rafael, have you seen Peter?' I asked.

'What? No, not Peter. It's Daniel.'

The cold sense of dread I'd felt when we'd realised that Peter was missing became even colder.

'Rafael, where is Daniel?'

'He fell.'

'What happened?'

'He was slow,' Rafael panted. 'I think oedema. Cerebral. I got him down the slope and across the rope to the Bottleneck. He held onto a rock but it came loose. He fell off the cliff. He's dead.'

Anatoli then burst in with, 'Did you see Reinmar?'

'He summitted, but after that I don't know.' I passed Rafael another cup of hot water from our stove.

'Tell us what happened,' I said.

The Norwegian explained that Bidner had reached the summit shortly after I had started down, and that Reinmar had summitted some time later. On their descent, Jensen and Bidner had gone ahead of Reinmar. They had only one headlamp between them, so they climbed down together. As they descended, Bidner had succumbed to the effects of cerebral oedema (an altitude-induced build-up of fluid on the brain) and become unsteady on his feet. Jensen helped him down, but Bidner had fallen to his death at the top of the Bottleneck. Jensen had then continued down alone.

Bidner's death was tragic, but we'd still not accounted for Peter or Reinmar. In the emerging dawn, we searched the slopes above us for several hours, but there was no sign of either of them. There never would be.

It seemed most likely that Peter had lost his hold on the mountain on that same desperate slope from which I'd nearly toppled, since we knew he'd reached that point with Anatoli. If he'd reached the fixed rope at the traverse under the serac, he'd have been able to safely move to the top of the Bottleneck. Had he fallen from that point, he would probably have ended up on the slopes above Camp 4, where we could have seen him.

Reinmar had probably suffered the same fate. His was the second headlamp we'd seen as he descended the fatal ramp at 2.30 a.m. The single headlamp that I'd seen at 3 a.m. had belonged to the Scandinavians. Like his friend Peter, it appeared that Reinmar had fallen before reaching the safety of the fixed-rope traverse.

*

An expedition that had been an amazing success just hours earlier had turned into a disaster. Half of the six of us who'd summitted had been killed on descent.

Anatoli was distraught. Reinmar had been a close friend of his. He wanted to wait at Camp 4 in case some miracle of survival occurred. I held no such hopes, but in any case my decision was soon made for me. Jensen, who'd been standing outside our tent, suddenly toppled over and lay still on the snow. He too had fallen victim to cerebral oedema. His only hope for survival was descent.

While Anatoli stayed at the camp a little longer, I crammed my sleeping bag into my rucksack, tied Jensen's rucksack on top of mine and hauled him to his feet. With an arm around him, I forced him to walk down the slopes towards Camp 3. I wasn't gentle but the situation was desperate. I had also been at extreme altitude long enough to be affected by oedema, and if I collapsed we were done for. Anatoli wouldn't have been able to carry both of us, even if he found us in time. With that in mind, I pushed, cajoled, dragged and carried Jensen down the mountain.

Peter and Reinmar had been carrying our two radios, so I was unable to call Base Camp and tell them what was going on. I knew that the British team members were on the way up to Camp 3 that day, and I needed them to climb a little higher to meet me as I brought Jensen down. By this time I was faltering from exhaustion, and I started to worry that we'd be caught by the night before we reached camp.

I searched through Jensen's pack and found a radio. I called the Swedish base camp, but trying to relay a message in my exhausted and dehydrated state was difficult, especially as I didn't speak Swedish. After numerous calls, the first few of which were answered by their Pakistani cook, I finally made them understand that I needed them to pass a message to the British expedition's base camp, that I needed help to get Rafael Jensen down to safety.

Whether the message would get through to the British climbers high on the mountain, I did not know. Nor did I know if they would even help. Jensen's condition was deteriorating and I had no choice but to push on. There were still a couple of crevasses to be negotiated. I kicked a deep hole in the snow, sat him in it and tied all my climbing slings together, one end of which I clipped to his harness, the other to mine. I had to jump the crevasse and hope that, if I missed the other side, his body weight would stop me from plummeting into the abyss.

Fear gave me wings and I made it to the other side okay. I then had to pull Jensen from the hole and cajole him to stand at the edge of the crevasse. The moment he stepped forward, I took a running jump down the mountain slope, trying to use my momentum to pull him over the crevasse. It worked well enough. Rafael was jerked from his stance and most of the way over the crevasse but crashed into the far side, where he hung precariously, connected to me, and therefore his life, by the thin slings between us. I threw myself to the ground to stop him dropping any further into the hole, and then dug my feet into the snow. With all my remaining strength, I heaved on the slings until I'd pulled him out of the crevasse and onto safe ground. In my oxygen-starved state, I almost blacked out from the effort and I lay on the snow for fifteen minutes, as comatose as Rafael.

While I recovered my breath, I remembered that I was carrying a small vial of drugs for illnesses brought on by high altitude, such as the oedema that Jensen was suffering. I had dexamethasone,

Diamox, nifedipine, aspirin and a few others, but I couldn't remember the correct dosages. Forgetting I was carrying the drugs was a clear sign of my own cognitive impairment, but an even clearer one was that I didn't see that the dosages were written on the outside of the vial. I decided that anything was better than nothing—in fact, everything was better than nothing—so I tipped the entire contents down Jensen's throat. Not surprisingly, he perked up a bit and we continued.

After we had descended another hundred metres or so, I was relieved beyond words to see a couple of the British climbers making their way up from Camp 3 and I gratefully handed Jensen over to them. Another hour of descent and I was in the snow cave that Reinmar and Anatoli had dug on their way up. Anatoli appeared shortly after and we spent a subdued night, too tired and too saddened to talk much.

The weather turned for the worse that night, so the British abandoned their summit push and took Jensen all the way down to Base Camp. Their descent was not without incident, though. At one point, as their leader Roger Payne led Jensen down, the fixed rope to which they were clipped broke. Thankfully, Payne was able to arrest their fall and save them both.

Anatoli and I also descended to Base Camp, where we were met by a tearful Ernst. We could tell him little of how his two close friends had perished. He was wracked with sorrow, compounded by the thought that, having given his sleeping bag to Peter, he had enabled Peter to continue the climb with its tragic consequence.

A new storm pounded the mountain that evening. My stomach had shrunk due to the past strenuous week of climbing, so I could only nibble at the food our cook offered me, but I was severely dehydrated and drank innumerable cups of hot juice. Soon, I staggered gratefully to my tent, where I dropped into the deepest of sleeps. The next morning I awoke long enough only to have a drink and a quick toilet stop, then returned to my sleeping bag and slept soundly right through until the following day. I got up again for a quick drink and fell back into bed until, finally, after another twenty-four hours, I emerged. I had never before been so tired.

In the interim, Captain Rashid had created two plaques from stainless-steel dinner plates. We sombrely walked over to the Gilkey Memorial and added them to the much-adorned rocky monument.

Our ascent of K2 had been achieved within just twenty-four days of our arrival at base camp, which was very fast. However, that speed had perhaps contributed to the tragedy we'd experienced. Both Anatoli and I were still acclimatised from our climbs a few weeks before this expedition, but it seemed likely that Reinmar and Peter had forced their bodies to cope with the extreme altitude at a faster rate than they should have. Our success in summitting was absolutely due to their insistence that we climb hard on the mountain's lower slopes during the bad weather, so we could make best use of the good weather when it finally arrived. It was just a shame they didn't get to enjoy that success.

No further expeditions would summit K2 that year, and it was probably just as well. Of the twelve climbers who reached the summit that season, five were killed on descent. Three of those deaths occurred during my own summit climb and, while I hadn't contributed to the accidents, they were very much a part of my experience. The deaths had little immediate impact on me, though. On the descent from Camp 4 to Camp 3, I'd been too focused on keeping Raphael alive. Once at Base Camp, I was too exhausted to think, let alone grieve.

When I finally awoke after three days of sleep and we placed the plaques on the memorial, I still didn't feel too much. I'd seen half my own team, and a member of another group, slaughtered, in a matter of hours. But the loss was theirs, not mine. My subconscious was in control. I could not allow myself to feel any emotion.

Postscript

In 1996 Anatoli Boukreev was instrumental in saving several climbers' lives in what is probably the best-known disaster on Mount Everest, when a storm trapped more than ten people above the South Col at 8000 metres. He climbed alone out into the storm's fury to locate and rescue climbers who'd collapsed and been given up for dead by others. His book *The Climb* described his life and those experiences. On Christmas Day in 1997, Anatoli was killed in an avalanche while climbing a difficult route on Annapurna, another of the 8000ers.

Roger Payne, the leader of the British team on K2, who'd survived the incredible avalanche I'd witnessed on Mount McKinley in 1991 and the fall on K2 while he was helping Rafael Jensen down, was killed in an avalanche in the European Alps in 2012.

4

FRUSTRATION

To put yourself into a situation where a mistake cannot necessarily be recouped, where the life you lose may be your own, clears the head wonderfully.

Al Alvarez

A FTER I RETURNED home from K2, I made a number of public presentations around Australia about the expedition, which were well attended. At the end of one presentation, a woman asked me, 'How do you feel about your friends' deaths?' Not being a particularly introspective person, I hadn't really thought about it since the expedition.

'Better than them,' I replied. She looked rather perplexed, perhaps justifiably so, but persisted.

'Yes, but how do you really feel?'

'I feel happy that I'm not with them,' I said. 'Any other questions?'

When I thought about this encounter later, I realised that I still really hadn't felt anything at all about the loss of life I'd witnessed on K2, or on my other recent expeditions. Consciously, anyway. By this time I'd been a police officer for twelve years, so I'd seen and dealt regularly with death. At work, we remained as objective as possible when dealing with deceased people and, while this situation was more personal, I suppose I'd just invoked that same approach.

The deaths were unfortunate, of course, but Lobsang, Peter, Reinmar and Daniel—even the two Norwegian boys on Pumori several years earlier—had all accepted the risks we'd faced and made their choices, even if, when we'd started, we hadn't really been aware of just how extreme those risks were. So I thought no more about it. Peter and Reinmar and all the others had died, and that was that. I was still working to achieve my long-held dream of summitting Mount Everest and I wasn't about to let the human cost affect my motivation.

*

Early in 1994 I was contacted by Goran Kropp, a Swedish climber who'd learned about the assistance I had given to Rafael Jensen the previous year. He was leading an expedition to Broad Peak and invited me to join the team. The other climbers were Mats Holmgren and Nicolas Gafgo. I agreed to go, and we met in Islamabad in May.

For the fun of it, our kindly expedition agent in Pakistan organised for our team to drive the Karakorum Highway to Skardu, rather than take the short flight. Clearly, he thought I hadn't had enough near-death experiences already. Our driver, who I'm certain had never been behind the wheel of any vehicle before, loaded all our equipment onto the roof of his dilapidated bus, making it ridiculously unstable, then drove at breakneck speed for the entire journey. He launched us around blind corners above vertical cliff faces, all the while chain-smoking his hashish cigarettes and yelling maniacally, '*Insha'Allah*, we die!' Thankfully, it wasn't Allah's will at the time, although he'd have been perfectly within his rights to rid the world of our driver.

At 8051 metres in altitude, Broad Peak is the twelfth-highest mountain on Earth but, being in the shadow of its larger neighbour, K2, it was ignored until the 1950s. Like many 8000ers, including K2, its summit ridge is the border between two countries—in this case China and Pakistan.

An attempt on Broad Peak in 1954 by a German expedition failed due to cold and violent storms. A joint German–Austrian expedition returned to the mountain in 1957 and attempted the climb under the most pure of climbing styles—without auxiliary oxygen or climbing porters. Included in the small team of four was Hermann Buhl, who had famously achieved a solo first ascent of another 8000er, Nanga Parbat, in 1953. Buhl and the team reached Broad Peak's summit on 9 June, remarkably early in the Karakorum climbing season. In doing so, Buhl became the first person in the world to have made the first ascents of two 8000-metre peaks.

The team didn't stop there. They split up to attempt two nearby peaks. On 19 June Marcus Schmuck and Fritz Wintersteller achieved the first ascent of Skil Brum (7360 metres) in pure Alpine style and in the extraordinarily fast time of just fifty-three hours. Buhl joined with the final team member, Kurt Diemberger, to attempt the nearby peak of Cholgolisa (7654 metres). Tragically, Buhl, the greatest proponent of lightweight high-altitude mountaineering of that era, was killed when he fell through a cornice on the summit ridge. Diemberger survived, however, and would go on to achieve other great ascents on the 8000ers.

Broad Peak is just 8 kilometres from K2, so our trek to base camp followed exactly the same route I had taken the previous year. This time, however, we went nearly a month earlier and there was considerably more snow on the ground.

When we arrived at Base Camp, our porter *sirdar* asked what date the porters should return to collect us. Goran nominated a date about four weeks hence, but I told him that it would be better to send a runner down to collect porters when we needed them, since booking them for a specific date would limit our ability to extend our time on the mountain if we needed to. Unfortunately, as it turned out, he stuck to his plan and set a fixed date.

Our intent was to make the first ascent of the mountain's unclimbed South Ridge, which to our knowledge had only been attempted once before. The climb began well and we opened the route to about 6500 metres through a near-vertical rock buttress that rose about 800 metres from its base. But the team lost its mojo when Nicolas received a letter advising that his girlfriend back in Sweden had been killed in a motorcycle accident. He went home immediately, of course, and the others in our team didn't have the heart to continue on this tough new route, so we switched to an easier line on the mountain's West Face.

This route was far less technical, and after three days of climbing we reached Camp 3 at 7000 metres. The following morning we set out for the summit. We climbed a steep face to a col between the main buttress and the central buttress, and then followed an exposed rocky ridge up and over a false summit—a point at which some climbers are alleged to have stopped and claimed to have reached the summit. But we wanted the real summit and continued the traverse.

The ridge, which sits at 8000 metres, is perhaps a kilometre long. As we made our way along it slowly and carefully, the wind picked up and cloud started to billow around us. When we were no more than 50 linear metres and just a few metres in height from the true summit, the wind suddenly built up to gale force. We were so close that it was hugely tempting to continue towards the summit, but prudence dictated that we retreat to safety. An Austrian woman who'd also been going for the summit that day, and who was climbing a short distance behind us on the ridge, also turned around and descended.

The storm continued for a couple of days so we retreated all the way to Base Camp. I felt strong enough to make another attempt a few days later, but at that point the porters who'd been booked to carry our expedition equipment back out of the mountains arrived. My chance to summit was lost—and the summit had been almost literally within touching distance.

Just as were preparing to start the trek back to civilisation, Goran told us that he'd arranged to join another team's expedition—he was friends with the leader of that group, it turned out—so that he could stay on and have another try for the summit. Incredible. While I'd have loved to stay to chat further with Goran about leadership and team spirit, the porters were already heading down the glacier with my equipment, so I shouldered my backpack and followed.

At camp on one of the final nights, I washed in a stream and then hung my towel over my tent to dry while I went to grab a cup of tea from the cook tent. When I returned, I saw that my towel was missing and immediately assumed that a porter had added it to his linen cupboard. As much as I loved Pakistan and its people, particularly the hardy folk of the Northern Areas, it was an unfortunate reality that any bit of equipment or clothing not locked away in drums or boxes would go missing during a trek. No matter how securely we packed the loads, our porters always managed to relieve us of something by the time we arrived at our destination. It was almost a sport to see who could outsmart the other.

I thought the porters were up to their usual tricks when I heard a rustle in the bushes behind the tent. *Right, you bugger, I've got you!* I thought. I sprinted through the scrub, ready to pounce on the thief, but as I emerged into a clearing I saw a zoe—a cross between a yak and a cow—chewing contentedly, the last few inches of my towel hanging from its mouth. I leapt forward and grabbed the remains and pulled for all I was worth, managing to retrieve about half a metre of saliva-soaked, chewed and stringy towel—my only victory in the mountains that year.

*

Frustrated by the failure to summit, I returned home. But far from being disenchanted with the mountains, by the time I stepped off the plane I was already planning a return to Pakistan in 1995. Having flown and driven past Nanga Parbat in the preceding two years, I couldn't get it out of my mind. It was an enormous black massif that commanded respect, and simultaneously struck both trepidation and excitement in me. And it had never been climbed by an Australian. All the previous 8000-metre peaks I'd been to had already seen Australians on their summits. I wanted to experience being the first. Joanne, however, had different ideas.

We'd been married for three years by this stage and she was desperate to start a family. My continual absences had done nothing to strengthen the relationship; indeed, we were on pretty rocky ground by now. She wanted me to play my part as a husband and gave me an ultimatum: it was her or the mountains.

I was torn. I cared for her greatly but I knew that if we had children, there would be no more mountaineering for me. It was too selfish a sport. I'd seen plenty of death up there and the odds were high that I would become a victim too. As a single man, and even as a married one, I could accept the risk, but I couldn't be so irresponsible as a parent.

The concept of no more mountaineering was abhorrent to me. In the long term, I still wanted to climb Everest but I was also coming to love high-altitude mountaineering purely for the sport. I'd never experienced such intense challenge and suffering, or such profound exhilaration. Rather than turn my back on it, I wanted more. It had become my life, more so than my marriage. I made my choice and we separated.

*

Newly single and raring for more adventure, I was pleased to be contacted by the English climber Victor Saunders, whom I'd met on K2 in 1993. Victor told me he was withdrawing from a predominately British expedition that was planning to attempt a new route on Nanga Parbat in the northern summer of 1995. The list of climbers who had signed on to the expedition read like a who's who of the world's top high-altitude mountaineers: Doug Scott, Voytek Kurtyka, Rick Allen and Sandy Allan.

Scott was an Englishman who'd had an extraordinary career of first ascents and epic expeditions. He was probably best known for his first ascent of the south-west face of Everest in 1975—and for breaking both ankles on Baintha Brakk (commonly known as The Ogre) in Pakistan in 1977, after which he'd still managed to descend the mountain, then crawl for miles across the glacier to get back to base camp. Kurtyka was from Poland and was a pioneer of alpine-style climbing on the 8000ers. One of his best was an incredible ascent of the West Face of Gasherbrum 4 with the Austrian Robert Schauer. It is regarded as one of the ten most notable ascents of the twentieth century. Rick Allen and Sandy Allan, both from Scotland had climbed together over a number of years in the European Alps and the Himalaya, including an attempt on the north-east ridge of Everest in 1987, which at the time was unclimbed. Doug had also been in that team.

Victor proposed to the team that I should take his place on the Nanga Parbat ascent, and they agreed. It was an incredible opportunity for me, and I leapt at the chance. I would be climbing with—and, more importantly, learning from—the best in the world.

Nanga Parbat is the westernmost 8000-metre mountain in the Himalaya, and the only Himalayan 8000er in Pakistan. The other four—K2, Broad Peak, Gasherbrum 1 and Gasherbrum 2— lie in the Karakorum Range, about 100 kilometres further north.

Unlike its 8000-metre neighbours, Nanga Parbat rises 8126 metres out of the landscape on its own, a solitary massif whose snow-fed streams irrigate the surrounding rural lands in an otherwise desolate region.

The ninth-highest mountain on Earth, it received some of the earliest attention of any of the 8000ers. Englishman Albert Mummery made an attempt in 1895 but disappeared on the mountain with two Gurkha teammates. Thereafter, the peak became the subject of German focus, and catastrophic tragedy. In 1932 an attempt was aborted due to bad weather, while a 1934 expedition ended when sixteen of the team were trapped at 7500 metres by a blizzard. Eight of the party died in that maelstrom, and most of the survivors were severely frostbitten.

A 1937 attempt on the same route, via Rakhiot peak, when seven Germans and nine Sherpas were killed by an avalanche that swept over them at Camp 4, resulted in the single worst disaster on an 8000-metre mountain, until it was equalled on Everest in 2014. A 1939 attempt, which included Heinrich Harrer, who had famously led the first ascent of the North Face of the Eiger in Switzerland, failed due to the outbreak of the Second World War. Harrer was interned in India by the British but escaped to Tibet, where he became a confidant to the Dalai Lama—his exploits are recorded in the Himalayan literary classic *Seven Years in Tibet*.

Thirty-one people had died on Nanga Parbat before it finally succumbed to the Austrian Hermann Buhl in 1953, just weeks after the British claimed Mount Everest. The two ascents could not have been more different. Buhl had continued alone to the summit after his teammates had turned back, thus making both the first ascent of Nanga Parbat and the only solo first ascent of any 8000er. In an epic of endurance, he reached the summit at 7 p.m. Caught by darkness on a narrow ledge as he descended, he was forced into a standing bivouac for the night. He survived and returned to his high camp forty hours after setting out for the top.

Nanga Parbat's history also includes the infamous 1970 Austro–German expedition to the mountain's Rupal Face, led by Dr Karl Herrligkoffer. The team members included the outstanding South Tyrol alpinist Reinhold Messner, who would go on to become the first in the world to climb all fourteen 8000ers, and his brother Gunther. After a protracted expedition marred by bad weather and very difficult climbing, Reinhold and his brother were positioned in the highest camp, ready to go for the top next day. It had been agreed that those at Base Camp would fire a green rocket that evening if the forecast was for good weather. A red rocket would indicate bad weather. Somehow, despite a good forecast, a red rocket was fired. Despite this, the Messner brothers struck out for the summit.

What followed was a messy case of claim and counterclaim, allegation and counter-allegation. Only Reinhold descended alive. He said that he and Gunther had reached the summit together, but that Gunther was exhausted and showed signs of oedema. They thought it was therefore safer for them to descend on the other, less technical side of the mountain. In a three-day epic they descended the entire Diamir Face without equipment or food, and had almost reached safety when an avalanche swept over Gunther.

Some claimed that Reinhold had abandoned Gunther on the way up to the summit in his quest for glory, and that if Gunther had really been sick, it would have been safer for them to descend on the known Rupal Face route, where there were fixed ropes in place and where they could get support from the other expedition members who were in nearby camps. Although Reinhold's version is generally accepted these days, he didn't get off lightly, losing six toes to frostbite, not to mention his brother. Whatever the facts, Reinhold would go on to establish outstanding alpine records for years to come, including the first ascent of Everest without oxygen and the first solo ascent of Everest. Without doubt, he is one of the greatest pioneers of high-altitude climbing.

Twenty-five years after that deadly expedition, our team met up in Islamabad on 17 July and had the usual mandatory briefings from Pakistan's Ministry of Tourism. We purchased food and kitchen equipment for our Base Camp, then travelled by road to Skardu—straight past the mountain we had come to climb. Our expedition had been sponsored by the Raleigh bicycle company, which had provided each of us with a brand new mountain bike so that we could cycle from Skardu across the world-renowned Deosai Plain back to Nanga Parbat.

The Deosai Plain is a 3000-square-kilometre national park. It's the second-highest plateau in the world, with an average elevation of over 4000 metres, and it was created to protect the indigenous Himalayan brown bear. While we didn't see any bears during our three-day bike crossing of the plateau, we did discover what must be the world's greatest concentration of mosquitoes. As we pulled up to camp each evening, the overwhelming hordes immediately drove us inside our tents, where, after killing the several thousand that had come inside with us, we'd lie awake as millions of the little beasts attempted to penetrate the tent walls.

Descending from the plateau with the few precious drops of blood we had managed to keep to ourselves, we completed the trip when we reached the picturesque village of Tarashing, close to Nanga Parbat. We planned to attempt the Mazeno Ridge, a route known as one of the great unconquered challenges of 8000-metre climbing. Most of its 10-kilometre length is above 7000 metres in altitude, and as narrow as a knife's edge.

After hiring porters, we enjoyed a very pleasant three-day trek across the alpine meadows below the Mazeno Ridge. At Base Camp our porters left us to fend for ourselves, with only a liaison officer and a cook for company, since we were on the far side of the mountain, away from the more popular Diamir Face. I appreciated the relative solitude because I could take in the spectacular landscape, undisturbed. Nanga Parbat absolutely dominated the flat terrain that lay all around it.

Some shepherds were grazing their sheep and goats near our Base Camp. It wasn't long before we reached an arrangement with them to bring us some fresh goat's cheese every few days. It was lumpy and runny, a bit like fresh ricotta. Since it wasn't pasteurised, we fried it up to kill the bugs and then ate it for brekkie. Absolutely delicious, although probably not Heart Foundation approved.

The first challenge of the climb was actually to get up onto the Mazeno Ridge, which sat about 3 vertical kilometres above us. We'd only brought a small amount of rope to fix to the mountain, which obliged us to solo most of the climb, unroped. This was totally new climbing to me. We had to be bold and commit ourselves to each movement fully, because there was nothing to save us if we fell.

It was absolutely exhilarating. I would look between my feet and see Base Camp thousands of metres below me, and I'd know that only the tenuous hold of the points of my ice picks and crampons lay between me and a rapid descent back there. Needless to say, it motivated me to focus. But the high I felt was like a drug. This was the unadulterated pleasure of pure climbing. I alone had absolute responsibility for my survival.

Early in the expedition, Doug became quite sick and left for home, followed soon after by Sandy. Although Voytek, Rick and I were disappointed to see them go, we chose to continue the climb. After establishing a depot of food and equipment at the start of the Mazeno Ridge, we descended to Base Camp to rejuvenate, await a spell of good weather and plan our summit attack. The ridge was so long, we decided we wouldn't be able to reach it and return the same way, so we'd have to traverse the mountain and find our way down the other side, very much in the way that Reinhold Messner had done with his brother Gunther many years earlier. This was a real risk, but it was the only feasible option if we were serious about reaching the summit.

Unfortunately, on our subsequent summit push, our climbing along the ridge was slower than we had anticipated. After climbing for several days we realised that we still had the most technical parts of the ascent ahead of us, and we felt that we didn't have the necessary food to complete the route to the summit, let alone down the other side. Discretion is the better part of valour, so we backtracked to Base Camp, our expedition over.

After a few days of rest, Rick and I decided to circumnavigate the mountain on foot, to explore the sides of the mountain that rarely see foreigners. We were still pretty exhausted from the climb, so we hired a local porter to help carry our camping equipment. At one point, as we crossed a narrow glacier, we had to descend a small block of ice. Our porter had no climbing equipment, so I lent him my ice axe for safety. Immediately, he began hacking at the ice to cut out some steps, but he only succeeded in breaking my axe—the one I'd taken to K2's summit! At the bottom of the ice cliff he gave it back to me and wandered off, not the slightest bit aware of why I might be upset. Possessions are a first-world problem.

The rest of the walk was incredibly beautiful, isolated and wild. And very hot. At one point, we walked for hours in baking temperatures without water, hoping at every bend to find even a puddle from which we could moisten our lips. Desperately thirsty, we finally came across a desolate village, comprising a few mud and stick houses in squalid condition. When we asked for water they produced a goatskin bag with fermented milk in it. Not only was it unpasteurised, it was full of dirt, goat's hair and goodness knows what else. It was lumpy, fizzy and rank, but we gulped it down like it was the freshest alpine stream.

While we hadn't summitted the mountain, the expedition had influenced me hugely. I had climbed with the best, I'd been pushed way beyond my comfort zone, and I'd learned much about risk and commitment. It was a positive step on my way to the top of Mount Everest.

*

Keen to have another go at Nanga Parbat, I wrote to my trekking agent in Islamabad to ask if he had any expeditions going there in 1996. He had. It was a Polish team. Two foreign climbers had joined the group and they were happy to have another. Of course, joining such an expedition flew in the face of my decision several years earlier to only climb with people I knew. But the problem was that I couldn't find people I knew, particularly in Australia, who wanted to climb the hard 8000ers, especially without oxygen and without Sherpa or high-altitude porter support. I rationalised my decision. If I wanted to climb high, sacrificing my ethics to do so was worth the added risk.

On paper, the leader of this expedition was the highly accomplished Polish mountaineer Krzysztof Wielicki, but in fact he had organised to climb on another mountain before Nanga Parbat and so did not arrive while I was there. In his absence, he'd appointed Jacek Berbeka, the brother of another proficient Polish mountaineer, Maciej Berbeka, to run the expedition.

Along with about six Polish climbers, there was the inter-national contingent: João Garcia from Portugal, German climber Berndt Hackler and me. I think the Poles had sought a few western members to help finance their expedition, but while we shared tents and equipment on the mountain, we pretty quickly split into two teams, the Poles in one and we three in the second.

The route that we chose to climb on Nanga Parbat was the same I'd intended to descend the previous year, had we summitted from the Mazeno Ridge: the Kinshofer Route on the Diamir (or western) Face. The trek to the Diamir side of the mountain is one of the shortest approach treks of any 8000-metre peak. From the village of Chilas on the Karakorum Highway, we walked through quite precipitous rocky gorges alongside thundering glacial torrents fed by Nanga Parbat's slopes. The path gains nearly 3000 metres between the KKH and base camp, which sits at 4000 metres. Given that radical altitude gain, it would have been prudent to allow three days for the trek in, to allow our bodies to acclimatise. But Berbeka was in a rush and demanded that our porters carry their loads all that way in just two days.

This was pushing the porters too hard, I knew, and it could well have detrimental effects on the rest of us, too. Sure enough, within a couple of days of our arrival at Base Camp, I suffered severe headaches and sleeplessness. While the others started climbing, I had to walk all the way out to the road head, then turn around and walk back in at a more appropriate pace, all of which took nearly a week. The better acclimatisation I gained, though, allowed me to catch up to the expedition—or at least with João and Berndt. By that time, the group had really split into two.

It was clear from the outset that the Poles lacked experience, and before long some of them went home. The work of opening the route, fixing ropes and carrying loads fell to our little group of three. That suited me fine. There is a particular thrill to be had when the path is unknown, and you must draw upon your skills and experience to determine the best line: *Should we climb up this gully or that? Does the top of the ridge lead onto easier terrain or is it blocked by ice and rock cliffs? What dangers are there en route? Is there rock-fall or avalanche danger? This cliff appears to have a weakness that will allow us to overcome it; that one does not.* All in all, I was happy to be out in the lead, making decisions about the route and safe sites for our camps.

We had constant bad weather with lots of rain at Base Camp and heavy snow dumps on the mountain. On 30 July, João, Berndt and I opened the route to Camp 4, but as we sat in the tent that evening, preparing for an attempt on the summit the next day, we were hit by a massive snowstorm that dropped a metre of snow in an hour. It was an incredible deluge, and our tent was crushed by the weight of the snow.

Desperate to save both it and ourselves, I went out into the storm and shovelled furiously, but I couldn't compete with the volume of heavy, wet snow pouring down and retreated back inside. We couldn't open the door due to the amount of snow blowing in, so we just lay there, the roof of the tent pressing down on our faces, wondering if we were being entombed or if we'd be swept away by an avalanche. We quickly ran out of fresh air and spent the rest of the night feeling really nauseated. By morning, the tent was a ruin. The storm continued, so we descended to Base Camp.

While we rested, the Poles went up for their own summit attempt. Somehow they got lost and tried to climb the wrong face of the mountain, constantly calling us on the radio, saying the slope was impossible to climb and wanting to know where the fixed rope to the summit was. There was no fixed rope to the summit, of course, so we gave them the best directions we could, if only to stop them climbing to a useless death on the wrong side of the mountain.

João, Berndt and I were keen to have another go at the summit, so we were very frustrated at having to wait at Base Camp while the Poles wasted days trying to find their way up the mountain. They occupied the tent that we had carried up to Camp 4, along with our sleeping bags and stoves. We'd agreed to let them use our equipment to save having to carry their own gear up the mountain, but only for as long as we rested at Base Camp. After a few days, we decided to go up. Berbeka had been sounding more and more confused on the radio, and we suspected the onset of oedema.

Setting out at midnight, we climbed directly from Base Camp to Camp 2, then the following day climbed through Camp 3 and up to Camp 4—a gain of 3000 vertical metres in two days, which indicated that by then we were very well acclimatised. On our way up we met the Poles descending to Base Camp. They were virtually dead on their feet with exhaustion and we were glad to see them go down.

The next morning we set out for the summit. After all the bad weather, the snow on the face seemed endlessly deep and we progressed only 150 metres in five hours. It was demoralising climbing. We tried to tiptoe over a very thin layer of windblown crust but constantly broke through to the bottomless snow beneath and then slid backwards down the hill. There was no way we could climb the 1000 metres to the summit at that rate, so we returned to Camp 4.

Tired but still determined to climb the mountain, João and I agreed to try again the next morning, but Berndt was too exhausted and descended to Base Camp. We were hit with yet another snowstorm that night, which buried the tent again. Worse still, it also buried our hard-won tracks of the day before.

Nevertheless, we set out in the middle of the night. Soon the wind picked up considerably. We were at serious risk of frostbite in the freezing temperature, so reluctantly we decided to turn around. It was the right decision, and we hoped that we might still have time for another attempt when the weather cleared. When we arrived at Base Camp, however, we found only Berndt there to meet us. The Poles had already left, he said, and were travelling back to Islamabad. They'd left us no food or fuel that might allow us another summit attempt.

Appreciative of another lesson learned about team spirit, we packed up the camp and started the trek out to civilisation. By the time we passed through the narrow rock gorges up which we'd trekked on the way in, it was blisteringly hot. It was the middle of summer and the polished rock escarpments that towered hundreds of metres above us reflected the heat even more. I measured the temperature at 50 degrees Celsius, meaning that we'd gone from minus 20 to plus 50 in just a couple of days. Our bodies simply couldn't cope, and João and I suffered severe heatstroke.

We staggered and searched for shade but could find none, and we eventually collapsed at the side of a canyon, unable to coordinate our limbs. I was conscious but unable to stand up, and just lay there for several hours, my ears ringing, barely able to breathe. Thankfully, with sunset the heat subsided and we recovered sufficiently to move.

We lurched down the valley until we reached a river, where we plunged ourselves into the ice-cold glacier-fed torrent. Later, we heard that a member of a Japanese trekking group that was trying to get through the same gorge that day had died from heatstroke. Having come from such cold temperatures just the day before, we were extremely lucky not to have suffered the same fate.

The delay, however, meant that by the time we reached Islamabad the Poles had left the country just a few hours earlier. While it would have been nice to catch up with them and administer a little summary justice, in retrospect I realised that we should have stayed on the mountain and finished the climb, even without food. Not summitting simply meant that I'd have to return all over again. I'd allowed myself to be distracted from my goal, and so had wasted an opportunity. I resolved not to let it happen again.

Postscript

Goran Kropp was killed in a fall while rock climbing in the United States in 2002.

In 1999, João Garcia suffered severe frostbite during his descent from the summit of Mount Everest. He lost many fingers and toes, his nose and other parts of his face.

5

TURNING THE KEY

On this proud and beautiful mountain we have lived hours of fraternal, warm and exalting nobility. Here for a few days we have ceased to be slaves and have really been men. It is hard to return to servitude.

Lionel Terray

BY THE END of 1996, I'd been on six 8000-metre expeditions in five years but had only succeeded in reaching the summit of K2 in 1993. While I'd developed a lot of experience, I'd not had the success I craved. As the 1997 climbing season approached, I forced myself to consider whether I should continue in the game or do something else altogether. I loved climbing at high altitude, but it was costing me a huge amount—financially, professionally and personally.

Genuine introspection was not one of my strong points, but it seemed that on my last few expeditions, while there had been a good reason to turn around below each summit, I could have pushed harder, really stretched myself. I had either allowed myself to become distracted or agreed for the sake of team harmony with decisions that I didn't support. I'd lost my focus.

I reminded myself that summitting Everest was my main aim. In order to gain the experience to do that, I needed to succeed in my shorter-term goals on other mountains. I made a conscious decision that I would start succeeding—start summitting—or else give up high-altitude climbing. To be clear, I wasn't advocating 'summit fever'—going for the summit at all costs—but rather that I would not give up unless I had no possible alternative. I knew I could push myself harder while still staying within my limits, especially as I gained more and more high-altitude experience.

With that newfound focus, I joined another Australian Army Alpine Association expedition in March 1997 to Mount Dhaulagiri in Nepal, the seventh-highest peak on Earth at 8167 metres. The AAA had attempted Dhaulagiri in 1993 without success, and by 1997 the mountain still hadn't seen an Australian ascent.

Like all 8000ers, Dhaulagiri has a fascinating history. Its Sanskrit name means 'White Mountain', but it is more frequently referred to as 'Mountain of Storms', due to the ferocious weather that constantly lashes its slopes. In the early 1800s it was believed to be the highest mountain in the world, probably because it stands isolated from the rest of the Himalaya and rises a full 7000 metres above the Kali Gandaki gorge. Reconnoitred in 1950 by a French expedition, the mountain was deemed to be impossible to summit. A few weeks later, that same team famously achieved the first ascent of any 8000er by climbing Annapurna. Dhaulagiri would wait another ten years for its first ascent.

Four members of a Swiss–Austrian team, together with two Sherpas, reached its summit on 12 May 1960. One of the team, Kurt Diemberger, had already completed the first ascent of another 8000-metre mountain, Broad Peak. Diemberger said after the expedition, 'It was technically challenging, it was difficult, but the main challenge was the weather. Storm after storm came in.' The expedition differed from all other first ascents of the 8000ers in that it used a lightweight ski-equipped aircraft, nicknamed the 'Yeti', to ferry supplies up the lower parts of the mountain. Ultimately, the Yeti crashed during the expedition. There were no injuries, but its wreckage remains on the mountain, buried by snow.

In 1969 a US expedition attempted Dhaulagiri's unclimbed south-east ridge. While the climbers were still very low on the mountain, a massive avalanche swept down, killing seven of the team. At that time, it was the worst disaster in Nepalese climbing history.

After several months of intense military-style planning, and the packing of several tonnes of food and equipment, our team flew to Kathmandu. We had ten members and were led by a long-time member of the AAA, Major Zac Zaharias, whom I'd known for some years. Since the expedition was being partly funded by the Australian Defence Force as an adventurous training exercise, we were required to include members with little Himalayan or no high-altitude experience. Adventurous training is a well-proven concept for teaching leaders to manage stressful situations in unfamiliar environments, but the risk of failure was certainly increased by the mixed experience of the team. The benefit of being an army team, however, was that we were well catered for. We had better rations on that expedition than any other I have ever been on.

Dhaulagiri lived up to its nickname of Mountain of Storms throughout our expedition and the tranquillity of our beautiful ten-day approach trek through numerous rhododendron forests in the Myagdi Kola Valley was quickly dispelled. Our final day to Base Camp consisted of a dash through a gorge on the flank of the mountain, whose snow-laden slopes teetered menacingly a couple of thousand metres above us. When we reached Base Camp, we could hear a deep, vibrating rumble coming from above. A permanent torrent of windblown snow arched across the sky from the mountaintop, signalling the gale-force winds that pounded the mountain's upper reaches. Those winds and the regular avalanches that swept Dhaulagiri's steep slopes had claimed many climbers' lives and been the cause of the failure of the previous Australian attempt.

To succeed we would need grit, while to survive we'd need careful risk management and a good degree of luck. We also needed the blessing of the mountain gods. A puja ceremony was conducted at Base Camp to ask the gods for permission and safe passage on the mountain. Having now spent six years climbing in the Himalaya, I looked forward to these rituals; indeed, I became uncomfortable if we didn't conduct them.

With the ceremonials completed, we started the climb and spent the first couple of weeks carrying loads on the lower slopes of the mountain to stock camps 1 and 2. During rest periods at Base Camp, we practised first aid and attended to our sponsorship obligations. One of those was to send a photograph of the team to the office staff at Thai Airways, who had kindly given us a discounted rate for our thousands of kilograms of baggage. For most sponsors' photos, we formed a ragged rabble while the cameras clicked. For the Thai Airways office ladies, however, we went the extra step. At 4000 metres and in a temperature around zero degrees, we stripped off completely, retaining only our ice axes to protect our modesty—it was very cold! The photo was duly delivered to Thai Airways and, I believe, mounted on the office wall.

We also introduced the less-experienced members of our team to the use of our Gammow bags. These are designed as a temporary and portable treatment for altitude sickness. The victim lies inside the bag, which is then inflated and pressurised by an external foot pump. The increasing internal air pressure effectively lowers the patient's altitude. To test the bag, one of the team jumped inside and the bag was zipped up and pressurised. The bags have a clear plastic window, so we could see the victim and he us. As luck would have it, he was quite the coffee addict, so naturally we opened a fresh packet next to the air intake on the pump, taunting him with the aroma for the next hour or so, while the rest of us stood around drinking fresh brews.

Another brew we had on hand was a homemade beer mix. Using one of our 200-litre equipment drums, we mixed up the ingredients and for the next two months waited with great hopes for a few lagers when we returned victorious from the top of Dhaulagiri.

The initial climbing was less fun, though, as constant storms forced us to move through deep snow and the team became very tired. To safeguard ourselves in the constant whiteout, we placed bamboo wands in the snow with compass bearings written on them, directing us to the next wand just 50 metres away. The huge precipices on both sides of the ridge we were climbing meant that keeping to the 'path' was essential.

Each time we returned to a camp, we would have to dig fresh snow away, and on occasion we had to dig down just to find the tops of the tents. In some storms the snowfall was so heavy that during the night we'd take turns to get out and shovel the snow off the tents to save us from burial and asphyxiation, which had killed many climbers on this mountain. Our expedition was becoming a war of attrition and we all lost significant amounts of weight.

My focus to succeed was not diminished by all these obstacles. In fact, it nearly caused me to have a blow-up with the leader. Zac's plan for the climb was more tentative than I'd have preferred. We spent a lot of time at Base Camp, whereas I knew I needed to spend time at higher altitude in order to acclimatise well. He was in a difficult position, having to safely manage a team with such disparate experience.

At one point, as we established the higher camps in preparation for a summit attempt, Zac wanted us to carry a load to Camp 3 at 7200 metres but then to return on the same day to a lower camp. That was to be the highest point we would reach before our subsequent summit push, and would complete our acclimatisation phase. While that was a safe approach, I knew that simply climbing to that height would not sufficiently acclimatise me for the summit. When I told Zac that I planned to stay at Camp 3 overnight, he wasn't in favour of it. While he didn't say it outright, I could tell he was concerned that I might just keep going and attempt to reach the summit by myself.

I knew that Zac was keen to be a part of the team's first summit attempt. Having been leader of the unsuccessful 1993 Australian expedition, he was doubly motivated to lead this expedition to success. I understood his concerns, but I also knew what I needed to do to acclimatise safely and sufficiently. I told him that I was going to spend the night at Camp 3 no matter what, but I gave him my word that I would not make an independent summit attempt. The mood was more than a little tense, but I was determined to give myself the best preparation for reaching the top.

Four of us, including Zac, did the load carry to Camp 3, then Zac and one of the other guys descended. Another teammate, Matt Rogerson, stayed on to acclimatise as well, which probably put Zac's mind at ease. I wondered if he'd ordered Matt to shoot me if I headed uphill the next morning! It was a difficult night, particularly for Matt, as we struggled with headaches in the high altitude. Matt proved the point by throwing up the cordon bleu dehydrated meal I'd cooked, straight into the spare cooking pot.

The next morning, in clear weather, we looked up at the summit, so close and beckoning, put on our crampons and descended to Base Camp. I had given my word.

With camps and fixed rope in place, the team was now ready to have a crack at the top. Major Zac announced who'd be in the first and second summit teams—it was a military expedition, after all. I was in the first team, as was he. All had been forgiven.

The newfound camaraderie didn't help much, though, as successive storms had dumped metres of snow on the mountain. Once again, we had to plough a track up to Camp 1, dig out the tents and do the same as we continued up. Camp 2 was also completely buried. The next night we experienced one of the heaviest snowfalls of the season, and by morning we had no choice but to give up the attempt and return to Base Camp to await better weather. I shall never forget the image of Matt, literally waist-deep in the fresh powder, pushing a bow wave of snow ahead of him as he forced his way down the hill.

Back at Base Camp, we sat out more storms as the days ticked by all too quickly. The pre-monsoon season in which we were climbing concluded on 31 May, and the Nepal Ministry of Tourism required us to be off the mountain by that date. It was already 19 May and the porters were scheduled to arrive in just one week to collect our equipment for the trek out to Kathmandu.

Tensions were running high, and Zac called a meeting to discuss our options. Everyone was thoroughly worn out by the constant storms, and the incessant bloody wind was driving us all nuts. Zac asked each of us what we wanted to do. Some spoke about wanting to go home, to enjoy the trek out, while others indicated that they might be interested to stay for another summit attempt. When it came my turn, I recalled my determination before the expedition not to give up until my last ounce of energy was expended.

'I don't care if everyone goes home,' I said. 'I'm staying until the last gas canister, if that's what it takes to summit.' I meant it. I was there to climb.

In the end, five of us decided to stay on. One man would remain at base camp, and four of us—Major Zac, Captain Matt Rogerson, Corporal Brian Laursen and the argumentative, undisciplined civilian, me—would make a final summit attempt.

When the weather improved, we set out and climbed over several days up to Camp 3. We'd set up this camp on our preparatory climb a couple of weeks earlier, digging a ledge into the face and erecting a small two-man tent. By now, however, one side of the tent had been buried by spindrift and was frozen into the side of the mountain. That meant there was only room for one person inside. I volunteered to sleep there, while the other three swapped war stories in a larger tent on a rocky prow about 20 metres away.

There was a howling gale that night. As I lay in my little half-collapsed tent, I listened to the storm raging outside. Suddenly, I heard the sound of an avalanche bearing down on me. The noise of the storm had hidden the usual distinctive 'crack, whumpf' of an avalanche releasing, and by the time I heard the snow approaching it was almost upon me.

I had only a split second to react, and quite instinctively jerked my knees up inside my sleeping bag. Doing this created an air pocket that would give me a few precious extra minutes of life—assuming I wasn't carried down the mountain and killed, of course, which, I'm pleased to say, I wasn't. The half of the tent that was frozen into the side of the mountain held it in place, but the avalanche crushed the tent poles and buried me inside.

Being buried in snow is like being buried in sand at the beach. I couldn't move my arms, my chest, my legs, anything. In fact, with the heavy pressure of the snow all around me, I couldn't even tell if I was facing up, down or sideways. But, for the moment, I could breathe. More worrying was the fact that small avalanches like this one—and it must have been small, or I would certainly have been given a free ride down the hill—are often followed by larger slides. That was definitely not on my agenda.

I was stuck until someone dug me out, but I didn't know if the guys in the other tent had also been hit. I yelled out a couple of times and waited. I knew that the storm and the snow above me would muffle my shouts, so I had to hope that they'd survived and would come to check on me. The main thing I had to do was conserve oxygen, so it was better for me to lie still and stay calm—not a natural response, when every sense was urging me to thrash desperately to escape that suffocating tomb. But I knew that thrashing around would just end things more quickly. It was better to stare down the threat than react to it, so I lay still.

I was there for about fifteen minutes—thinking about life, as one does in those situations—by which time the air was getting quite thick. It seemed as though this was to be my chilly end and I started to make my peace with it. Finally, though, I heard some scraping, and a few minutes later Brian dug me out. The avalanche had missed their tent. That first sweet breath of fresh air was the very taste of life itself. I guess I'd paid sufficient homage at the puja ceremony before we had started climbing, since the gods definitely gave me a second chance that day.

*

We continued the next morning, pushing up to Camp 4, which sat at 7500 metres on steep and exposed ground. The vista towards the Annapurna mountain range just across the Kali Gandaki Valley was stunning. This valley descends to 1000 metres above sea level, which, with the 8000-metre-plus summits of Annapurna and Dhaulagiri on either side, creates a vertical difference of 7 kilometres. It thus stands as the deepest gorge in the world.

We had two new tents for Camp 4. Zac and Brian were sharing one, while Matt and I occupied the other. We planned to make a 4 a.m. start for the summit, and duly rose at two in the morning to light the stove and commence the arduous process of donning all the necessary high-altitude clothing. It would have been better to leave at midnight, but we needed the light of day to find a specific weakness that would give us a passage through the cliffs above.

Right on 4 a.m., however, the wind picked up to gale force and trapped us in our tents, only easing off a little before eight. With the instability of the weather, there was no telling what the future would bring, so I called out to Zac's tent to see if they were still keen to start. They weren't. They preferred to wait a day, and, as it was late and we were all still tired from the exertions of the previous day, Matt and I agreed.

I felt a little uneasy, though, as once the wind died away it became a brilliant day on the mountain, a perfect summit day. Days like that are rare on Dhaulagiri and I wondered if we were throwing away our only opportunity. We were out of food, too, so if we didn't go for the summit the next day, the expedition would be over. As the day passed, I also became quite queasy. I'd eaten some tinned fish the night before and it wasn't agreeing with me. By evening I was really out of sorts.

We prepared again for a 4 a.m. departure, but right on four the wind whipped up again. It was furious, almost cyclonic—impossible to venture out into. There was nothing for it but to wait. Around seven, it started to die off and I yelled out to the other tent that we should prepare to go for it. They weren't too keen, but I insisted that if the weather turned out like yesterday, the wind should stop by eight and it would then be a great day. While we were likely to be caught by darkness on our return from the summit, there would be a full moon. They agreed.

At eight, the wind died away. I was out of the tents first and headed straight to the rock buttress above, which I bulldozed my way up, crampons flailing on the bare rock, and then flopped seal-like at the top of the cliff, trying to regain my breath. Walking at 7500 metres is completely debilitating, but climbing a pitch of rock brings on head spins, a heart rate above 200 beats per minute and a desperate heaving for oxygen.

The others took turns to climb the buttress, while I started up the slope above, post-holing in the nightmarishly deep snow. I managed to keep up a pretty good pace and made the track for about 200 metres—perhaps two hours of climbing—before Matt caught up with me and took over. Here the slope steepened, making the going worse. We took turns to break trail, but by 1 p.m. we were all exhausted, and we'd climbed just one-third of the face. It was going to be a long day.

Brian declared surrender and turned back for Camp 4. The rest of us pressed on. Constantly changing the lead allowed us a brief chance to recover, but we were getting weaker with every metre gained. Worse, I felt completely nauseated and dizzy from the food poisoning. I could barely stand up straight, let alone kick steps into the deep snow. At 3.30 p.m., that tinned fish finally caught up with me. I had no choice but to stop and attend to urgent business while the other two continued climbing. Everything takes time at that altitude. By the time I had undone my various layers of clothing, found the loo paper in my backpack and then redone everything, I was a full thirty minutes behind, with Zac and Matt about 50 metres above me.

That's a long way at such altitude, and it would have been almost impossible to catch up to them under normal circumstances. I decided to offload some weight to give me an advantage. I took out my water bottle, snack bars, spare mitts and headlamp from my pockets and pushed them into the snow. That weight saving gave me the advantage I needed, and after climbing hard for the next hour I caught the guys—just in time for them to let me go ahead and break trail again!

Just on dusk, we finally hit the ridge at the top of the face and could see all the way down to the Kali Gandaki River, 7 vertical kilometres below us. With the ridge only a couple of metres wide, it was not the place to slip. Clouds swirled below us and the wind blew strongly, so we had to push on quickly.

Dhaulagiri's summit ridge is infamous for having lots of bumps that appear to be the summit—all the more so in dying light—and it lived up to its reputation. Striking out hard for what we thought was the highest point, we ascended to its peak, only to see the ridge stretching out into the gloom, with numerous rocky outcrops above us. The gloom became night and we continued to climb along the ridge, past more buttresses of rock.

Finally, we found ourselves below the last buttress. Matt led the last steep and exposed climb to the summit. It was 9 p.m., thirteen hours after we'd set out from the tents. We snapped one quick photo before Zac provided appropriate leadership with the comment, 'Right, let's get the fuck out of here!' This time, I didn't argue.

We headed back along the knife-edge ridge as quickly as possible. Because I'd left my headlamp in the snow, I had no light as we climbed. I moved between the other two, using the light from the guy in front of me to see the general direction and the light from the headlamp behind me to see my feet. Given the sharpness of the ridge and the rather long drop to the valley floors on either side, it wasn't great, but it was the only option I had.

It was bitterly cold, around minus 25 degrees Celsius, and pitch-black. The full moon stubbornly remained behind the clouds. We were frozen and exhausted and the climb down was slow. When at last we made it back to the spot where I'd stashed my spare gloves and other gear, I found my headlamp, but it failed to work due to the cold.

The safest thing for me would have been to continue climbing between the other two guys, but this was really slow and I could tell that they were desperate to descend as quickly as possible. I told them to go ahead, and resigned myself to a long night of careful climbing, picking my way down the massive face in the blackness.

I'd been keeping diaries for the last few expeditions and I later recorded the events of this night:

> I was soon alone in the darkness but felt quite secure down-climbing. The only problem was the cold of the ice tool whipping the heat out of my hands.
>
> As I descended, I worked my free hand constantly to rewarm it, as my fingers were freezing solid every few minutes. When it was warm, I swapped the axe into the warm hand and then worked the freshly frozen one. The shells over my down mitts was useless and frozen and not even seam-sealed, so they were full of frost.

I had lost most of the sensation in my toes also, and they felt wooden and stiff, though not lost.

Over the next couple of hours, I down-climbed the face, picking my way step by step. Eventually, I reached the top of the rocky band, where I was grateful to find Zac and Matt waiting for me:

> Just as we were approaching the ridge, an unbelievable wind whipped out of nothing. From 0–100 mph instantly. Felt like it would blow us off and had to crouch to hold on. Absolutely freezing and whipped up snow crystals lashed us constantly.
>
> I was wearing my goggles, thank heavens, but they soon iced up. I couldn't take them off or I'd have been blinded by the stinging bite of the crystals. I had an ice beard in seconds and Matt's eyelashes had frozen together.
>
> Every now and then I would lift my goggles for a better view and my own lashes would freeze. I tried to peer through a window in the frost on my lens but was basically blinded. Without a headtorch it was hopeless.

Groping blindly, we forced our way down the cliff and the final snow slopes to our tents, into which we immediately dived. Inside, they were covered in frost and snow—the carnage of having been whipped by wind since we'd left—but they seemed like a tropical paradise compared with the bitter wind outside. Our water bottles were frozen, but despite our incredible thirst we hadn't the energy to light the stove. We simply collapsed into our sleeping bags. It had taken us thirteen hours to climb to the summit and about four and a half to return. A good day on the hill

*

Next morning, the wind eased and we stumbled down to thicker air. Zac and Brian were too exhausted to go below Camp 3, but Matt and I kept on to Camp 2. Yet another brutal storm blew in, and we were soon climbing almost blind in the maelstrom. In our exhaustion, we moved painfully slowly and the hours ticked by. I realised that we'd became separated in the cloud, and as night approached I started to wonder if I'd passed the tent. I prepared for a bivouac, knowing it would be a life-and-death struggle in that storm. Then, out of the gloom, I spotted the faint colour of tent fabric and scrambled desperately over to it. I collapsed inside, onto a pile of rope, climbing equipment and other detritus, but it felt like a feathered bed. I was asleep in seconds. Matt found another tent and he too escaped the tempest.

Zac and Brian joined us next day. It took another two days to descend to Base Camp, as we packed up our camps along the way. There we found that our porters had been waiting for us for a couple of days. One of the more entrepreneurial of them had brought in half a dozen bottles of beer, which he offered to us at an exorbitant price. We still had our 200-litre drum of homemade beer, but the freezing temperatures had prevented proper fermentation, so it had little alcohol and tasted nothing like beer. We paid the asking price for the 'imported' beer, and donated our own brew to the porters, who immediately hooked in and drank the lot without ill effect.

We set about packing up the camp so the porters could leave the next morning, as there wasn't any more food for them at Base Camp. Rather than taking the long trek out with them, though, we decided to take a shortcut over two high passes that would bring us down to a village with an airstrip, from which we could fly back to Kathmandu in a light plane. It would be an extremely long day, but worth it if we made it. Unfortunately, we didn't have a map, and the only person in the group who'd been over the passes previously was our cook, Prem. But we were simply too exhausted to face a

10-day trek out with the porters, when one big day could have us back in civilisation.

It took until midnight to finish packing the camp, after which we grabbed a couple of hours of desperately needed sleep. Up again at 3 a.m., we had a quick bite to eat and started walking. We pushed hard to cross the first pass by 8 a.m., then raced for the second pass before the inevitable afternoon cloud stymied us with a whiteout. We made it by the skin of our teeth, as cloud billowed all around, but then struggled to find our way down in the complete whiteness. Plodding on as the hours ticked by, we fought to at least get below the snowline, as we had no tents, food or stoves. Shortly before nightfall we dropped below the cloud, but with the darkness we lost the track. We searched carefully around the sodden, precipitous cliffs, but by 9 p.m. and after eighteen hours on the go, had found nothing, and admitted defeat.

Being below the snowline meant that the falling snow had turned to freezing drizzle. We crawled into our sleeping bags and sat in a circle with our backs together underneath an umbrella. I was exhausted beyond words after such an epic summit push and the long days since, but we had no food, so sat there bleary eyed, soaking and cold, trembling with fatigue but happy to be alive. Then, to our absolute amazement, Zac reached into his backpack and produced a full bottle of peach schnapps. Consuming alcohol in our utterly shattered state, half-frozen with hypothermia, probably broke all the survival rules. But we drank it and we loved it. I shall never forget the incredible morale boost it gave us—probably as much for the insanity of it, but no doubt also because it was packed full of much-needed sugar.

In the light of day, we found the track down to the village, where we dried out, warmed up and ate. And ate. Back in Kathmandu soon after, we met up with the other guys from our team. Noting how much weight we'd all lost, we held a Mr Puniverse competition. Zac and I shared the award for 'Most Puny'.

Our ascent of Dhaulagiri was the first-ever Australian summit of that mountain, a major achievement in Australian Himalayan mountaineering. It was particularly significant for me. Before the climb, I'd made a conscious decision not to give in to fear, hardship or fatigue. The mountain had thrown numerous barriers at me, but I'd overcome them and succeeded. That was a huge boost to my confidence as a mountaineer. It was my second successful ascent of an 8000-metre peak and the first time that I'd made a first Australian ascent of an 8000er.

The team's success was not without a price, however. Zac and Matt both suffered frostbite to the fingers of their right hands. I realised afterwards that it was probably because, after they had left me on the way down from the summit, they'd made as fast a descent as possible with the benefit of their headlamps. The route down was a long right-hand curve, and they had faced out from the slope as they descended, meaning that they held their ice axes in their right hands. In their haste, they probably hadn't stopped to warm their fingers. They each lost minor bits of a couple of fingers, nothing too serious. Matt also lost bits of a couple of toes. I'd survived uninjured because, having been without a light, I'd been forced to face into the slope and to climb slowly, swapping the ice axe between my hands every couple of minutes.

*

In June 1996, while at my Rawalpindi hotel en route to the crazy Polish Nanga Parbat expedition, I'd bumped into the Scottish climber Rick Allen, with whom I'd climbed on the Mazeno Ridge of Nanga Parbat in 1995. He was on his way to K2. I liked Rick's climbing style and we agreed to make an expedition to Broad Peak in 1997 to attempt the still unclimbed South Ridge, which had not seen another expedition since my brief attempt on it with the Swedes in 1994.

Back then, Pakistan's Ministry of Tourism only issued permits for a maximum of six expeditions per mountain—a sensible limit that the Nepalese and Chinese governments would do well to adopt today—and our application for a permit to climb in 1997 was refused, as six permits had already been issued.

I wrote a letter to the Ministry of Tourism, requesting an exemption on the grounds that we'd be attempting a route well away from the rest of the expeditions. No response was forthcoming, but elections in Pakistan in February 1997 brought a change of government. I wrote a letter to the new prime minister, Nawak Sharif, graciously offering him the opportunity to exercise his new powers in the interests of a worthwhile cause—well, a charitable one at least. I'd not heard anything when I left for Dhaulagiri in April 1997, but, when I arrived home eight weeks later, the permit was waiting for me.

There followed some fast talking with my boss, and perhaps another nail in the coffin of my police career. In truth, I think he was glad to see me go again. I had no annual leave left but had racked up enough years in the job to take a little of my long-service leave at half pay. Having finalised my divorce only a short while before, and having then outlaid a chunk of money for Dhaulagiri, my bank balance was getting a little low. But after searching under the last moths in my hidden shoebox, I managed to scrape together the funds. When I flew out of Australia again, just two and a half weeks after getting home from Dhaulagiri, I had six dollars left in the bank.

*

The Pakistani climbing season is the northern summer—June to August—so the Dhaulagiri expedition during the Nepalese pre-monsoon season, March to May, was the perfect preparation for me. I still had considerable acclimatisation and fitness, although I was somewhat lighter. After completing the official necessities in Islamabad, Rick and I were soon ready to head for the mountains.

I prayed that the weather would let us fly to Skardu because the thought of another 24-hour hellride up the KKH in a bus definitely didn't appeal. After a short delay we took off. There seemed to be a lot of cloud, and I knew that the pilot needed clear sight of the airstrip at Skardu where there wasn't radar. The cloud increased, and halfway through the flight the intercom crackled into life to announce that we were returning to Islamabad. Clearly, we hadn't said enough *Insha'Allahs* at takeoff; we certainly said a few as we came in to land, with the plane bouncing around in the increasing turbulence.

While I argued with every airport official I could find about a refund of the fees for our excess baggage, on the apparently absurd notion that the airline hadn't actually delivered us to our destination, Rick went in search of a bus. After some hours we were both successful, and we also managed to get the driver to let us pack our gear inside the bus and lay off the hashish until at least halfway.

About eighteen hours into the drive, the road to Skardu turns off the KKH and heads north-east, towards the Karakorum Mountains. We'd only gone a few kilometres when we were stopped by a long line of traffic. The road was obstructed by large rocks put there by angry villagers, who were demonstrating against the government's failure to build a promised mini hydroelectric power supply for their village. They had blocked the road and were telling all the vehicles' occupants that there were snipers in the surrounding hills who'd shoot at any vehicle that tried to get past. We were about thirtieth in the queue, and they weren't letting anyone through.

The villagers told us that they'd communicated their issue to the government, who had sent a representative the previous day, but that they still didn't have electricity. I guessed that there was a slight misunderstanding as to the time it takes to build a hydro

Matt Godbold looks out from our camp on the West Rib of Mount McKinley.

Tengboche Monastry, the spiritual capital of Tibetan Buddhism in Nepal, watched over by the majestic peak of Ama Dablam.

Mount Everest (at left), Lhotse (middle) and Nuptse (right) bask in the evening glow, as seen from our camp on Pumori in 1988. Images like this inspired me to take on the 8000ers.

Watchful eyes oversee distribution of meat rations in the porters' butcher shop at Paiju campsite, en route to K2 in Pakistan.

Reinmar Joswig, Daniel Bidner and Rafael Jensen emerge from the 'bottleneck' beneath the monstrous ice serac on K2 on summit day.

K2, generally described as the hardest mountain on earth. It was the first 8000er that I successfully summited.

Peter Mezger at the end of the icy traverse below the 'endless couloir' on K2 summit day. Both Peter and Reinmar fell from this point later that night. Broad Peak and the Gasherbrum Ranges are behind.

On the top of K2, my first 8000 metre summit, with Anatoli Bukreev in red.

Triumph turned quickly to tragedy with the loss of two of our team on K2. Our Liaison Officer, Captain Rashid, made these memorial plaques out of dinner plates.

En route to Broad Peak with the Swedes in 1994 on the 'suicide bus'.
Our driver smoked hashish constantly and drove at breakneck speed, despite
the huge load on the roof.

Rick Allen and Voytek Kurtyka climb unroped on the huge face leading up the
Mazeno Ridge on Nanga Parbat in 1995.

Brian Laursen digging out the crushed tent on Mount Dhaluagiri.
(Photo courtesy of Zac Zaharias)

Major Zac (centre) wins gold from Matt Rogerson (at left) and me, in the
Mr Puniverse competition, after our successful first Australian ascent of
Dhaulagiri.

Broad Peak. Rick and I attempted the right hand skyline ridge. I subsequently soloed the face leading up to the col and bivouacked, on descent, at the left end of the horizontal ridge at centre top. The summit is at the right end.

The road block en route to Skardu. which threatened to stop my Broad Peak expedition in 1997. Shortly after this shot was taken, an army convoy passed through and we seized the opportunity to run the blockade.

plant, even a small one, but the villagers were adamant that they—
and we—weren't going anywhere until the power was switched
on. Amazingly, given the would-be assassins he had to negotiate
with, the government official returned after a couple more hours.
Unfortunately, though, he didn't have the magic switch, and the
discussion soon became a shouting match. As if to prove their
intent, the villagers started to let down the tyres of the waiting
vehicles to further immobilise them.

Nobody carries a tyre pump in Pakistan and I could see us
sitting there for days, with the lost time potentially costing us our
summit chance. As the mob approached our bus to let down the
tyres, I instructed our driver to offer them our car keys instead,
as we'd have no way to reinflate the tyres once the blockade
was lifted. The mob's representative accepted the proposal, but I
actually gave him an old padlock key, knowing that he wouldn't
recognise the difference. I felt no guilt whatsoever at exploiting his
naivety, given that Rick and I had just invested about $20,000 in
his country's economy.

We sat around on the side of the road for several more hours.
Some of the vehicles ahead of us had been there for a couple of
days, and the government representative was clearly struggling to
reach an agreement with the locals. Late in the afternoon, a military
convoy arrived at the blockade from the other direction. They took
no side in the argument but instructed the villagers to allow them
to pass. This was our chance. As the locals rolled back some of the
boulders, I grabbed our driver and we piled into our bus. As we
still had the real car keys, we used the noise of the passing military
convoy to disguise the sound of our vehicle's engine starting.

At the moment the last military truck passed us, our driver
slammed the bus into gear and we charged around the queue and
towards the roadblock, while the villagers raced to roll their boulders
back into position. They were too slow and we tore through the
gap at the last moment, with villagers shouting and throwing rocks

at us. We drove like crazy in case the threat of snipers was real, but no shots came. We were the only private vehicle to get through the blockade until it was finally opened some days later.

From Skardu we jeeped to the village of Askole, purchased the mandatory goat and started the 10-day trek to Base Camp, with thirty porters to carry our fuel, food and equipment. About three-quarters of the way there we suffered a porters' strike. These were becoming increasingly frequent in the region. Despite the contracts they had signed, they demanded additional wages or they wouldn't continue. It wasn't because the loads were too heavy or the track was too difficult; they simply knew they had us over a barrel. These strikes can be quite tense. If we'd refused to pay, they could have done as they threatened, which was to abandon us and all our equipment on the Baltoro Glacier, leaving us without any means of getting to Base Camp. Or they could have stolen our equipment—there'd have been nothing we could have done about it.

Most expeditions just paid the ransom. But we were running a low-budget trip and simply didn't have the money to pay the additional wages. I decided to play them at their own game and agreed to pay the additional money they demanded. We continued the trek, arriving at Base Camp three days later. When it came time to pay them, I counted out the wages for each porter according to their signed contracts. There were shouts and threats as they demanded to know why I hadn't paid the additional money.

'It's simple,' I replied. 'You broke your contract and demanded extra money. I broke my contract to pay you that extra money. We are even.'

It was a risk, I knew, but I preferred to take it at Base Camp rather than halfway there. They had no tents or food, so they couldn't stay at Base Camp longer than the hour it took them to drop off their loads and get paid. After a bit more shouting, they actually saw a bit of humour in having been outplayed. They accepted the contracted wage and departed.

It was 6 July when we reached Base Camp, and we were amazed to find another expedition already there. They were the Inurrategi brothers, Felix and Alberto, of Spain. These guys were hardcore and highly accomplished climbers. They had already been on the mountain for a couple of weeks and it was incredible that a route that had only had two or three previous attempts in history was suddenly hosting two expeditions in the same season.

Rick and I were pissed off that the Ministry of Tourism in Islamabad had not advised us about the other expedition and given us the chance to change our permit to a different route. The South Ridge was so steep and razor sharp that there would be few places to site our tents and sharing the ridge with another team would only exacerbate the problem. Worse, the Inurrategis were several weeks ahead of us and could potentially achieve the first ascent of the ridge before us, thus wasting our time and money and the extreme risk that the climb would involve. As it turned out, it didn't matter because within a week of our arrival, while we were acclimatising on the lowest parts of the mountain, the route became ours alone when the Inurrategi brothers decided to abandon their attempt due to its length and difficulty.

At Base Camp we set up our meagre facilities. Our expedition was very, very lean. We had a cook, Sher Afzal, and the obligatory liaison officer (or LO), a Pakistani Army officer, Captain Shahid. While the heavily sponsored Inurrategi brothers had brought house-sized canvas tents for their base-camp kitchen, dining and sleeping tents, and at least a couple of cooks and all possible luxuries, our expedition kitchen was a low pile of rocks on the glacier with a tarpaulin stretched over the top. It was cold, dirty and uncomfortable. Sher Afzal and Captain Shahid must have felt really ripped off.

Given that there were just four of us, and that Sher Afzal could speak just a couple of words of English—which I admit was better than my Urdu—the four of us agreed that in order to avoid long

nights with no conversation, we would take turns to tell a story—
one person each night. Captain Shahid would translate for Afzal.
The subject was entirely up to the storyteller. It was a great idea
and we enjoyed many interesting nights, with insights into each
other's lives, books we'd read, hobbies, subjects studied at university
and so on.

One night, Rick related the history of the Scottish royal family.
This won't take long, I thought. I couldn't have been more wrong.
He proceeded to recite every detail of every person even remotely
connected with the Scottish throne for the last two thousand years,
maybe longer—I think there were even some dinosaurs thrown
in. Now, I'm of Scottish heritage, but after two hours the LO and
I were praying for a merciful end that neither the gods nor Rick
would bestow.

On the odd occasion when someone found it difficult to think
of a story, or when Rick offered to tell us a few more obscure
facts about the Scottish royals, I took great delight in raising the
topic of religion. The LO was a devout Muslim and Rick a devout
Christian, so this would always spark some lively debate between
them. Luckily, they were both quite able to discuss their faiths
without getting hot under the collar.

Like most liaison officers assigned to expeditions in the Baltoro
region, ours was a Pakistani Army officer. Captain Shahid's role
was to ensure that we climbed the mountain and the route we'd
been assigned, and that we didn't photograph any military bases or
bridges, given the proximity of the mountains to the Indian border
and the ongoing Kashmir conflict. Most LOs were majors, but ours
was a captain, and one day I asked him about his career and what
he saw as his future.

He was quite candid, telling us that he didn't see any promo-
tions for himself in the near future, because he'd been in a bit of
trouble recently. He'd been in charge of a platoon of soldiers in
some part of Pakistan, where he'd been tasked to capture a local

bandit. His orders were to capture the bandit alive, as the authorities wanted to interrogate him. As his platoon surrounded the bandit's house, a shot was fired from within, hitting one of his men. Shahid was so enraged that he ordered his platoon to fire on the house with all weapons. Needless to say, the bandit was not captured alive and our LO's career prospects were curtailed, at least temporarily.

*

Rick and I decided that the best way to climb Broad Peak was alpine style. This meant climbing it in one push from Base Camp to the summit, carrying everything we'd need for all the camps, rather than the siege style of climbing up and down, establishing and stocking a series of permanent camps. The route was so steep and technical—and therefore slow—that it would take us too long to descend from any point, get a fresh load of equipment and food, and climb back to our previous high point. The only way to do it was in one long push, and so each morning, over a week or ten days, we'd pack up the tent and all our equipment and carry it up with us. The risk, however, was that if we needed to descend due to injury, altitude sickness or bad weather, we wouldn't have fixed safety ropes in place to facilitate a quick escape. It is a more pure style of climbing but also a more dangerous one.

Climbing in this way requires you to be acclimatised before you start the ascent. To achieve that, we walked around to the easier West Face of the mountain, and over two days we climbed up to 7000 metres, where we slept a night before returning to base camp. With this done, we felt well enough acclimatised to attempt the unclimbed South Ridge.

Back at Base Camp, we rested for two days, using the time to prepare our loads for the assault. Going alpine style meant that we had to trim every luxury from our loads or they'd be too heavy.

We had food and fuel for a week, tent, sleeping bags, climbing equipment, water bottles and all the little extras—it added up fast. Our packs weighed around 25 kilograms each. To save a few critical grams, I threw out my toothbrush and plastic pee bottle. Pee bottles are essential if you want to avoid struggling out of your sleeping bag into the freezing cold of night, particularly when the tent is perched on a tiny ledge over a huge abyss, with no room to stand outside. But saving weight was critical on this climb. I still wasn't going to go out into the night, though, so if I needed to pee, I'd just have to use my cup.

While we were physically prepared, the climb presented us with a severe psychological challenge. We'd be climbing alone, on a very technical route, without communication with our Base Camp or anyone else. Any accident or prolonged storm would almost certainly be fatal. The only way to overcome our self-doubt and trepidation was to stay absolutely focused and committed to our goal. And, to get on with it.

We planned to start the climb on 21 July. After dinner the night before, I fiddled with the final adjustments to my load, and then completed an entry in my diary:

> Have a small moosehead good-luck charm that Alex gave me at the airport. Mustn't forget to take it … Just had dinner—everyone is a bit nervous, including Shahid (our LO). Have agreed to send an 8 p.m. torch signal of 3 flashes = ok; 10 flashes means coming down for some reason.

I finished the page with my last will and testament, and settled in for a few hours of sleep.

As if to test us, though, the weather the next morning steadily deteriorated. It was both a reprieve and a great frustration, as our nervousness only increased while we lay in our tents. We prepared for a start the following morning but were again stopped by rain and sleet. I was getting edgy, so I applied my nervous energy to construction, building a frame under the kitchen tarpaulin to prevent the rainwater from running inside.

On 23 July we awoke to patchy cloud. It appeared to be clearing and we could wait no longer. We called out to Sher Afzal to get the kitchen stove going, and he duly produced an inventive concoction of chocolate muesli. At least, I think that's what it was. Shahid gave us a couple of little food bars for good luck, a genuine and heartfelt gesture that I greatly appreciated.

The route took us up a rising glacier, on which we placed Camp 1, then up a steep and exposed ice face. We soloed the first 250 metres of 60-degree ice before facing a bulge that steepened to the vertical. Rick went first and trailed a rope, but he climbed so quickly that I couldn't catch it. I picked my way up very carefully, still solo and unroped. The face narrowed to a rock and ice gully, where the climbing was technical but fun, and we reached the ridge above at about 10 a.m.

We'd hoped to keep climbing another 500 metres higher, but it was too hot. We spent the remainder of the day resting and rehydrating and set out again at midnight, hoping for firmer snow conditions. The route led us over a jagged and exposed ridge before joining up with a long snow ramp, up which we took turns plugging steps for endless exhausting hours with our 25-kilogram rucksacks. We finally hit the South Ridge proper at 4 p.m., sixteen hours after setting out that morning. These mountains are so big that our two days of tough climbing had only brought us to the start of our intended route.

From our vantage point we could see major rock buttresses on the South Ridge, so we soloed below them, across a very steep and exposed face. The drop was a couple of thousand metres—not the place to slip. We traversed to where the rock blocked our way, and then climbed up to the massive buttress above us. With our limited equipment, continuing meant crossing the point of no return.

We wouldn't be able to down-climb back through that buttress if things went bad, but we'd known in advance that this would be the case. Our plan was to climb over the summit and then down the West Face, on which we'd previously acclimatised.

Normally, this was a risk we'd have accepted, but on this occasion we both felt apprehensive about the situation. It wasn't that the rock buttress was impossible, although it was clearly highly committing; it was more a feeling of unease, almost dread. We decided to descend. It was a big decision to give up because it meant the end of our attempt on that route, but to me it felt like we were being given a second chance. My inner voice speaks loudly when I'm on a mountain, and I'm not inclined to ignore it.

Despite having started climbing at 7 a.m. that day, we descended well into the evening, not stopping until we reached a lower camp-site at midnight. Such are the days on big hills. The descent was not without challenges. An avalanche had stretched a section of rope left by the Inurrategi brothers that we'd hoped to use, so that it was too tight to clip on to. We were forced to solo again, above the steepest sections. When we clipped to the rope a little lower, we saw that it was frayed and worn thin in places from abrasion against the rock. Thankfully, the darkness of night hid the abyss below us and we could turn our minds away from the danger.

Rick started to abseil. Suddenly the piton that anchored the rope to the cliff yanked out of the rock. With a startled yelp, he fell. *He's a goner,* I immediately thought, and watched on, aghast but helpless. Incredibly, the rope snagged on a tiny knob of rock, just long enough for Rick to regain his purchase on the mountain. Our small team of two had almost become a smaller team of one.

The next day we continued our descent, however the heat of the preceding couple of days had caused considerable rockfall. The rope had been nicked in a dozen places, but, without a replace-ment, we were forced to rely on it. I gingerly rappelled down a steep gully, using the points of my crampons on every little edge to try to take some of the weight off the cord, but in the end I had to commit myself and swing out over a cliff.

I found myself hanging in free space, the seriously damaged rope stretched thin and taught as steel, its worn sheath rubbing vigorously on the sharp cliff edge above. Below me was a steep face that fell away for another 800 metres. My heart was pounding and, with my full body weight plus my 25-kilogram backpack pulling on that frayed thread, I fully expected it to break at any instant and send me tumbling down the face, bringing an untimely end to my high-altitude aspirations. I did everything I could not to bounce as I descended.

I thought momentarily about how I might stop my fall if the rope snapped, but in reality I knew I'd be killed within seconds. For reasons known only to the gods and that rope's manufacturers, it didn't break. When at last my feet touched the slope below me, even though it was still steep and exposed and I had to down-climb very carefully, it felt as flat as a football field.

We reached Base Camp in the late afternoon and collapsed gratefully into our tents. Soon afterwards, a storm blew in, and it lasted for days. Had we continued climbing through that rock buttress up on the ridge, we'd have been caught by the storm at 8000 metres. That feeling of unease, our inner voices, had saved us.

*

Rick was out of time and decided to go home, which left me in a difficult position. I was still highly motivated to climb Broad Peak, but without Rick as my partner I would have to climb without a rope. That would mean greater risk, but my determination to succeed or take up another sport meant I had to take every possible opportunity to summit. I would have to climb a route that was less technical than the South Ridge, though, so I decided to wait out the storm and attempt a solo ascent of the West Face.

Ten days of snowfall meant a heightened avalanche risk, but a basic rule is to wait at least a day for avalanches to clear before setting foot on the slopes. I passed that day walking around the mountain to the Base Camp below the West Face. A more pressing issue was how best to attempt such a big mountain without a climbing partner to share the load of breaking trail and carrying equipment. I knew that lugging a heavy load in all that fresh snow would destroy me, so I decided that my only possible method of reaching the summit was to leave everything, including my tent, sleeping bag and mattress, behind. My only climbing equipment would be the crampons on my boots, an ice axe in my hand and a stove so I could melt snow to rehydrate. I figured that with the light load, and assuming I didn't freeze, I might just make it.

When I reached the West Face Base Camp, I found two expeditions there. One was American, whose members told me that I would have no chance of climbing through all the fresh snow. They had given up on the mountain and had called for porters. The other team was Spanish, although not the Inurrategi brothers. They felt the same way but were going to wait a week for the deep snow to settle or avalanche off, and then have a go. I was determined to try, however, so I borrowed a down suit from the Americans and a radio from the Spanish.

I set off at five the next morning and climbed quickly through Camp 1 and towards Camp 2. The snow was deep but negotiable. All signs of previous expeditions and fixed ropes were well buried. I revelled in the feeling of being alone, powering up the slopes. I was fit, acclimatised and well rested after my prolonged wait at base camp. Stopping only for an occasional snack, I continued all the way up to Camp 3, which sat at 7000 metres, a good 2000 metres' continuous climbing above Base Camp.

Arriving there at 4 p.m., I started my stove and drank several cups of tea over the next couple of hours, and snoozed in the luxurious warmth of the bulky American down suit. Waking at

11.20 p.m., I lit the stove for one last drink. It was a clear night, but there was a mild breeze and it was bitterly cold.

I started climbing at 12.20 a.m. There was no moon, and after a couple of hours in the pitch-dark, I couldn't tell if I was on the right heading to get to the narrow couloir that would give me access to the ridge above. At 2.30 a.m. I stopped and waited until first light, which came around four, so that I could find my way up. So bitter was the cold that my 1-litre water bottle froze solid, despite being in a pocket inside my down suit.

The light made it easier to see the way, but as the face steepened the snow became much deeper. I sometimes plunged thigh-deep, sometimes waist-deep, and other times I actually slid backwards down the slope. That wasn't great for my motivation. Worse, I knew that there were two large crevasses to cross. Being unroped, I was at great risk of falling into them. There was no one on the mountain to rescue me if that happened, and I'd die either from the fall or from asphyxiation, crushed deep inside the icy fissure. Added to that risk was the considerable avalanche debris all around me, and my subconscious started asking the inevitable questions about the sanity of the task I'd embarked upon. I hadn't listened to the others on this point, I decided, so there was no point in listening to myself either.

The fresh snow must have been very deep because I didn't ever find those crevasses, but the work of clawing my way up the bottomless muck in the ever-steepening gully was desperate. Hours ticked by and I seemed to be making hardly any progress. I had hoped to be on the col, a saddle between the Main and Central Buttresses, by 8 a.m., but that hour came and went and I was still well below it. I was comfortable being alone on this massive mountain, but I could feel my legs starting to tire. My wish for company at that moment was more to do with sharing the trail breaking than for the human contact.

To counter any waning of my motivation, I reminded myself of my ultimate goal: Everest. Broad Peak was a step on the way, and exhaustion was simply not an excuse to quit. Nor was cold, self-doubt or loneliness. I pressed on and, finally, pulled up and onto the col at midday. When I'd set out from my bivouac twelve hours earlier, I'd hoped to be on the summit by this time, but there were still hours of climbing ahead of me in the rarefied air. I set my mind to yet another epic day at high altitude.

At least the ridge was more solid than the slopes below had been. It was heavily corniced—windblown snow on the edges that concealed the limits of the solid ground—so I tried to stay above where I thought the rock was. I climbed over some knobs of snow and rock and was going okay, when suddenly the ground fell out from underneath me and I plummeted downwards.

Instinctively I knew I'd strayed too far onto the cornice and had fallen through it. I threw my arms out sideways—like a crucifix—to stop myself from falling through the hole. Luckily the cornice held my plunging weight. My feet were dangling in space and when I looked through the hole my body had created in the cornice, I could see straight down the sheer vertical East Face of the mountain, thousands of metres down into China. I didn't have a visa for that country, though, so considered it best not to keep falling.

As I looked down, I saw an old ice axe sticking out of the snow a couple of feet below me. *I'll have that, thanks*, I thought, and gently reached down with one hand to retrieve it while hanging rather precariously from the other. I'm guessing the previous owner had had a similar experience to me but continued down into China, also without a visa, and liked it so much that he stayed. If, on the other hand, the Buddhists are right, then I still have that ice axe at home and he's welcome to have it back.

I was able to get some footing and crawled back onto firm ground. The near miss had taken a toll on my confidence, though, and I felt even more alone and exposed, totally beyond any kind of help. My mind was playing games with me and I was starting to listen to it.

The ridge steepened and I was forced to climb across very exposed rock pinnacles. I picked my way gingerly around them, feeling really unprotected without the safety of a rope. Near the top of the ridge, a large pinnacle forced me further out onto the face, and I found myself delicately traversing on loose rock with enormous exposure beneath me. The Base Camp tents that I'd left at dawn the previous day were 3 vertical kilometres below the soles of my feet.

At this point my self-doubt welled up, and every sense screamed at me to turn back. I stopped, clinging to life by my mittens and crampon points. I had no rope, no friendly, encouraging voices with me, no one even to notice my passing if I slipped. I looked around. I was completely alone on the mountain, had just nearly fallen through a cornice, was mentally strung out after a day and a half of climbing solo without equipment, and had been without food or water since midnight. Above me lay danger, perhaps even death. Below me, safety, comfort and warmth. And people.

I looked again at the steep rock to which I clung. If any of my hand or footholds broke, or even slightly slipped, I was gone. The only sensible thing was to go down. I'd given it my best shot, but this was beyond acceptable risk. I started down.

Wait a minute, my inner voice reminded me. *Remember: you decided to start succeeding or take up another sport. After this, it's lawn bowls.*

I stopped again. *Acceptable risk.* I looked once more at the rock, still feeling very, very exposed, and willing it to give me an answer. *Actually, the climbing isn't so difficult*, I thought. *Okay, so there's no rope. And nobody to see me fall. But what would they do anyway? Wave good-bye?* I suddenly understood that it was the environment that was intimidating me, not the climbing. The climbing was well within my capability. At sea level I'd do it with my eyes closed. Sure, if a hold broke I'd have a bad day, but that wasn't actually likely. It was unlikely. The climbing was within acceptable risk.

With that realisation, I was able to control my fear and continue. I began moving up again. I later wrote in my expedition diary:

> Decided to go for it. Did not want to fail again. This was really a psychological point in the climb! Once committed, I knew I would make the summit. I wasn't going to stop. I knew that I would be caught by the darkness but I was no longer concerned. I would take the obstacles as they came. Moved up ... all the while clinging to the rock pinnacle like a cat to a tree branch.

This was the most significant epiphany I'd had in my climbing career. The previous few years of expeditions had all failed on the summit push, and while there'd been a good reason to stop each time, in retrospect I believe I could have better assessed the risks involved and pushed harder to succeed.

This time I did push on. I overcame the rock step and continued up the ridge, climbing over ice seracs and a couple of little pinnacles before finally breaking out onto the false summit. It was 3.30 p.m. I knew that many expeditions had stopped at this point and claimed to have reached the true summit because it is still a daunting distance away along the ridge, but I wasn't interested in claiming the summit; I wanted to achieve it. Logically, perhaps I should have turned around, since the night would be on me in a couple of hours, but I was so far past my own turn-around time that it didn't matter any more. Either way, I would still be climbing when darkness fell. And I wanted that summit.

*

The summit ridge of Broad Peak is very long, close to a kilometre. It undulates by 15 or 20 metres but is pretty much on the same contour except for a couple of seracs along the way. I edged carefully along the crest, which dropped sharply down the West Face and absolutely vertically on its east side, then climbed over a large serac and started the long traverse to the true summit.

It took another two and a half exhausting hours, as I plodded just a few steps at a time and then bent over my ice axe and gasped for breath for several minutes. Finally, after ascending a short rise to a snowy pinnacle, I was on top. It was 6.05 p.m. on 7 August 1997.

It was a balmy and clear evening, with spectacular views across the Karakorum Mountains, over the Gasherbrum Ranges to Masherbrum and back to K2. I turned on the borrowed Spanish radio and called them at base camp. They were cheering and congratulating me and said that they'd watched me through their telescope. I took a few photos, then balanced my little camera on my ice axe to take a self-portrait.

I spent fifteen minutes on the summit and then started back, six and a half hours behind schedule. By 7 p.m. it was dark and I climbed by the light of my headlamp. It would be a long night. I was incredibly tired, and hadn't had a drink in twenty-one hours of extreme physical effort in the dry and cold atmosphere, nor any food.

I climbed back along the ridge as fast as I could, but the hours ticked by quickly. My exhaustion must have been extreme because it took longer to climb down the ridge than up it. At 11 p.m. I found myself at the top of the rock step that had almost stopped me on the way up. By then I was so frozen and dehydrated that I didn't have the dexterity to climb back down the rock and so I was faced with a dilemma: risk climbing down without being able to hold on properly, or bivouac at 8000 metres without tent, sleeping bag, stove or water.

Bivouac! That most fearsome of words to high-altitude climbers. I'd once watched a documentary about Mike Rheinberger's successful but tragic ascent of Everest in 1994, in which a climber at Base Camp watched through a telescope as Mike and his guide were preparing to bivouac.

'*Bivouac*,' he'd said. 'French for mistake.'

That comment rang loudly in my mind. This was a far more serious situation than my brief bivouac the night before, 1000 metres lower, where I'd had a stove and where the air was exponentially thicker. Bivouacking at this altitude meant prolonged exposure without the oxygen I so desperately needed, which brought a much greater likelihood of falling victim to pulmonary and/or cerebral oedema. If they got me, I'd be dead. My dehydrated state also meant that my blood was thickening dangerously, leaving me at great risk of a stroke. And, in the extreme cold, my body would try to prevent hypothermia by cutting the blood flow to my fingers and toes, so I'd also be risking serious frostbite. If that happened, I'd be stuck above the rock step for good. Bivouacking above the rock step was all bad news, but I simply couldn't down-climb the cliff without falling. Put simply, my choice was to stay up and risk death, or to climb down and guarantee it. I chose the bivouac.

It would be the longest night of my life to that point—interminable, freezing at minus 25 degrees Celsius, a strong wind blowing and nowhere to shelter. I scraped a seat in the snow, then took off my crampons so they wouldn't draw the heat from my feet and forced myself to stay awake so that I wouldn't just go to sleep and die.

I worked my fingers and toes throughout the night to stave off frostbite. To kill time, I dreamed of cooking meals and eating them. I even went as far as making up a recipe, shopping for the ingredients, preparing the meal, cooking it and then eating it slowly, savouring every bite. All in my mind.

The time passed so slowly that it was depressing to look at my watch, so I'd try to estimate how much had elapsed. When I thought it was about an hour, I'd refuse to look at my watch and force myself to wait another hour, just to be sure. When finally that hour had passed in my mind, I'd allow myself to peek, only to find that just five minutes had elapsed since I last looked. Five minutes when it felt like two hours! It was soul-destroying. The night just wouldn't end. I told myself stories, mumbled songs with chattering teeth, rolled from side to side to keep from freezing, and visualised warm things.

I forced myself to break the night into chunks and focus only on each chunk. When an hour had passed—a real hour—I told myself that I was one-sixth of the way through the night—*That was an hour. Now we'll do another one. Just another hour.* After the second hour I was one-third of the way there—*One-third. That wasn't so bad. Only twice that still to go. I can do this.* After three hours I was halfway there—*Okay, you're over the hump. Everything still to go is less than you've done already. It isn't so bad. It isn't so cold. Wiggle your fingers. Wiggle your toes. I can do this.*

Finally, there was a faint lightening of the sky to the east, but I had to wait until the sun actually rose to feel some warmth. With the caress of those first life-giving rays, I regained some dexterity in my fingers—enough to climb with.

I picked my way down the cliffs with the greatest care, as I still had only limited feeling in my hands. I felt very clumsy, like I'd been drugged by exhaustion and the altitude. Once off the rock face, I staggered down the corniced snow ridge to the col and, from there, plunged down the deep, steep snow face to where I'd left my stove, reaching it at 10 a.m.

I called the Spanish and assured them that I was okay. They were greatly concerned that I might have been frostbitten, but I could feel my toes so I knew that any damage would be minor. It took another hour or so to boil some snow for a drink, as everything I did was in slow motion—just lighting the stove took a weight of concentration and effort. That first drink, thirty-eight hours since my last, was a weird mix of excruciating pain and pure bliss as I tried to swallow. But the pain eased and I kept the stove going until I'd drunk enough and filled my water bottle again.

I then struck down for Base Camp, pushing myself through my exhaustion. By now I was desperate to get off the hill. Yet I was so spent that I'd fall back onto the snow and sit there panting for five minutes until I regained my breath. Eventually I passed some members of the Spanish team who'd decided to make their own summit bid.

I had no desire to spend a third night in the open, so I pressed on without a rest, reaching the glacier around 7 p.m., where I wheezed and staggered in the gloom, anxious not to be caught in the maze of ice cliffs and crevasses there. My legs felt like dead weights and my almost empty rucksack like a bag of concrete. The final obstacle was a few small ridges of ice, but even the smallest rise now seemed Everest-like in size and reduced me to a crawl.

At last I arrived at the Spanish Base Camp. It was about 8 p.m. Someone handed me some food, but it was fluid that I needed, and I sat there, speechless, drinking endless cups of tea and warm juice. In the afterglow of success and safety, I slumped into a tent; however, sleep escaped me—probably due to adrenaline, caffeine and the physical pain that was racking my body.

Shahid had walked up from the South Ridge Base Camp to meet me. He'd made up a sign congratulating me and welcoming me back to base camp: 'Welcome to Base Camp safe and sound after successful, courageous, wonderful and above all alone climb of Broad Peak.' It was a really lovely gesture and I was very touched.

With that, the expedition was over. While my little team of three waited several days for our porters to collect us, the Spanish summitted and returned to Base Camp safely and I pondered my latest success. Broad Peak was my third ascent of an 8000-metre mountain. By reaching its summit a few months after summitting Dhaulagiri, I'd become the first Australian to successfully summit two 8000-metre peaks in one year. More importantly, though, I had turned the corner on failure and endured two very tough expeditions, both of which had tested me to the limits of my psychological and physical endurance. Both had almost killed me, but I'd persevered and succeeded. And I'd learned that risk management is more than just knowing when to turn back; it is also about knowing when *not* to give up. I knew then that I could, and would, cope with whatever challenges I faced in the future. More than that, I looked to them with anticipation.

That trek back to civilisation was glorious. I was on a high from my success and I was alive, fabulously warm, and safe. I luxuriated in every little experience, my senses in overdrive—a cup of tea, the first smell of vegetation, a friendly conversation. These were the real rewards for having put myself on the very edge of existence, for having risked my life on what many would see as a useless lump of rock and ice. For me, these intangible rewards were of exponentially more value than anything money could buy. I was the richest man on Earth and positively glowed with spiritual energy.

Postscript

Felix Inurrategi died in an avalanche on Gasherbrum 2 in 2000. This was a real tragedy because Gasherbrum 2 is one of the easiest 8000ers and he was a very gifted and accomplished climber.

6

SUMMITS AND BETRAYALS

*To those who have struggled with them, the mountains reveal beauties
that they will not disclose to those who make no effort. That is the
reward the mountains give to effort. And it is because they have so
much to give and give it so lavishly to those who will wrestle with
them that men love the mountains and go back to them again and
again. The mountains reserve their choice gifts for those who stand
upon their summits.*

Sir Francis Younghusband

WHILE 1997 WAS the turning point in my climbing career,
1998 was a pivotal moment in my working life. I'd been
operating for a number of years in covert police taskforces between
expeditions, investigating highly organised crime. Suddenly I found
myself, together with a number of the best detectives in the police
force, the subject of an aggressive investigation by our own agency
due to an accusation of corruption. It came as a terrible shock to
all of us—not so much that we were accused, because many people
accuse police of wrongdoing in attempts to undermine criminal

cases against them, but because the police hierarchy treated us as though we were guilty before we'd had a chance to prove otherwise. We felt terribly betrayed. We fought hard to clear our names and subsequently were fully exonerated—we were even awarded medals for our work. But I'd seen the organisation that I'd faithfully served for nearly twenty years turn on me, and I lost all confidence in its leadership.

I'd also been pursuing a new love interest in Australia for a while, but just as things were getting interesting, Lynda was injured in a motorcycle accident. By the time she'd recovered, her ardour had cooled and I was flying solo again.

I decided the best thing to do was to take an extended leave of absence—a sabbatical, if you like—from the police force to think about my future. I enrolled in a part-time disaster-management degree at university and applied for a position as a training officer with the Australian Antarctic Division, which ran scientific research expeditions in the deep white south. I also thought about big hills.

The call of the mountains was stronger than ever. While I needed a break from the recent stresses in my life, more than anything I just wanted to re-experience the savage yet intensely honest existence of high altitude. With the successes of 1997 and my newfound understanding of managing risk, I was keen to return to my adversary of recent years, Nanga Parbat. Coincidentally, British climber Alan Hinkes called me early in 1998 to ask if I'd like to climb it with him that year. At the time, Hinkes had climbed more 8000ers than me, so I hoped we'd work well together.

The day before I left Australia was frenetic. I had a university exam—in psychology, ironically enough—then I went to town to buy duty-free and foreign currency and rushed home to pack my belongings, which were going into storage because as soon as I returned from the expedition I'd be heading to Antarctica for seven months. I moved boxes until midnight and started again the next morning, not finishing until midday. I then headed for the shops for some last-minute purchases for the expedition, before driving to the airport and getting on the plane.

We trekked into the Diamir Valley, on the same side of the mountain as I'd been with the mad Polish expedition when we'd attempted the Kinshofer Route in 1996. The Base Camp there is truly lovely, with grass underfoot, marmots all around and wild ibex in the surrounding hills. At 4000 metres in altitude, it is one of the lowest of any 8000-metre base camps, and you can recover much more effectively at this altitude than at, say, Everest's Base Camp at 5300 metres. It wouldn't be right if there wasn't a down-side, though. On Everest, one has to gain approximately 3.5 vertical kilometres from Base Camp to the summit. On Nanga Parbat, it is over 4 vertical kilometres.

There were two other drawbacks. First, there's a large rock cliff on one side of the valley, from which truck-sized boulders regularly crash down onto the valley floor, before rolling around randomly, much like the trucks on the KKH. And second, the frisky little ibex, lithely bounding across the rock slabs above us, were good eating, which inspired the base camp staff, liaison officers and locals to prove their manhood. They also proved the worthlessness of AK-47s as hunting rifles, and how well military ammunition ricochets around valley floors and through nylon tents. *Insha'Allah.*

Ours wasn't the only expedition on the Diamir side of the mountain that year. I was excited to learn that Kurt Diemberger, one of the world's most famous 8000-metre pioneers, was there to do some filming. It was an incredible thrill for me to meet the German because he had been a member of two expeditions in the 1950s that made the first ascents of Broad Peak and Dhaulagiri, and I'd just climbed the very same two peaks in 1997. He was totally supportive of me as one of the 'next generation' of climbers having my own go on the 8000ers.

Alan and I coveted a route on the mountain known as the Mummery Rib, named after the British climber Alfred Mummery, who was immortalised in 1895 on this very hill. Infamous for the frequent avalanches it experiences, the route forces its way up an improbable looking line below, between and around some enormous cliffs of ice. Shortly after we arrived at Base Camp, one of the cliffs released what we would learn were daily examples of why people don't successfully climb the Mummery Rib. Including Mummery. The avalanche, which was a couple of kilometres away from us, was of such epic proportions that it shook the ground we stood on as it crashed down the mountain, sweeping everything before it. It thundered into the glacier below for several minutes, sending a billowing cloud of ice particles over our camp. We watched until the avalanche debris cleared, then agreed to climb the Kinshofer Route instead.

This season was much warmer than in 1996, and on the steep mountain face between our Camp 1 and Camp 2 we were under constant threat from rocks that melted out of the ice above us and fell. As we 'front-pointed'—using the front spikes of our crampons—up the steep ice face, hundreds of metres above the glacier, rocks came screaming past us, often missing us narrowly. It was Russian roulette. The high temperatures that were melting out the rocks caused us other problems as well. It's easy to dehydrate in the very dry air of altitude and the heat compounded the effect. On one load carry up to the lower camps, I began suffering from painful kidneys and strong headaches and I suspected dehydration. I drank four litres of water that evening, but by morning I'd peed only about 200 millilitres.

The climb progressed well enough, but I soon learned that Alan wouldn't break trail—he preferred to follow. That meant I had to do the hard work of kicking fresh steps whenever we were on new ground. While I had always enjoyed being out in front, as the altitude increased I knew I was taking the risks and sacrificing my own fitness while Alan preserved his. He knew it too. Nonetheless, we overcame the major technical obstacles of the route to place our Camp 2 on a rock rib above the steep Kinshofer Face.

While resting there and waiting for a bit of bad weather to clear, I saw something buried in the ice underneath my feet. I hacked at the ice for hours, and eventually uncovered a large object that seemed to be wrapped in a tarpaulin or old tent. Tied to the outside of the object were several old bamboo ski poles. I was able to recover three of them, and assumed that the object was a stash of climbing equipment or rubbish left over by an early expedition. I didn't attempt to open the frozen tarpaulin. After I returned home, I learned that the German expedition that completed the first ascent of the Kinshofer Route in 1962—which was named after one of the team, Toni Kinshofer—had lost one of its members on the mountain. The leather handles of the old bamboo ski poles were stamped clearly with a German manufacturers' mark, Desgleffs, suggesting that they were probably from Kinshofer's expedition. To this day, I've wondered if I disturbed the last resting place of the lost member from that expedition. I certainly hope not, but I still have those ski poles.

Our cook on this expedition, Sher Raman, was an engaging and friendly young man whose English skills far surpassed my basic grasp of Urdu. One cool night, he appeared in the dining tent wearing a most extraordinary coat. It was knitted from undyed handspun wool, full-length, with oversized sleeves and colourful embroidered patterns. It had been made by an elderly couple in his village and the task had taken them three months. They'd sold it to him for 3800 rupees (approximately US$70 at the time). It was quite the fashion statement, and the other local men eyed it off enviously. For people who owned virtually nothing, this was a most-prized possession.

After two and a half weeks we'd established our way up to Camp 3. Following a few days' rest at Base Camp, we climbed back up and opened the route up to Camp 4 at 7200 metres, from which we could make our summit attempt. Also going for the summit were five other climbers: two teams of two Koreans, one of which had a Pakistani high-altitude porter named Rosi Ali. One of the Koreans was Park Young-Seok, a highly accomplished 8000-metre veteran who was well on his way to climbing all fourteen peaks of that height.

We set out at first light from the high camp, around 4 a.m. I led and broke the trail for the first hundred metres, then Park took a turn for 30 metres, before handing over to Hinkes who led for 20. Ali and I then alternated the lead for a few hundred metres before stopping to wait for someone else to come up, but Hinkes, Park and the other Koreans all stopped about 30 metres below us and rested. So Ali did another stint, as did I, and again we stopped and waited. Again the others stopped below us. I called out to them to come up and do their share of the work, but they stood there mute. When Ali and I started moving again, they did too.

This would be the pattern for the entire day. Ali and I pushed out the route and broke the trail in deep snow, and at every point the others refused point-blank to do any work, even when I yelled some artistic encouragement towards them. Without their help, the going was slow, and by 1 p.m. we'd only reached about 7700 metres. Ali and I were completely shattered and could barely put one step in front of the other. We'd been going for eight hours, and those other bastards refused to do their share.

As we lay down to rest, a strong but brief blizzard blew in. We hunkered down for about 30 minutes until it passed, and as it eased the others finally climbed up to us. Ali and I shouted at them to take the lead, but they all averted their eyes. I then declared that I wouldn't break another step, as did Ali, who was sobbing on his knees at that point, exhausted confusion on his face. The Koreans' response was that if we wouldn't break the trail, they'd go back down to Camp 4 and give up the summit. That suited me fine. Hinkes remained in the background and waited to see what would happen.

Despite my exhaustion, I had a sudden rush of blood to the head, and in a fit of anger I grabbed Ali and told him we could make it to the top ourselves. If I had to do the work alone, so be it. I would summit this mountain anyway. Fuck the others!

We jumped up and almost forced marched ourselves up the final slopes. Luckily for us, the face had turned from deep snow to mixed ground—rock and snow—and we were able to get a better purchase. At 5.50 p.m. we staggered onto the summit. Needless to say, the others all followed us to the top, at which point they hugged each other and celebrated like they'd actually earned it. Hinkes actually asked me to take photos of him, and then to hold the video camera while he narrated what a great climb it had been and how hard it was.

In later years, I reflected on what motivated these people to come to a mountain like Nanga Parbat if they didn't want to participate fully in the climb. Where was the fun in just follow- ing? I came to appreciate the difference between them and me. I climbed for the love of it and to challenge myself, to see if I could do it. It was their loss, I decided, because I had become part of that mountain. I felt it, knew it. But this was just the start of the drama on Nanga Parbat in 1998.

*

We'd arrived at the top shortly before dusk, so we needed to descend as quickly as possible. At 7 p.m. we started down, but I was so tired from the climb that I had to stop and rest every couple of steps. Before I knew it, Hinkes took off down the mountain, leaving me behind in the growing darkness. Both pairs of Koreans also passed me by, with Ali in tow. Good riddance, I thought. I'm better off without them. Alone and with only my headlamp for light at the top of this mighty and remote Himalayan massif, I started a slow plod down the slopes, following the tracks to safety.

I took my time, because my headlamp was quite dim and there was absolutely no moon. I didn't expect to see the others until I reached the tents but after just an hour, I caught up to them all again. They'd stopped at the point where the blizzard had hit us on the climb up, at around 7700 metres. Below that point, our tracks had been buried by fresh snow. They were unsure of the way and were also concerned about avalanche danger. Hinkes wanted me to lead. I didn't say a word, just pushed past them and kept climbing down, followed immediately by Hinkes, and behind him, the Koreans. I was able to find the way down the mountain reasonably well, but was very slow as I'd burned all my reserves on the ascent. When we reached safer ground I told Hinkes to go ahead and he led until we were in the vicinity of Camp 4 around midnight.

When we'd sited the camp the day before, we'd placed it below a serac, in the hope that it would provide some protection should an avalanche sweep down, as was common in that area. But that meant our tent was hidden from our view as we descended. All we could see were lots of seracs spread across the face, to both sides and below us.

Hinkes lay in the snow and waited while I descended about 80 metres to look below some seracs that I could just make out in the gloom. Two of the Koreans and Ali arrived at Hinkes' position, and in the stillness of the night I could hear them talking. From my position, further down the face, they appeared to disperse.

It was about 1 a.m. when I got to the seracs below me, but the tents weren't there. I looked up and could see headlamps spread out across the face, and it appeared the others were searching for the camp. Not long after, the lamps disappeared and I assumed they had bivouacked. I searched a little longer but without success. I called out a number of times but received no response. At 2 a.m.,

I decided to bivouac also. I climbed to a safe spot and hacked out a small ledge with my ice axe, then settled there to await the dawn. I was frozen, exhausted and dehydrated, and I knew that I was in for another brutal night, as I recorded in my journal:

> Was feeling exhausted but okay and figured it was only until first light at four a.m. Sat for a while then lay but too cold. Almost immediately all my warmth was sapped out. Knew I should take off my crampons to prevent heat drainage, and also had my down vest still on my harness which I could put on, but both were too much effort. Bad sign.
>
> Felt lucid, just exhausted. Probably should have put on vest. Thought I might lose a bit of heat putting it on. In the end, just sat there wriggling my toes and rocking back and forth. Luckily, I had carried my down mitts as spares and I put them on to save my fingers. Didn't allow myself to sleep as I would have fallen off the ledge. Used my ice axe to anchor myself but not sufficient on that slope. Kept nodding off and jerking awake. Then would work my toes and fingers again and rub my shoulders to warm up.

At this point the most amazing thing happened: a light appeared down in the valley, 3.5 kilometres below me. Our Base Camp cook had hung a small kerosene lantern on the outside of the cook tent. That dull glimmer seemed a tangible link to life, which gave me an incredible boost. It was like someone holding out a hand to me. I focused on that lantern for the next few hours.

Of course, the time still dragged by. It was desperately freezing—around minus 30 degrees Celsius—and I was so exposed to the elements that I should have been severely frostbitten, but somehow I made it through largely unscathed.

At 4.45 a.m., in the grey light of dawn, I climbed back up the slope to where I'd left Hinkes. To my surprise, he wasn't there, nor could I see any of the other climbers. I looked around and found a trail in the snow that led off to some nearby seracs. I followed the trail, and there were the tents—just 100 metres from where I'd bivouacked. I was disgusted that the others had found the camp and not let me know.

When I reached my tent and opened the door, there was Hinkes, in the tent, wrapped up in both of our sleeping bags. I doubted that the flushed look on his face was from overheating but I was still shaking almost uncontrollably from the bitterly cold bivouac and desperately tired, so I blundered into the tent, snatched back my sleeping bag and collapsed inside it, fully dressed.

Waking at 8 a.m. for a few much needed drinks, I wallowed in the faint warmth of the sun as it hit the tent, grateful to be alive and uninjured. We were still at 7200 metres and needed to get off the mountain, so after packing our equipment, we descended through Camp 3 to Camp 2, arriving about 5 p.m. In the thicker air I actually felt quite good and managed to eat a big dinner, if only to lighten the load going down.

The next day I reached Base Camp and was delighted to receive a congratulatory garland of flowers from our cook staff. Somehow they seemed to know there'd been underhandedness on the climb and they took extra care of me in basecamp. Sher Raman was more excited than I was, as our summit maintained his record of only ever having worked for successful expeditions.

Hinkes went on to claim all fourteen of the 8000ers, but his assertion was discredited by the main historian of 8000-metre ascents, the American journalist Elizabeth Hawley. A resident of Kathmandu since the 1960s, Ms Hawley, as she is known to one and all, has for over fifty years chronicled expeditions to the Himalaya and, in particular, to the 8000ers. She is the world's undisputed statistical expert on the big hills, and the authority on who has and who hasn't actually climbed the peaks they claim to have ascended. Ms Hawley recorded Hinkes' claim to have successfully summitted Cho Oyu, one of the fourteen 8000ers as 'disputed'. This meant that when I completed the fourteen peaks, I would actually be the first member of the British Commonwealth to do so, an achievement that Hinkes had previously claimed.

Hinkes' own book about climbing the 8000ers was published in 2013. In it, he wrote that he'd made a solo expedition to Nanga Parbat in 1998 and was totally independent. I wasn't mentioned in any part of his account. I wonder if he's forgotten that I actually survived that bivouac? He also wrote that from where he lay in the snow a short distance from Camp 4, on his descent from the summit, he'd seen the tents but had waited for two hours until some others arrived and led the way across some dangerous ground. Sure wish he'd told me that at the time.

My ascent—and survival—of this peak were particularly satisfying, as mine was the first Australian ascent of that mountain. It was my fourth ascent of an 8000-metre peak, and my second first Australian ascent. The perpetual rockfall between camps 1 and 2 had been extraordinarily dangerous. Indeed, a day after we returned to Base Camp, a Japanese climber was hit and killed on that very face. It was almost inevitable that someone would die there. I was just lucky that it hadn't been me.

The disappointing aspect of this expedition was that I'd once again found myself with a climber whom I didn't really know, and whose company I really didn't enjoy. It didn't put me off climbing any more than the death of the Japanese climber had, but it would have been nice to have shared the experience with a mate, someone who valued the spirituality and sanctity of the big hills. The camaraderie of sharing and overcoming significant challenges with a friend is incredibly powerful. The mountains were my escape from jerks. I certainly didn't go there to be partnered with them. I'd rather climb solo than team up with someone whose motivation and ethics are diametrically opposed to mine.

The frustration for me was that there simply weren't any Australian mountaineers who wanted to climb either as regularly as

I did, or on the tougher 8000ers such as Nanga Parbat. I'd become the most active 8000-metre climber in the country, despite not yet having climbed Mount Everest. On the plus side, I'd met one of the Himalayan greats in Kurt Diemberger, and he'd invited me to climb with him in Europe. I felt I was coming of age as a high-altitude mountaineer.

*

After returning home from Pakistan, I took up the offer to spend seven months on Macquarie Island in the Subantarctic. I worked as a field training officer, using my alpine skills to teach the research scientists and support staff how to stay alive in that harsh and wild environment. I was still on leave without pay from the police force, but ultimately I would never return to work with them, an agreement that I believe suited us both.

I came home from Antarctica in April 1999 and was immediately keen to make a fresh expedition to the Himalaya. I'd missed the start of the pre-monsoon climbing season in Nepal so decided to head back to Pakistan. I'd climbed three of the five 8000ers in Pakistan and I wanted to finish them off, particularly as the remaining two peaks—Gasherbrum 1 and Gasherbrum 2—were right beside each other.

Once again, my agent in Pakistan found an expedition that was willing to have an outsider on its permit, so I joined a Latin group comprising Brazilian Waldemar Niclevicz, Italians Abele Blanc and Christian Kuntner, and Pepe Garcés from Spain. They were a highly experienced team. Blanc and Kuntner had previously summitted seven 8000ers each, while Niclevicz and Garcés had three apiece. My agent assured me that they were a great bunch of people, so I took a chance and accepted the invitation. Waldemar was heavily sponsored and had hired Abele to guide him on G1 and G2. If all went well, they hoped to move up the glacier and finish off with an ascent of K2. It was a very ambitious plan. I had no desire to climb K2 again, so I joined the team only for the first two hills.

While resting in our hotel in Skardu, after another death-defying journey up the Karakorum Highway, the hotel owner gave me a letter that had been posted from Japan. It asked that expeditions going to Gasherbrum 1 look out for any sign of four Japanese climbers who'd disappeared there without trace the year before. Clearly, G1 would not be a pushover.

The Gasherbrum group of mountains lies in the Karakorum ranges immediately beside Broad Peak and within sight of K2, at the head of the Baltoro Glacier on the border of Gilgit–Baltistan province, Pakistan, and Xinjiang, China. They are also just a few kilometres from Pakistan's disputed border with India. There are six peaks in the group, but only G1 and G2 rise above 8000 metres. At 8068 metres' elevation, Gasherbrum 1 is the eleventh highest peak in the world and was first summitted by an American team in 1958. Gasherbrum 2, being the thirteenth highest at 8035 metres, saw its first ascent in 1956, by Austrians Fritz Moravec, Josef Larch and Hans Willenpart. All the peaks except Gasherbrum 1 are easily sighted from the Baltoro Glacier, up which you need to trek in order to access them. For this reason G1 is often referred to as Hidden Peak.

Our trek to the mountains followed the same route as the one for K2, past isolated villages amid barren hills, then onto the Baltoro Glacier and past the sheer rock spires of the Cathedral, Trango Towers and Lobsang Spire. At many points the track is forced onto the sunbaked cliffs above by the wild torrent of the Shigas River. Bereft of vegetation, the rock is so sheer that in many places, logs and branches have been jammed into small fizzures, providing a platform for yet more branches and then flat rocks. All of these pile up to form a teetering pathway that constantly threatens to tip porters and climbers alike into the icy river below. Numerous tributaries flow into the river from side glaciers and we were frequently obliged to wade through waist-deep water that was barely above freezing or to pick our way over newly erected but highly suspect bamboo bridges. At least they were better than the flying foxes they had replaced!

A Korean expedition joined us at the campsite of Paiju. Actually, they overwhelmed us, as its twenty-five members were accompanied by 340 porters! Rather than take the usual rest day there, we pushed on for a kilometre to get away from the masses.

Four days later, Concordia, the wide-open expanse surrounded by mighty peaks where the head of the Baltoro intersects with the Godwin-Austen Glacier, became the site for our penultimate camp before we reached Base Camp. With K2 and Broad Peak just up the glacier to the left, Concordia sits under the shadow of one of the most beautiful mountains in the region, Gasherbrum 4. Just shy of 8000 metres, it has the classic pyramid shape of the perfect mountain.

I was reminded of a funny story that Voytek Kurtyka, the outstanding Polish mountaineer from my 1995 Mazeno Ridge expedition, told me about his own climb on Gasherbrum 4. He and his climbing partner had trekked along the same path that we'd just taken. One of their porters had been tasked with carrying the eggs for the whole expedition. Hundreds of eggs were stacked in layers of twenty, within a rough metal frame, which the porter carried on his back. At every stop, Voytek rushed over to the porter to help him set down his load, fearful of losing the lot, while all the time berating the unfortunate porter: 'Careful, careful, be gentle!' When they finally reached the base camp of Gasherbrum 4, Voytek again rushed over to the porter as he gently took off his load. No doubt both the porter and Voytek were equally glad that the trip was over, and the porter walked away. Voytek then picked up his backpack and slung it over his shoulder, in the process knocking the egg load over and breaking every single one.

I came close to similar disaster while walking towards Base Camp. Recent snow had disguised the safe route over the glacier, and as I took a step forward I suddenly found myself falling through the snow. I immediately flung my arms out to the sides. Together with my bulky backpack, they stopped me at chest level. I'd punched through a snow bridge over a crevasse. After using my ice axe to pull myself out, I slid across the snow to firmer ground. When I widened the hole so it was clear to the group following me, I saw that it descended more than 15 metres.

I survived the trek, as did our eggs and some other delicacies. These Latin types eat well and my muesli bars paled in comparison to their cryovacked pork knuckles, some seriously stinky cheese and even fresh coffee. It became an afternoon ritual to gather in the dining tent while one of the coffee aficionados used an empty oxygen bottle to pound what looked like a kilogram of coffee into the tiny coffee basket, then brewed it over the gas stove, producing such a thick syrup that just a single centimetre in the bottom of my cup would make me buzz around the camp until dinner, looking for things to fix. Perhaps it was their cunning way of ensuring that our equipment was maintained.

When not drinking coffee or hand sewing torn tents faster than a Singer, I found it an absolute delight to walk about the South Gasherbrum Glacier. We were surrounded by the six Gasherbrum peaks and across the glacier sat the Golden Throne, which earned its title in the evening glow of sunset. Next to it was Chogolisa, which had claimed the life of Herman Buhl, the legendary alpine master who'd soloed the first ascent of Nanga Parbat in 1953, backing that up with the first ascent of Broad Peak just a couple of weeks before his death on this peak in 1957. Perhaps that tragic outcome added to the surreal but savage beauty of these mighty peaks. Despite the perpetual threat, which simmered just below their austere surfaces, occasionally these grand and majestic monoliths would lift their veils briefly and treat the lucky few to tantalising glimpses of their beauty. Our cameras clicked like machine guns.

As did actual machine guns, it turned out.

Our Base Camp was just a few kilometres from Conway Saddle, the highest permanently occupied outpost in the world. Every few weeks, an unlucky contingent of Pakistani soldiers dutifully trudged up the Baltoro Glacier to occupy this tiny frozen garrison, from which they could look down upon the Siachen Glacier in India, the scene of many years of bloody conflict between the two countries. So brilliant were the strategists in this useless battle of egos that over 2000 young men, probably quite a few women and certainly a lot of unlucky donkeys have perished in the contest for this strategically worthless lump of ice. The majority died from the inhospitable environment, rather than actual fighting, yet we frequently listened to their best efforts to add to those statistics. Big guns sent shells across to each side and I just hoped their aim was better than that of their ibex-hunting compatriots at Nanga Parbat.

I preferred a more peaceful contest: my Base-Camp ritual of getting together with the liaison officers to listen on our little radios to the cricket World Cup. None of the Koreans, Americans or Latins who shared our base camp was even vaguely interested, but for me it was a great way to establish a bond with the LOs. I enjoyed many lively discussions about famous players, past competitions and who'd win this one. Needless to say, they were quite certain that Pakistan would triumph. And throughout the tournament it seemed likely that they'd be right.

Cricket on the subcontinent is second only in importance to religion—and sometimes that order is reversed. Every patch of grass, dirt or bitumen that you walk past in the cities has teams of ragged urchins playing the game with enormous enthusiasm. Whenever I joined them, having declared myself an Australian, the tempo of the game would pick up even further.

One night at base camp, the BBC broadcast the final of the World Cup, with Pakistan and Australia as adversaries. Pakistan was the favourite and Australia the underdog, so the LOs were showing plenty of bravado, teasing me about the whipping Australia was about to endure. As the match progressed, however, the situation reversed and the tent went quiet. Shortly before the end of the match, I retired to my sleeping tent to hear the Australian victory in private, and I didn't see the LOs for a couple of days. When they finally emerged from their tents, there was talk of prosecution and incarceration of their treacherous cricket team. They were really dispirited and felt their nation had been shamed.

I often took a cricket bat to base camps on expeditions in Pakistan, in the hope of having a game with some of the locals. It seemed that the only way to break the LOs' mood was to replay the match: the Pakistani LOs versus the Rest of the World. I conscripted a team of disinterested climbers from the four corners of Base Camp and the match began. Our LOs were talented to a man, and within a short time they'd destroyed the international team. Relations were revived and their honour restored. The climbs could continue.

*

Initially, I climbed with Christian, as he was also 'extra' on the team. He was very competent and extremely fit and I enjoyed climbing with someone who was prepared to share the work and the risks. Waldemar, Abele and Pepe climbed as a team of three, enhanced by the assistance of two high-altitude climbing porters. Without the luxury of such assistance, Christian and I carried all our own equipment and several hundreds of metres of rope to contribute to the work of fixing a safe line up the mountain.

This was probably the hottest expedition I'd ever been on. Despite the altitude and massive mountain peaks all around, the sun blazed down, making the snow treacherously soft, triggering avalanches and opening hundreds of crevasses. To beat the heat we often started climbing at 1 or 2 a.m., so that we could reach our destination, usually a higher camp, by mid morning. That same strong sunlight, however, often provided the most extraordinary sunrises and sunsets. Brilliant pink, purple, gold and blue hues converted harsh and icy monoliths into artistic masterpieces, almost too outlandishly colourful to be real.

Being right beside each other, Gasherbrum 1 and 2 share both Base Camp and Camp 1. We had intended to climb Gasherbrum 2 first, using the easier peak to acclimatise before taking on the tougher challenge of Gasherbrum 1, but, as we were opening up the route on the mountain, several commercial expeditions arrived at Base Camp and set about occupying some of the lower camps. We had no desire to battle with inexperienced climbers or have our adventure overwhelmed by teams of tents, so we switched our attention to Gasherbrum 1.

From Base Camp to Camp 1, and then on to Camp 2, the challenge was simply to find a route through the crevasse-ridden glacier. Once above Camp 2, we moved on to a steep face of ice and rock. We overcame the technical difficulties pretty easily, but as we climbed towards our intended Camp 3 location, at 7200 metres, the weather deteriorated and we were forced to drop our loads on a tiny ledge at 7000 metres. Waldemar and Pepe descended straight away, but by the time they were off the rope the storm was on us, so Abele and I set up the tent and took shelter for the night. Christian also stayed there.

When the storm eased the next morning, Abele and Christian decided to make a summit push, which was a bit of a surprise to me as the weather was still unsettled and our acclimatisation was barely sufficient. I wasn't keen to go for the summit so soon in the expedition and in questionable weather conditions. When they set off in the wee hours of the morning, I climbed a little way to recce the route for later and then returned. In the morning light I descended from Camp 3 all the way to Base Camp, having left in the tent my down suit, warm overboots and high-altitude mittens for my summit attempt. Abele and Christian reached the summit that day and descended to Base Camp over the next couple of days.

On 8 July the weather indicated a fine spell of just two days. That was not enough time to climb Gasherbrum 1, I knew, but mountaineering demands flexibility. Sticking doggedly to your original plan is a great way to fail. Or die. Pepe and I felt that the patch of good weather would be sufficient for us to climb the much easier mountain, Gasherbrum 2, even though it would be difficult because much of our climbing equipment and clothing was now at the higher camp on Gasherbrum 1. We decided we could make do with some spare clothing but had to climb as fast as possible, leap-frogging camps in order to expose ourselves to the extreme cold for as little time as possible.

We set off immediately and climbed up to Camp 1, where we stopped for a few hours to rehydrate before continuing through Camp 2 to Camp 3, where we again stopped for a few hours in the evening. Setting off again at midnight, we climbed straight through Camp 4 at 7300 metres and pushed on for the summit.

Not surprisingly, after such a fast ascent of more than two and a half vertical kilometres, Pepe was a bit slow, but I couldn't wait for him as I was absolutely freezing. I was climbing in only lightweight fleece pants with a wind shell over the top, my base-camp down jacket, which was about half the warmth of my climbing suit, basic boots, and gloves with plastic bags over them to block the wind. It was still bloody freezing, and I had to stop every ten minutes and swing my arms and legs wildly to try and force some blood into my extremities.

Despite the cold, though, I thoroughly enjoyed the day. The mountain was well within my abilities and I felt strong and in control. With Pepe lagging behind, I was essentially on my own and I loved that. I was unencumbered by responsibilities to others. I was free to enjoy the climbing purely for the fun of it. I established a rhythm that let me climb as hard as I could without actually exhausting myself, a feeling that I'd come to crave. I was in the zone and, as the day dawned, I saw that nearby peaks were dropping well below me.

I climbed so fast that I caught up with British climber David Hamilton, who'd left his high camp some hours before I passed through it. I overtook him and kept going for the summit ridge, making good height as the horizon began to lighten. Once I was on the ridge I had to slow down due to deep snow, but I pushed on and eventually reached the top at 8.40 a.m. on 9 July. I waited up there for about half an hour until David arrived, and we took a few photographs before descending.

On the way down I passed Pepe, who was still coming up, and promised to wait for him at Camp 3 while he went to the summit. We then descended together all the way to Base Camp. The entire climb from Base Camp and back had taken us just three days, a pretty quick ascent of an 8000-metre peak.

We spent the next few days resting and socialising at Base Camp. At one point I visited the American commercial expedition that was climbing on Gasherbrum 2. Its leader, Christine Boskoff, was the new owner of Mountain Madness, an expedition guiding company that had been founded by Scott Fisher, who'd died in the big disaster on Everest three years before. Christine was good fun and happy to share her bourbon with a stray Aussie. She was a keen climber and was hoping to climb other 8000ers after Gasherbrum 2. Our paths would cross again.

One afternoon, as I lay dozing in my base-camp tent, I heard an ominous rumble from the other side of the glacier. It didn't sound like the usual afternoon exchange of pleasantries and artillery fire between our hosts, so I poked my head out of the tent. A massive avalanche was thundering down the Golden Throne. Although it was a kilometre or two away, I knew it was big enough to cause a strong wind blast.

I yelled a warning and zipped up my tent door, but even before I finished I was hit by an enormous wind gust that flattened my tent and knocked me sideways. As I lay there holding onto the sides of the tent, looking out through the partially open door, I saw the blast sweep through base camp like a tornado, flattening tents and blowing clothes into the air as it went. Much to my amusement, a toilet tent was ripped from its anchors and flung across the glacier, its startled occupant getting more than a little wind chill while clutching at his trousers.

*

After four days the weather indicated another good spell, this time a bit longer. As Abele and Christian had already climbed Gasherbrum 1, and Waldemar had said that he didn't want to, Pepe and I set off on our own. We made good time up to Camp 3 and from there we headed for the summit at 2 a.m.

The climb from our tent at 7000 metres to the summit at 8068 metres was a huge distance, one of the biggest altitude gains from a high camp to a summit of any 8000-metre peak. Again Pepe was slower than me, so I broke trail almost all the way to the top. The route doglegged through some rocks after a few hundred metres, then opened out onto a major face. When the snow conditions are firm, some teams go straight up the face or onto a snowy ridge to the left, but on this day the snow was deep. I needed to conserve energy, so I headed for a rock ridge to the right. It was a longer route, but the rock was easier to climb.

The day ticked by slowly, but we gradually gained altitude. About 100 metres from the summit I was stopped by a rock face. It was steep and unconsolidated, and in my exhaustion I didn't think that I could overcome it. Luckily, Pepe caught up to me. Still having some strength, he threw his energy at the rock and found a way over the buttress. I followed him up.

Above the barrier, Pepe stopped on a ledge to take off his boots and warm his feet, at which point I caught and overtook him. I climbed another 20 or 30 metres, then realised that I was just 10 metres from the summit. I stopped and called to Pepe to come up. It was about half an hour before he caught me, and we walked the last few metres to the top together, reaching the summit at 4 p.m. It was very important to me that I didn't step on the top before Pepe. It seemed fair that we share that moment; indeed, it was a far richer experience for me that we did. It was just eight days since we'd stood on the summit of Gasherbrum 2.

Strangely, I found a chocolate bar on the top, but I guessed that Abele and Christian must have placed it there. Their motivation for doing so wasn't completely clear, but I had no desire to leave rubbish on the summit of this beautiful peak, so I put it in my pocket. We made it back to Camp 3 around 11.30 p.m. and over the next couple of days descended to Base Camp. We'd seen no sign of the Japanese climbers we'd been asked to look out for. I suspected they'd missed the dogleg turn on the way down from the summit. Pepe and I had had enough difficulty locating it in the dark of night, even with our tracks in the deep snow. If the Japanese climbers had continued straight down the face and missed the dogleg through the rocks, they'd probably have climbed down into such steep ground that they'd either fallen or been unable to make their way back up again.

Once Pepe and I reached the glacier above Base Camp, we saw that it had changed completely in the few days we'd been up high. Crevasses had opened up everywhere. At one point we sat on the snow to rest, with about 8 metres of rope tied tightly between us. All of a sudden Pepe disappeared with a yelp, as the snow he was sitting on collapsed and he dropped into a massive crevasse. As he plummeted, the rope jerked me towards the hole. I managed to roll onto my stomach and use my ice pick to stop the slide, but Pepe was already 6 metres down the crevasse. Normally, a climber is able to climb back up the rope using prussik loops—short lengths of cord that can slide one way up the rope—but Pepe wasn't carrying any. So I made a pulley system with the remainder of the climbing rope to hoist him out.

Even with my knowledge and experience, it was all I could do to pull him up and out of the crevasse, such was the exhaustion I felt after climbing two 8000ers in a just over a week. His enthusiastic encouragement—'Pull harder, Andre! Harder!'—didn't actually assist me very much, but finally I hauled him out. I collapsed face-first onto the snow. His rescue was testament to the value of those mountaineering courses I'd done in New Zealand fourteen years earlier.

Back at Base Camp, Christian, who wasn't the friendliest guy in the world, doubted our claim to have summitted. He thought it was too tough for us and said he'd left something in the snow on the summit and demanded we describe it, to prove to him that we'd made it. I pulled out the chocolate bar that I'd found on the top and handed it to him. There were no further questions.

Waldemar, Abele and Pepe moved on to K2 but weren't successful in climbing it. Christian walked out to civilisation, and I followed a day or two later, taking an interesting route over a pass called Ghondogoro La, which went out via a different valley system than the Baltoro Glacier. As far as I know, ours was the only team to summit Gasherbrum 1 that year. For Pepe and me, it was a really great expedition. We'd become good friends, worked well together and achieved two tough summits—my fifth and sixth ascents of 8000-metre peaks. In addition, my climb of Gasherbrum 1 was the first Australian ascent of that mountain, my third such honour. As well as being the second time that I had summitted two 8000ers in a single year, summiting these two 8000ers just eight days apart was a personal record.

More than the statistical achievements, the climbing style and my performance on the climbs were of most significance to me. I'd made the summit of Gasherbrum 2 in extremely fast time and in barely enough clothes to keep warm at base camp. On Gasherbrum 1, I'd led virtually the whole way on the summit day, breaking trail in steep, thigh-deep snow for more than twelve hours nonstop. Not because I had to but because I could and I wanted to. On both climbs I'd felt absolutely in my element. I'd relished the hardship and felt almost at one with the peaks. I realised that the mountains were becoming a part of me, or me a part of them. They were no longer just an object for challenge and adventure; they were my life. I feared them and I respected them, but I also loved them.

Postscript

Park Young-Seok, the highly accomplished Korean climber I met during the Nanga Parbat expedition, was killed in an avalanche on the South Face of Annapurna in Nepal in 2011, the same face on which Anatoli Bukreev was killed several years earlier.

My friend Pepe Garcés fell to his death while attempting to climb Dhaulagiri in Nepal in 2001.

7

A DREAM REALISED

It is not the mountain we conquer but ourselves.

Edmund Hillary

B ACK HOME, I found that the media were starting to take an interest in me. Outdoor magazines reported my successes and requests for interviews became more frequent. While that was an interesting new element to my mountaineering life, it also signalled a change: my climbs were no longer my own. People wanted to know the stories behind the climbs; they wanted a piece of me. The personal purity of the experience was just a little eroded by this. Inevitably, questions were asked of when I would tackle Everest and whether I was actually chasing the fourteen big ones. While I hadn't given much thought to the fourteen, Everest was clearly in my sights.

I won another contract with the Australian Antarctic Division as a field training officer over the southern summer of 1999–2000, this time to work on the Antarctic continent. Interspersed between my own expeditions and the Antarctic work, I led groups of people on treks and easy climbs in the Himalaya and Karakorum, and the Tien Shan and Pamir mountain ranges in Central Asia. My life had become one great adventure. Girlfriends came and went, but the mountains remained constant.

While in Antarctica, I received an invitation from a British company, Jagged Globe, to lead a commercial expedition on the south side of Mount Everest in the pre-monsoon season of 2000. I was pleased to discover that David Hamilton, the British climber with whom I'd summitted Gasherbrum 2 the year before, had recommended me to the company. While the invitation was welcome, leading a commercial expedition was not how I'd planned to return to Everest. In the seven years since my last attempt on the mountain, I'd gained a wealth of experience, and success, on more technical and more remote high-altitude mountains. I was confident that I had the skills needed to take on Chomolungma with a fair likelihood of success. In the interim, however, the cost of an expedition to Everest had skyrocketed.

When I first went to Everest, in the post-monsoon season of 1991, the peak fee was US$3000. In 1993, by which time the first commercial expeditions were coming to Everest, the fee had gone up to US$10,000. Now, in 2000, it was US$70,000 for up to seven foreigners, including guides—Sherpas, as Nepali citizens, didn't need a permit. This was now well out of my price range, so the opportunity to get paid to go back to Everest was a tempting alternative. The quandary was that, in order to lead a commercial expedition, my personal goals would have to be subservient to the goal of getting the paying clients to the top and back down safely. I would be climbing as a business entity, not for the pure love of mountaineering. But at the end of the day, I wanted to climb Mount Everest and I was prepared to do whatever it took to achieve that goal. I accepted the job.

The ship bringing me back from Antarctica was delayed by sea ice and we had to make several resupply stops at other Antarctic bases en route to Australia. I emailed my deputy leader on the Everest team, Tim Bird, and requested that he meet the clients in Kathmandu and take a slow and leisurely walk to Base Camp, so they would achieve maximum acclimatisation. I would have to hurry as quickly as possible to meet them there.

I did what I could to improve my fitness, spending a couple of hours a day on the ship's rowing machine. Each evening I climbed the outside ladders, five or so levels to the top deck and down again, with a heavy backpack, 100 times. The Southern Ocean is a maelstrom at the best of times and when it was really blowing, the ship lurched and bucked about. With great sheets of freezing water blowing over me, it actually felt quite like I was in the mountains!

Eventually we docked in Tasmania and I flew straight up to Sydney, raced home to pack my expedition equipment and flew out to Nepal the following day. On 2 April 2000 I started a fast trek towards base camp, popping lots of Diamox to aid my acclimatisation. Six days later I arrived, having stopped for a couple of hours at the Thyanboche monastery to attend a puja ceremony, in case I'd missed our expedition puja. I am not a Buddhist but I have always felt spiritual in the Himalaya, and with each expedition, this feeling has increased. There is an energy, a sense, to which I've become very accustomed in those mountains. Perhaps I've become a little superstitious, too, having survived avalanches, plummeted unroped into crevasses and had multiple bivouacs at extreme altitude without equipment or oxygen—situations in which so many others have perished. Puja ceremonies are a part of life in the Himalaya, and I feel much more at ease if I abide by the spiritual customs of the locals.

Our expedition team was made up of me, my assistant leader Tim, seven paying clients, four climbing Sherpas and a couple of Base Camp kitchen staff. Somehow, as I raced up the Khumbu Glacier on the final day of my trek, I took a different trail and passed the clients without seeing them, so I actually beat them to the camp by about half an hour. Our Sherpas and staff were already there, and the kitchen was functioning when I arrived. By the time the rest of the team traipsed into camp, I was sitting outside the kitchen tent with a cup of tea, so I took full advantage of the opportunity to rib them for taking so long to get there!

Having spent the last two summers teaching inexperienced people to survive in Antarctica, I wasn't about to allow any accidents on this expedition. We spent several days practising basic climbing skills in the Khumbu Icefall, which allowed me to evaluate their abilities and to lay down some ground rules about the way we'd climb and use our equipment. This was important because I wouldn't be able to watch every one of the clients all the time, and I needed them to be able to look out for each other and spot any potential problems themselves. Our climbing Sherpas were very strong at altitude but didn't possess the same technical skills as most western guides, so I wanted to make everyone in the team responsible for each other.

It quickly became clear that most of the group had 'enhanced' their claimed experience when they'd applied to join the expedition. I was stunned to see that one of them didn't even know how to use his crampons. But the company had accepted them all, so the onus was on me, as leader, to help them reach the summit. This is the dilemma of guided climbing on these mountains, and it's something I've thought about a lot over the years I've been climbing in the Himalaya.

Is it appropriate for inexperienced climbers simply to pay big dollars to be virtually hauled up Everest and other big peaks? Guiding has been around since climbing began in the European Alps, when Swiss guides led tweed-jacketed punters up hills they wouldn't have been able to climb on their own. But where do you draw the line? Should guided clients be limited to certain altitudes—5000 metres, 6000 metres, 7000 metres? When I decided all those years ago that I wanted to climb Mount Everest, I spent a year learning to rock climb, then went to New Zealand for alpine training. After that I spent several more years climbing in New Zealand and on progressively higher peaks around the world, until I felt I was ready to take on the 8000ers. And even then I still had a lot to learn.

The number of climbers on the 8000ers in those days was very small because everyone went through a similar lengthy process to develop their skills, and only the most highly skilled attempted the biggest and toughest peaks. Since about the mid 1990s, guided climbing has enabled anyone with enough dollars to access these peaks, and this has massively increased the numbers of people climbing them, which has forced up the costs and effectively shut out the amateur enthusiast who might have real skills. Those enthusiasts either have to go further into the wilderness or climb harder routes on the big peaks, or else turn professional in order to fund their own 8000-metre aspirations.

For my team of seven clients and two guides, officially we needed two permits at $70,000 each—an awful lot of money for a piece of paper. On top of the permit was the cost of all the infrastructure, transport, food and staff. Each of the clients on this expedition had paid US$50,000 to join. When the Nepali government put the price up from US$10,000 to US$70,000, the intention was that only one expedition would be allowed on each route per season. Only commercial groups could afford the massive fee, and since their clients were almost always inexperienced, the commercial operators only wanted permits for the *easiest* route. The one-expedition-per-route mandate was then never implemented. This is why there are regularly thirty or more expeditions on the 'tourist route' during the pre-monsoon season these days, with hundreds of climbers, hundreds of support Sherpas and hundreds more base-camp staff. The Nepali government has simply failed to regulate the numbers, and poor old Everest has been greatly diminished by the circus that commercial guiding has brought to her flanks.

But while the government hoards the revenue from the permit system, which rightly upsets the population, the guiding business still injects huge income into the local economy. Sherpas can earn a year's salary during a single expedition, villagers sell accommodation and meals to climbers and trekkers heading to base camp, locals are hired as porters and others lease out their yaks. The Khumbu (Everest) region of Nepal is by far the most affluent in the nation, precisely because of all these expeditions and commercial trekking groups.

What is the solution? In 2000, as the leader of my own expedition, I hadn't worked through this whole conundrum. I hoped that guiding the Jagged Globe team would provide me with an informed perspective on the issue. More importantly, however, leading the expedition gave me another chance to climb the mountain that I'd wanted to summit ever since I'd been inspired by a slide show years earlier and which I could no longer afford to climb on my own.

Our team was international, with members from the United States, the United Kingdom and Germany. Almost from the start there were some significant problems to deal with. The equipment supplied by the company's agent in Nepal was in very poor condition. Our base-camp gas lantern didn't work, and nor did the generator that could have provided electric lighting. I was surprised to find that while Tim was a highly experienced mountain guide, having led climbing expeditions around the world for a number of years, he had not been to high altitude. It was unclear therefore whether he would be able to cope with Everest's altitude and be in a position to assist me on the summit push.

The leader of our four climbing Sherpas advised that, as *sirdar*, he would not climb, leaving me with only three climbing Sherpas to support nine foreigners. The clients wanted everything carried for them, including their sleeping bags, which weighed virtually nothing. I wasn't sure what the clients had been promised, as the company hadn't sent me any of the 'joining information' that they'd been given. We had been provided with a satellite phone, but that too failed to work, so I couldn't easily contact our head office for information.

Back in the 1950s and 1960s, when expeditions were organised by national climbing bodies, often with the support of their governments, a single team member reaching the summit was counted as a success for the entire expedition. The expeditions took a 'pyramid' approach to logistics and support up the mountain, and higher camps were smaller and had less equipment, because they only had to support the climbers who would try for the summit. On modern commercial expeditions, however, every client pays a large amount of money to be there, so everyone expects to get to the summit. Commercial expeditions need pretty much the same amount of equipment all the way up the hill, to give every team member an equal chance of reaching the top. There is some attrition along the way, of course, but you get the picture.

Despite my own preference for climbing without oxygen, it was my rule that everybody, including me, use it on this expedition. It would give us the best chance of summitting, keep our minds sharper and, most importantly, help to ward off frostbite and altitude sickness. For seven clients, three Sherpas and two guides, that amounted to around fifty bottles to be carried up the mountain. The only way we would succeed was if we had the infrastructure in place all the way up the mountain. My intention therefore was to have the Sherpas carry tents, stoves, fuel, food, oxygen and rope. The clients would have to carry their own personal gear.

Many commercial groups have at least one climbing Sherpa per client and we were woefully understaffed with just three. Part of our base-camp logistics was actually being provided by another commercial expedition through an arrangement between the two companies. I managed to strike a deal with the other expedition for their Sherpas to carry a few of our loads up the mountain—including, in my benign soft-heartedness, the clients' sleeping bags.

Despite the equipment issues and the very different style of leadership required of me on this expedition, I revelled in being back on Mount Everest. It was sixteen years since I'd decided to climb this peak and much water had passed under the bridge in getting to this point, but here I was again on the mountain of my dreams. As well, I now felt very comfortable in the environment. I felt physically capable, powerful almost, and in control.

I doubted that all my clients would make it to the summit; in fact, I was quite sure that several of them wouldn't. Given the poor equipment, limited Sherpa support and a deputy leader who was unproven at high altitude, my first priority was ensuring that everyone went home alive. I would send home anyone who seemed too great a risk. But I was confident that both the more capable clients and I, would, if the circumstances allowed, come to stand on the summit of the world's highest peak.

*

With my clients' basic training completed and having achieved sufficient acclimatisation, we were finally able to start the climb. We were going with pure siege style: ferrying loads up to higher camps and returning to lower camps to sleep. We interspersed these day trips with rest days at Base Camp, as some of the clients were pretty unfit and needed plenty of time to recover.

Within a couple of weeks, the stress of climbing at altitude had exposed a few frailties. One of the guys struggled to acclimatise, and another twisted his ankle quite badly in the Khumbu Icefall. Both were incredibly slow on the mountain and were looking for an opportunity to go home but didn't want to be seen as quitters. I arranged for them to see a doctor at Base Camp, who confirmed that they were unfit to continue with the expedition, due to injury.

This allowed them to save face, and they were soon on their way down to Kathmandu.

The stress of high altitude also revealed people's characters, and one of the team, David, soon showed his true colours. Due to the collective inexperience of the group, I had made it a rule that they should never get ahead of me or Tim. As we prepared one morning to climb from Camp 2 to Camp 3, I saw that David had snuck out of camp and gone ahead of the team. He was nearly at the steep ice slopes of the Lhotse Face.

This was incredibly dangerous, as the face had several old ropes hanging down it, which had been seriously weakened by ultraviolet rays. I doubted whether David could tell the difference between the old and the new ropes, and if he hauled on an old one it could be disastrous. I raced towards the face, but David had started up it. As I approached I lost sight of him. He had fallen. I radioed the other members of the team and told them to stand by to help out with a rescue.

Our Sherpas had set off before me and were soon at the scene. As anticipated, David had clipped onto an old rope but thankfully had only climbed up about 20 metres when it snapped, so he hadn't fallen far. He wasn't badly injured but was shaken and very scared and had hurt his wrist. The incident stopped us from climbing to Camp 3 that day, because we had to escort him back to Camp 2 and tend to his wrist—and his bruised ego. The following day it snowed heavily and we were unable to reattempt the climb up to Camp 3, so we descended to Base Camp, having lost our opportunity. Such is commercial expeditioning.

A few days later we returned to Camp 2 and completed the climb to Camp 3. The climb to this altitude, around 7300 metres, is I think, the coldest part of the mountain, except perhaps the summit night. The Lhotse Face is west facing, meaning it doesn't receive the sun's warmth until late morning and a constant wind sweeps its broad, icy slopes. I implored the team to take care of their fingers and toes because frostbite could be a very real risk on that hill. The mistake that many climbers make in this situation is to continue to the destination with the intention of rewarming their freezing digits in the shelter of a tent, but that can be hours away and far too late to stop serious damage. Prevention is better than cure and rewarming en route is far preferable to waiting until later.

Unfortunately, one of the guys ignored the advice and froze his fingers quite badly. Not only did he sustain the injury but he also hid the fact from me and I only noticed it when he struggled to hold a cup of tea in his tent that night. Back at Base Camp the doctor confirmed frostbite. Despite the client's great protestations that he could continue, I had to order him home. It gave me no joy to do so but, once frozen, tissue is far more likely to refreeze. If he'd frozen those fingers again during that expedition, he'd almost certainly have needed amputations. That was unacceptable to me, irrespective of the fact that he was prepared to risk it.

I knew that sending clients home would annoy the company. It wanted statistics of success to attract future business, but I wouldn't risk leaving bodies, or fingers, on the mountain for the sake of the summit.

Despite these minor issues, it was still lots of fun being on Mount Everest and Base Camp gave me plenty of opportunities to socialise with friends. Rick Allen, whom I knew from Nanga Parbat in 1995 and Broad Peak in 1997, was guiding a team. Christine Boskoff, whom I'd met on Gasherbrum 2 the previous year, was also there, as was Piotr Pustelnik, with whom I'd climbed on Mount McKinley in 1991. Sandy Allan, also from Nanga Parbat in 1995, was guiding a client on Lhotse, right beside Everest, and was sharing the same base camp.

The season progressed and so did our climb. We were ready to make our summit push on 15 May, although Tim had pulled out due to ill health and was waiting at Base Camp. There were actually four expeditions going for the summit on this night. The leaders met and we agreed that each expedition would take its turn to lead the way and fix rope over all the difficult or dangerous spots, in order to safeguard their members' ascents and descents. A total of 800 metres of rope would be taken, 200 metres per expedition.

As we readied ourselves in our tents at Camp 4 on the bleak and barren South Col at 7950 metres, one of our three Sherpas suddenly declared that he had bad headaches and could not continue. This left me with significantly reduced support for our four climbers, plus me, and we had a fair bit of necessary equipment to carry—oxygen, rope, medical kit and spares. The clients and I were using the normal allowance of oxygen per person—a pair of 3-litre POISK oxygen bottles, each providing the climber with six hours of supply, and a single 4-litre bottle with eight hours' worth of oxygen. That gave us a total of twenty hours of climbing time to get from the high camp to the summit and back. The Sherpas used two 3-litre bottles but at a lower flow rate, which gave them about the same climbing time.

I'd planned that each climber would carry two of their allocated three oxygen bottles, while the Sherpas carried both of their own bottles plus a climber's third bottle. As we were left with only two Sherpas for four climbers, each of the Sherpas now had to carry four bottles, and each bottle weighed about 3.5 kilograms, giving them a load of 14 kilograms of oxygen, plus their personal gear. That's a big load at that altitude. In those circumstances, I couldn't ask the Sherpas to assist with my load, so I carried all three of my own oxygen bottles, as well as the first-aid kit and the rope. When we set out from Camp 4 that night, my load was 25 kilograms! I'd frequently trekked with that sort of weight at sea level, but at 8000 metres it felt like a tonne.

We set out from our tents on the windswept South Col at 11 p.m., aiming to get to the summit by midday the next day and then return to Camp 4 that afternoon. We climbed steadily, although my load put me under extreme stress and it was all I could do to keep up with my own team. We reached the point where it was my team's turn to fix our rope, so I handed it to the Sherpas. With the loss of that weight from my pack, I immediately felt like I had a new lease of life.

Dawn came as we reached a point on the ridge at 8400 metres known as the Balcony, at which time we changed to our second oxygen bottles. It was a stunning day, with little wind. Everybody was doing well, so we pushed on. At nine-thirty in the morning we reached the south summit, at 8750 metres, just 100 metres below Everest's summit. I was over the moon. Not only did it look like I'd get my team to the summit, but I was about to realise my own dream of climbing Mount Everest, which had been sixteen years in the making.

It was now time for the fourth team to fix their ropes across the final ridge. We called them forward and waited for them to do their bit. But they just stood there. They hadn't brought the rope … They hadn't brought the rope!

I was dumbfounded. What were they thinking? Neither we, nor they, could go on without the rope. Experienced climbers could possibly have continued, but our clients absolutely could not. And we couldn't pull up the rope from below, as it was essential in case anyone had to descend quickly in an emergency. We were left looking wistfully at the top of the world, just 100 metres away.

It was cruel, but I had to turn my team around and take them down the mountain. The other teams did the same. As we descended, David fell constantly on the fixed rope, a combination of his extreme exhaustion and the effects of altitude. It was probably a good thing for him not to have gone on to the summit, as he may well have collapsed up there without hope of rescue.

We spent a night at Camp 4 but had neither the strength nor the oxygen supplies to reattempt the summit immediately. The next day we descended the mountain. It was a very disappointed team that straggled into Base Camp the following day.

I was just as shattered as everyone else, if not more so. My dream to summit Everest had been crushed by a most incredible act of idiocy. But my focus wasn't on our failure; it was on what I would do next.

*

After climbing to such a high altitude as we had, most people are so physically exhausted that they can barely stagger around Base Camp, let alone consider climbing the mountain again. The body is so burned out that even the slightest exertion is exhausting. To walk on the flat may be fine, but the slightest uphill, just a few metres on a gentle track, will stop you dead as your lungs heave away again. Your legs feel like dead weights, like nothing will get them going. It takes a few days for that completely debilitating exhaustion to go away and a number of weeks to recover fully.

The other teams that had attempted the summit with us that day packed up their camps and trekked out to civilisation, but I could see no reason for our team to give up. We were tired but healthy, and we had just enough time left in the season to continue the expedition. And, importantly, while we were resting at base camp other teams were climbing and fixing that final length of rope.

I talked with the team about going up again. Having been well inside the 'death zone', we needed several weeks to recuperate. With the approaching monsoon, though, we had very little time in which to re-climb the mountain. In fact, we could take just two rest days before starting our next attempt. I didn't know whether we could re-climb Everest with such little recovery, but I was adamant that we should at least try. I implored them not to give up. If we only made it as far as Camp 1 before we collapsed from exhaustion, we'd at least have given it our best effort.

Interestingly, the three members of the team who'd worked well and climbed within the guidelines I'd set were willing to try again. The less team-oriented member withdrew from the second attempt. The group performed exceptionally well on the climb back up. Although we had to physically dig deep, we made it through camps 1 and 2 and, after a rest day, continued up to Camp 3. It snowed heavily when we got there, a product of the rapidly approaching monsoon—so heavily, in fact, that I almost called a retreat because of the danger of avalanches. To assess the conditions, I led all the way to Camp 4, plugging steps in the fresh snow. It seemed okay to continue, and we arrived in the late afternoon, with Christine Boskoff and her Sherpa coming up shortly after for their own attempt.

After rehydrating and resting for a few hours at Camp 4, we set off at 10 p.m. and climbed through a cold and blustery night. Christine and another larger team had moved out just ahead of us, but we quickly caught and overtook them. We were climbing much more quickly than on the attempt a few days before—despite being physically exhausting, it had probably greatly enhanced our acclimatisation. We reached The Balcony at 2 a.m. and by 5 a.m. were approaching the South Summit, our previous high point.

It was not anywhere near the beautiful day we'd had the week before as a bleak dawn clawed through swirling clouds to lighten our way. The wind was so strong that I had to kneel on the ridge and haul in the rope, which was stretching in a great arc out over the void of the mighty Kanshung Face. Windblown frost encased my goggles to such an extent that I couldn't clean them, and I had to go without. That caused the fluid in my eyes to freeze, so I could neither see nor blink. I had to cover my eyes with the sleeve of my down suit to allow them to thaw again:

> Conditions on the ridge from the south summit over to the
> Hillary Step were better, so I led across. The step was a mix of
> rock and snow. Once across, it was relatively straightforward but
> not the place to lose your footing. The wind felt like 60 knots

or so. Plugged on but the ridge seemed to go on forever. Lots of false humps. The rope finished at a big boulder on the south-west side. Staggered on towards the final rise.

It's several hundred metres or more from the south summit to the top. Took over an hour. Finally reached the top at 6.30 am. Very windy and cloud only 50 metres below, but blue sky above.

I'd forged about 50 metres ahead of the team to kick steps in the snow as they plodded slowly but steadily along the final summit ridge, so I had ten minutes to myself on the top of the world. It was an intense and deeply personal moment. After sixteen years and a near miss just a week before, I'd finally realised my dream. Better still, I'd led my team safely to the top.

Christine and her Sherpa joined us and we took a few photos, but the wind was really blasting and it wasn't the place to swap stories. By 7 a.m. we had to escape the wrath of the storm, so we beat a hasty retreat down to Camp 4. Having summitted so early in the day, we were able to down-climb all the way to the relative luxury and comfort of Camp 2 on the same day, before hitting Base Camp next morning. After just a day at Base Camp, we packed up and left.

*

We trekked into Lukla, from where we planned to fly back to Kathmandu, and were told that the airport would close the following day to allow the dirt runway to be tarmacked. The stormy weather of the monsoon had caused lots of flight cancellations that week, so the airport was overflowing with literally hundreds of climbers and trekkers clamouring to get on the last flights. Everyone was desperate to avoid an additional few days' trekking, followed by a 12-hour hell ride on a local bus back to Kathmandu.

Our trekking agent had managed to obtain seats on different flights back to Kathmandu, but only some of the scheduled flights managed to get into Lukla due to the bad weather. One of my clients had an international departure the following day and needed to get back to Kathmandu, but his flight out of Lukla was cancelled. It's the luck of the draw—sometimes your flight arrives, but just as often it doesn't. My plane arrived, but I had plenty of time up my sleeve, so we swapped boarding passes and I resigned myself to a few days of hard trekking and dhal baht for dinner, rather than the cold beers and yak steaks I'd been dreaming about.

As I stood there watching the passengers board the very last flight of the season, I decided to try to bluff my way onto the plane. The Twin Otters could seat about eighteen passengers, but I knew they always kept an empty seat or two at the back—probably something to do with the load limit at altitude, although I didn't know for sure. I walked over to the plane, climbed aboard and just sat in the back.

My new boarding pass was for a different company, let alone flight, and the poor Nepali stewardess frantically tried to explain that I had to get off the plane. I played dumb until she went to get the pilot. He too told me that I couldn't go on that flight. I replied that the seat was evidently empty and I wouldn't be getting off. Perhaps because of my slightly crazed, just-summitted-Everest look, he didn't immediately summon any of the numerous armed police and soldiers at the airport, but muttered something about crazy Americans—heh, heh—then strapped himself in and away we went. Best flight of my life.

Back in Kathmandu, and after several yak steaks and cold beers, I reported the details of our climb to the Nepali Ministry of Tourism. Interestingly, the other expeditions that had summitted on the same day as us had advised the ministry by email from base camp, which meant the official statistics listed their ascents as having happened ahead of ours, whereas in fact we'd reached the summit some hours ahead of them. In the records of who has climbed Mount Everest, therefore, we are listed about fifteen positions lower than we should be. But in the scheme of things, that matters little, and I shall forever remember those ten minutes I had alone on the summit of the world, early in the morning of 24 May 2000.

8

A HIGHER GOAL

Mountains have a way of dealing with overconfidence.

Hermann Buhl

CLIMBING EVEREST WAS the realisation of a dream born in 1985 in the back room of a country pub. Having finally achieved it, what next? I hadn't tired of climbing the big peaks—indeed, I enjoyed it more with each expedition. While the goal of summitting Mount Everest had finally been realised, my need for high altitude had in no way been sated. It was time for a new goal.

Despite my successes to that date, even with seven 8000-metre summits under my belt, I'd never really considered attempting to climb all the 8000ers. It was the absolute grand slam of high-altitude mountaineering and has been likened to winning successive gold medals over numerous Olympics.

The early 1980s saw the first concerted effort by individual climbers to reach the summits of all of the 8000ers. The leader of that charge was the indomitable Reinhold Messner, a truly innovative and daring climber from the Tyrol in Europe. Messner had been the first to climb Everest solo and, with Austrian Peter Habeler, the first to climb it without oxygen. Messner's goal was threatened, however, by a supremely tough Polish climber, Jerzy Kukuczka, who started the chase several years later but attacked the peaks in rapid succession and, on all but Lhotse, climbed either a new route or in winter. The race culminated with Messner claiming his fourteenth summit in 1986, while Kukuczka claimed his just a few months later.

A blog site called Everest Book Report, referring to the race by these extraordinary climbers, states that, 'if Messner broke down the psychological barriers of 8000 metre climbing, then Kukuczka was the man to break down the physical ones'. That sounds about right to me. Tragically, when Kukucka returned to Lhotse in 1989 to climb it by a new route, he was killed in a fall when his rope broke.

While Messner and Kukuczka were the first to climb 'the fourteen' and their race was well publicised, there were other regular climbers in that era and the years following who claimed the Holy Grail. Even so, by the time I'd climbed Everest, only half a dozen of the world's very best climbers had achieved it. I certainly didn't consider myself to be in their league, but I started to wonder if maybe, just maybe, a boy from the suburbs of Sydney really could do it. To me, the end of one adventure has always been the starting point for the next one, and this would certainly be a major challenge. The more I thought about it, the more excited I was by the idea. And apart from a few risks like frostbite, death, bankruptcy and permanent bachelorhood, I couldn't come up with any reason not to try. I decided to go for it. I called the project Summit 8000.

An important aspect of this project, though, was that it should be fun. While I lived for the challenge of climbing these mountains, I wanted the rest of the project to be as much fun as possible. No doubt, I'd have some very tough experiences and meet some unsavoury characters along the way, but as far as possible I'd seek to climb with friends—or, at the very least, with mountaineers who shared my passion for the spirit of the adventure.

Another major decision was also forced on me at this time. I'd used up all possible sources of leave from the police force and had to either return to work or resign. My sense of betrayal at the treatment I'd received in the force had not diminished. Although I'd coped with the inevitable trauma of policing for twenty years, I'd been irreparably wounded by the organisation and I could not find it in myself to forgive. I realised I could not work there again, and so I was discharged.

*

I started making plans to climb Mount Manaslu in Nepal in the post-monsoon season of 2001. It is the world's eighth-highest mountain, standing at 8156 metres tall, and it had never been climbed by an Australian. Manaslu sits wholly within Nepal, to the north of the historic fortress town of Gorkha, from where the last kings of Nepal launched their conquest of the country during the eighteenth century. Its name is derived from the Sanskrit word Manasa, meaning 'Mountain of the Spirit'. The valleys that lead up to the mountain are inhabited by snow leopards, red pandas and the Tamang people, who are the original horse traders of Nepal.

Manaslu's first ascent was the goal of four unsuccessful Japanese expeditions between 1950 and 1955. The summit was finally achieved in May 1956. Like the other 8000ers, the mountain has taken a lethal toll on those who have sought to know her summit. In 1972, fifteen members of a Korean expedition were killed when an avalanche buried their camp. In 2012, eleven climbers were killed by an avalanche that swept through Camp 3, where numerous teams were sleeping. In addition, Manaslu is infamous for its terrible storms, particularly on the summit plateau, where many climbers have perished while trying to return to their High Camp after reaching the top. Even the famous Italian climber Reinhold Messner lost two climbing partners when they became lost in a high-altitude whiteout.

In May 2001, as I was making plans to climb Manaslu in September/October of that year, I was invited to join an Australian expedition to the same mountain that was scheduled for the pre-monsoon season of 2002. I knew, or knew of, all the proposed members of the team, and since I hadn't yet firmed up my own expedition for 2001, I agreed to join them. I cancelled my plans and had a year off from the 8000ers. I travelled to South America, where I guided a few treks and climbs and enjoyed the hospitality of the locals. Great steaks, fabulous wine, pretty girls. Very pretty girls.

I was also approached to work with a small adventure-tourism company that was hoping to expand its operations around the world. Unfortunately, as I found out later, it would be in direct competition with the business of one of the other members of the proposed 2002 Manaslu expedition. At the very first planning meeting for the 2002 expedition, held at the Oaks Hotel in Neutral Bay, Sydney, that person made it clear to me that he took the business issue as a personal attack. I was left with no doubt that it would create significant animosity during the climb. Expeditions can be tense enough without pre-existing troubles, so I immediately withdrew from the team. By then, though, it was too late for me to revive my own expedition to Manaslu in 2001 and it seemed that I'd missed my chance to be the first Australian to ascend it.

In February 2002, with the pre-monsoon climbing season fast approaching, I was sitting at home feeling rather sorry for myself when Alex, my old mate from Everest 1993, called me up. As we chatted, he asked what my climbing plans were, so I told him about the Manaslu debacle. Alex knew Manaslu well, as he'd been a member of a 1984 Yugoslavian expedition that had achieved a new route up the mountain's towering South Face to the plateau at

7500 metres. Bad weather had prevented them from completing the final few hundred metres to the summit, so he still had unfinished business there. In his inimitable way, he said, 'Ah, Andrew, mate, this is bullshit, mate. I'll go with you. Can you organise?'

I could and I did. Within a few short weeks we were at Sydney airport, preparing to board a plane to Kathmandu.

*

After years of climbing, I'd established a fairly large store of equipment in Kathmandu, which I'd either leave at a hotel or with a friend so I could use it again the next time I was there. This helped me avoid hefty excess-baggage costs on flights to and from Nepal. My luggage from Australia usually comprised a little special food for high altitude, some Vegemite, cheese and replacement equipment for whatever I'd destroyed on the previous trip. This expedition, however, was different—it had the 'Alex' element. I knew how much he loved his food and drink, so I wasn't surprised when he suggested that we bring a few 'essential' items. Knowing the horrendous cost of excess baggage, I advised him to keep it to a bare minimum.

'Andrew, don't worry, mate,' he replied. 'Just the basics, mate.'

When we met at the airport and pooled our gear, I was stunned to see that we were 200 kilograms overweight! Most of that was cured meat and tins of sheep's cheese, not to mention Alex's father's special homemade spirit—'Macedonian firewater', as I called it. With some frantic repacking, and Alex's roguish charm working overtime on the lady at the check-in counter, we managed to get away with being charged for only 20 extra kilograms. Short in stature but larger than life, Alex has a gregarious nature that wins the heart of anyone who meets him.

Part of our repacking, though, involved stuffing as much meat, cheese and alcohol as we could into our carry-on luggage.

By the time we'd finished, they must have weighed 25 kilograms apiece. In the time-honoured tradition of climbers attempting to sneak massively overweight carry-on baggage onto the plane, we sauntered through the departure lounge as lightly as we could, trying to mask the pain caused by the loads we were carrying. We headed down the ramp towards the plane and I was just starting to think we'd got away with it, when a voice called out, 'Excuse me, sir ...'

Alex had been pinged, possibly because the daypack he was carrying was starting to burst its seams, or perhaps the bewitched girl at the check-in counter had snapped out of her Alex crush and advised the attendants to look out for a stocky man with a daypack of similar dimensions. The attendant asked Alex what was in the pack.

'Camera gear, mate,' Alex replied without a second's hesitation.

The attendant politely asked if he might just check the camera gear, so Alex unshouldered his pack, which crashed to the floor with such force that the tunnel bounced a little. As he started to unload the contents, a pile of food and alcohol suitable for a small corner store grew, much to the amusement of our fellow passengers—and to the amazement of the attendant. With each contribution to the pile, the attendant shook his head and muttered, 'Camera gear, huh?'

'Yes, mate,' Alex replied each time.

When Alex finally reached the bottom of his pack, by which time the path to the plane was all but blocked by a small delicatessen, he produced a tiny disposable plastic camera, worth about $10. With the greatest sincerity, he patted the nearly hysterical attendant on the shoulder and said, 'See, mate, I told you it was camera gear!'

Luckily for us, the plane was ready to depart. It would have been more expensive to argue about the cost of the excess than to simply let us go. With a look of stunned disbelief, the attendant offered some no doubt wise counsel and told Alex to repack and board the plane. I confess that I felt a little sorry for the official—he'd just been 'Alex'd'.

*

Joining us for the trek to base camp were two of Alex's friends from Macedonia, Alexander and Stoly. They weren't serious climbers but were keen to experience the Himalaya with their expat mate. The walk to Manaslu is one of the most scenic in the Himalaya, but at the time it was seriously affected by the Maoist insurgency against the Nepali monarchy. The conflict had escalated significantly since 2001, with armed attacks against police and military garrisons throughout Nepal. All outposts had been abandoned in the isolated Manaslu region as they were small and easily overrun by the Maoists, who were ruthless in their treatment of prisoners. As a result, very few trekkers ventured there.

Other institutions were closed too. Our plan to change our dollars into rupees at a bank in one of the small towns en route to Base Camp, so we could pay our porters, was thwarted. The bank had closed four months earlier, in order to prevent the Maoists from robbing it. The Nepalese are nothing if not entrepreneurial, though, and we found a pharmacist who was prepared to make the exchange at a surprisingly reasonable rate.

We passed the entire 10-day trek along the old salt-trading route between Nepal and Tibet without seeing another foreigner, but we did see firsthand the barbarity of the civil war. As we walked through one village, we came across a particularly brutal scene: a local village mayor had been beheaded by the Maoists, simply because he was a figure of authority. Not only had they murdered him in cold blood, they had also ordered the villagers not to move his body from the path where it lay, so that all who passed would see it.

At the last village before we reached the mountain, Sama Goan, we paid off our lowland porters and engaged some local men to carry our gear up to the Base Camp of the mountain. It was a tough trek and would involve pushing through deep snow, which the lowland porters were not equipped for. It was also the policy of the villagers at Sama Goan to deny other porters permission to carry loads to Manaslu's Base Camp. There were no laws as such, but there would have been violence if we'd tried to use our lowland porters all the way. In any case, we were happy to share the employment among different villages.

We took a couple of rest days in Sama Goan to acclimatise and repack our loads before heading up to the mountain. This also gave us time to explore the village and its surrounds, which I was keen to do. In centuries past, Sama Goan was a part of Tibet, but in an effort to crack down on illegal trade between the two countries, Nepal had annexed this valley. The locals had retained their traditional customs, though, so the village provided us with a wonderful insight into Tibetan life before the Chinese occupation. Inside their houses, the villagers maintained a strict hierarchy around the fireplace, with the matriarch of the household in prime position, and the remaining members positioned according to their place in the family.

We ate with the family in whose house we stayed. *Dhal baht* was the main meal, but I couldn't stomach the accompanying beverage. Each day the lady of the house prepared traditional yak-butter tea—literally, tea with butter in it—in a long wooden cylinder, stained dark with age, smoke and rancid butter. Living with the family in such close quarters was enlightening and very personal, and I felt very blessed by the experience.

Ours was the first expedition into Manaslu that season, and the route from Sama Goan to base camp was still buried in snow. We decided to do a reconnaissance the next day, before taking all the equipment up with our porters. Wary of the avalanches that had thundered throughout the night, we plugged our way up a steep track. After some hours, and nearing the top of the hill, we had to cross a shallow gully. Alex and I both recognised the gully as an obvious chute for avalanches and yelled back at the others not to dawdle, just in case.

Sure enough, there was an almighty roar from above us, followed by an avalanche crashing down. Without the need for words, Alex and I instinctively darted forward a hundred metres to escape the fall zone, then looked behind. To our horror, we saw that both Alexander and Stoly were in the path of the avalanche. This was not a massive powder avalanche, such as you see in Europe, but an avalanche caused by the collapse of a major ice cliff. It was more like a river of ice blocks, and most definitely fatal.

The two Macedonians had just seconds to react. Although neither had any rock-climbing experience to speak of, they threw themselves at the cliff beside them and scampered up the vertical rock face as if it was a set of stairs. The river of ice crashed down and roared past for another thirty seconds, before slowing and finally coming to rest. Thousands of tonnes of ice had poured down.

Shaken and well stirred, Alexander and Stoly scrambled down the backside of the cliff because they couldn't down-climb what they'd just ascended. In fact, none of us was able to climb that cliff, as it was a near-blank vertical wall. Fear is a great motivator, apparently.

After identifying the rest of the route to Base Camp, we returned to the village. We'd have liked to have started the trek again the next day with a full team of porters but were concerned about further avalanches, having set off several more on our return to the village, so we decided to wait to let them clear from our route. It was a wise decision. The next afternoon we heard an enormous avalanche near the base of Manaslu, and shortly afterwards the Buri Gandaki River, which passed Sama Goan, became a flooding torrent. A huge ice cliff, which had overhung a great glacial lake that fed the river, had collapsed into the lake, causing it to flood its banks.

We'd likely escaped death had we set off on the route, but all the bridges over the river had been washed away, and we were told that we might be stuck in Sama Goan for a couple of weeks until a new bridge could be built. We were dismayed at that prospect, but there was little we could do. The next morning, however, we awoke to find that the ice-cliff collapse had been so enormous that it had blasted all the water out of the lake. Once the flood had passed, the river dried up, so we simply walked across the dry riverbed and trekked up to Base Camp. We could only imagine how many thousands of tonnes that ice cliff must have weighed. Once we were at the mountain, Alexander and Stoly trekked out, leaving just Alex, me, our base-camp cook and a local villager as a base-camp assistant. We had the whole mountain to ourselves.

Manaslu's reputation as one of the most beautiful peaks in the Himalaya was well deserved. Its two pointed peaks, reminiscent of a bull's horns, soared into the clouds above. Climbing alone with Alex on this striking mountain was a real joy, as was having such an extraordinary wilderness to ourselves. Quite deliberately, we'd not brought a map, so we were obliged to find a way up the mountain using our alpine skills and experience. It was a great adventure.

After two weeks we'd forced a route up the glacier, around crevasses and through some big ice cliffs to establish Camp 1 at 5300 metres and Camp 2 at 6800 metres, despite the regular snow-falls that buried our tracks. It was sustained work, with just the two of us having to kick new steps each time we carried a load. Alex had been suffering considerable back pain throughout the climb and at this point decided that he was unable to continue—he was later diagnosed as having kidney stones. I was willing to carry on but knew it would be extremely challenging trying to open the route up the steep ice cliffs to Camp 3 on my own.

Just as Alex had to withdraw, two Norwegian brothers turned up at the mountain with their own expedition. Sven and Jon Gangdal, both of whom had completed a number of Himalayan expeditions over the years, were climbing with two support Sherpas, Dawa Tshering and Kili, and they invited me to climb with them. I preferred to climb alone, but we shared much of the work of opening up the route to Camp 3 and fixing ropes where they were needed. Several more expeditions also arrived at the mountain over the next couple of weeks, although the other Australian expedition, from which I'd withdrawn at the first planning meeting, was not one of them.

While I continued the climb, Alex waited at Base Camp. He refused to leave, having committed to wait until I was finished. This was really magnanimous of him because he was in serious pain. Luckily, all the excess baggage we'd brought with us was able to sustain him, and he spent several weeks working his way through the portable delicatessen, repeating his own special mantra: 'Eat, drink, relax.' I'd have loved to have done that too, but I wanted this summit and needed to keep pushing hard on the mountain.

Together with the Norwegians, I planned to fix a small amount of rope on the steep ice face below Camp 3 at 7500 metres. Having fixed the rope, and after depositing some supplies at Camp 3 for a later summit attempt, we would return to Base Camp for a rest before launching the summit bid. At Camp 2, however, the night before we started the rope fixing, the Norwegians declared that after establishing Camp 3 they would keep going for the summit, rather than descending to Base Camp to recuperate. I couldn't join them as I didn't have my down suit with me, but I wasn't about to miss out on a summit chance, so as they prepared to sleep, I raced down the mountain to Base Camp to collect my summit clothing. Next morning, as the Norwegian team made its way towards Camp 3, I climbed the mountain from Base Camp to Camp 2, and then continued up, trying to catch the others.

At one point I could see Dawa and Kili on the steep ice approaching Camp 3, but when I looked up a moment later, they were several hundred metres back down the slope. Neither was moving, and it was clear that they'd fallen. I feared the worst and continued to climb towards them, but a few minutes later both figures stood up and started slowly downhill. When I reached them they told me that a strong gust of wind had literally blown them off the mountain face. They were both shaken and bruised but otherwise unhurt. This summit attempt, though, was over. They descended to Base Camp with the Norwegians.

Having just reclimbed to Camp 2, I wasn't inclined to descend again so quickly, so I decided to enhance my acclimatisation by spending another night there. What an experience. I was the only person on the entire mountain. The sunset was fiery red, with monstrous black lenticular clouds above me. The air had such a feeling of menace that I thought I might be in for some kind of super storm, so I dressed in my summit clothing in case the tent was destroyed. But it was just a colourful show and the night passed calmly. The next day I joined the others at Base Camp, and after two rest days we were ready for the summit attempt.

*

To avoid becoming lost in Manaslu's notorious summit clouds, I'd brought a GPS. It was the first time I'd used one on an expedition. On a bitterly cold morning, Sven, Jon, Dawa, Kili and I left Camp 3 at 7500 metres, crossed the plateau and ascended the final face to the top. As with many mountains, what looked like the top from below was a false summit. There was still a very sharp snow and rock ridge to traverse before we reached the exposed and precipitous peak. The mountain has one of the sharpest of all the 8000-metre summits, and I literally wrapped my arms around it to stop from toppling off the side.

It was very blustery, and low-pressure cloud was forming right where I was. After a couple of minutes at the top, I backtracked to the col and we climbed quickly down to the plateau. The wind was getting stronger and it looked like it would blizzard. As we crossed the plateau, Camp 3 was out of sight and the snowstorm obliterated our tracks. There was some disagreement about the direction to follow, but I placed my trust in the GPS, and after some tricky down-climbing found the camp.

The others were too tired to continue, but I've always adhered to a principle of getting lower than the highest camp as soon as possible, so I packed up my gear and continued on my own down the mountain. A short distance before Camp 2, the storm worsened and I lost the way in the whiteout. Here the GPS didn't help, because although it pointed out the general direction of the tent, the unseen path zigzagged through a crevasse field. Being unroped, I had to follow the path exactly or I'd meet my demise at the bottom of a cold, dark crevasse—not my preferred ending to the expedition.

To confuse things, I had no idea what time it was, as my watch had malfunctioned. I couldn't tell if the increasing gloom was a result of the cloud overhead or the encroaching darkness. I had no option but to stop and hope that the cloud would lift enough for me to dash through the crevasses, but it became darker and I resigned myself to yet another high-altitude bivouac.

This time it wouldn't be too uncomfortable because I had my down suit, sleeping bag and some food, although no tent. Most of all, though, I needed a drink, having consumed less than a litre of water since starting out at twelve-thirty that morning, some fifteen hours earlier. It's difficult to describe just how thirsty you get at high altitude after days of climbing in the cold, dry air, but you rarely have the fuel or the time to melt enough snow to satisfy your thirst. Your kidneys ache, your throat swells, your head pounds, you cannot swallow and you cough constantly. You crave liquid more than anything else.

I placed a little snow into my water bottle, which I then put inside my down suit to melt. I was getting ready to pull out my sleeping bag when the cloud lifted temporarily and I glimpsed the tent—it was just 100 metres away. Despite my exhaustion and clumsiness, I stuffed everything back into my pack and scrambled as quickly as I could around the crevasses and into the protective nylon cocoon.

It is incredible what a sense of security such a tiny, flimsy shelter as a lightweight summit tent can provide. Immediately as you enter, the biting wind is cut and the intimidating precipice below is shielded from your view. No matter the frozen ground beneath, or the congestion of stinking clothes, food scraps, climbing equipment and bodies within, it is better than being outside. I collected enough snow to fill an oil tanker and soon had the stove purring, with glorious liquid forming in the pot. Within a few minutes I was ensconced in my sleeping bag, gnawing on a muesli bar and sipping a hot brew. Five-star luxury.

*

High on adrenaline, courtesy of having reached the summit of my eighth 8000er, the next day I forced my way down through the fresh snow, accumulating a load of 35 kilograms as I cleared my camps. I wrote in my diary:

> Had to cross a widening crevasse at the bottom of a steep slope, and with my heavy load I thought the snow bridge might collapse, so I sat on my bum and slid down over it. After that, no worries, except on one slope where I had to self-arrest after slipping.

I was greeted at Base Camp by several people, each of them giving me a different reception. Alex was overjoyed, of course.

We'd cemented a special bond of mateship, having succeeded on the mountain in such a small and lightweight expedition. For Alex to have stayed on, despite his illness, was truly the action of a great friend. The moral support he'd provided while I climbed played a major part in giving me the confidence to continue and succeed.

Also at our base camp was Gerlinde Kaltenbrunner, an Austrian woman with whom we were sharing our climbing permit and base-camp infrastructure. She had arrived with an Italian climbing friend. They would summit several weeks later, and Gerlinde would go on to become one of the world's leading 8000-metre mountaineers. She has now climbed all fourteen of the 8000ers, the second woman in the world to do so, but she did it in much finer style than the first. She is probably the strongest high-altitude female climber in the world, willing to climb very technical routes, carry her own loads and break trail. She's also absolutely gorgeous and has a wonderful personality, so naturally I fell in love with her immediately.

Unfortunately for me, one of the other expeditions on the mountain that year was a commercial group led by the highly accomplished German mountaineer Ralf Dujmovits. Gerlinde fell in love with him, not me, and they are now married and virtually inseparable in the mountains. I console myself with the knowledge that everybody falls in love with Gerlinde, so mine is only one discarded heart on a pile of many.

The third was the Australian expedition, which had finally arrived at Base Camp on the day I summitted, as it happened. I'd intended to send a message to them before I left Australia, to let them know about our little expedition, but I simply hadn't done it in the mad rush to organise everything. Needless to say, that didn't win me any fans. Some were disappointed, and others were even angry that I'd stolen *their* summit.

I have little sympathy for that point of view. It was unfortunate that things had turned out as they had. If there hadn't been the tension at the first planning meeting, I'd have been there with them. It took a few years to repair the relationships with some of those guys. At the time, however, I was exhausted and had no desire to argue with them. Alex proved to be an impenetrable barrier to their attempts to 'discuss' the situation. I was simply happy to enjoy the success of another summit. It had actually been the first ascent of any 8000-metre peak for that season anywhere in the Himalaya, as we'd summitted on 20 April, very early in the climbing season.

*

Alex needed medical treatment for his kidney stones, so we caught a helicopter back to Kathmandu rather than make the long trek out. After three days in the madness of Kathmandu's tourist suburb of Thamel, where we did our best to 'eat, drink, relax', Alex flew back home to his family and business. I flew to the mountain airstrip of Lukla, which was looking resplendent with its new bitumen tarmac, as I had another mountain to climb.

Before going to Manaslu I'd booked a permit for Lhotse, the fourth-highest mountain in the world. It sits just to the south of Mount Everest. Indeed its Tibetan name means 'South Peak'. The Swiss pair of Ernst Reiss and Fritz Luchsinger were the first to reach its 8516-metre summit on 18 May 1956, but Lhotse has since received far less attention than its taller sibling, to which it is connected by a precipitous ridge that sits above 8000 metres for its entire length. Despite this, Lhotse has seen its share of tragedy and controversy.

Polish legend Jerzy Kukuczka had climbed all the 8000ers but Lhotse either in winter or by a new route. In 1989 he returned to Lhotse to forge a new route up its extremely technical and at the time unclimbed South Face, arguably the hardest mountain face in the Himalaya, which would give him an outstanding ascent of every peak. Near to the summit, however, he fell to his death when his rope broke. Thus the Himalayan climbing fraternity lost one of its greats.

In 1990 a Slovenian climber, Tomo Cesen, declared that he'd achieved the first ascent of the South Face, solo. His claim was disputed and he subsequently retracted it, but the inquiry led to many of his claimed ascents also being disputed.

The trek from Lukla to base camp normally takes about ten days, but being acclimatised from Manaslu, I charged into Base Camp in just three days, two porters struggling behind with my climbing equipment. My existing acclimatisation wasn't the only advantage I had from having climbed Manaslu so recently. When booking the permit for Lhotse I knew that, in addition to being acclimatised, I'd also have the right psychological mindset for climbing hard at altitude. I would need to be in the zone, because I was planning to solo the mountain's steep West Face. Lhotse is some 500 metres higher into the death zone, and considerably steeper and more technical, than my solo climb on Broad Peak.

Lhotse shares its Base Camp with Everest but, despite the number of expeditions there, the mood was sombre when I arrived. Just that morning a British climber had been killed in a fall on the Lhotse Face. This was the same face down which Michael Groom had been avalanched back in 1991, although he'd somehow survived.

I spent two days resting at Base Camp and then climbed quickly up the mountain to test my acclimatisation. It was good. In just six hours I climbed through Camp 1 and on to Camp 2, and the next day I continued to Camp 3 at 7300 metres in five and a half hours. After leaving a deposit there of my down suit, stove, fuel and food, I returned to Base Camp and spent another six days resting and watching the weather. When it looked good, I started back up the mountain.

My route on Lhotse followed the same path as the normal route on Everest to a point a little higher than Camp 3. A number of climbers were pushing up to the South Col on Everest, so I shared the climb with them. At one point, I looked down the slope but could see no faces, only oxygen masks. I was the only one climbing without gas.

After crossing the Yellow Band of rock a few hundred metres above Camp 3, I branched off and headed straight up the Lhotse Face, making my own Camp 4 at 7800 metres. It was perched on the side of the Lhotse Face, with a massive drop down to the Western Cwm, some 1300 metres below.

The next morning I set off alone at 1 a.m. and pushed up the face into an ever-narrowing couloir, which was the Achilles heel in the mighty rock buttress above me. It didn't receive the morning sun until 8 a.m., so it was bitterly cold, but that kept the snow nice and firm, and I cramponed quickly up the steepening slope, using my two ice tools as fists and punching their picks straight into the snow.

The crux of the route is where the couloir narrows, and I had to bridge across a small rock step before it opened out again onto firm snow. It was absolutely fantastic climbing. I was completely alone on the world's fourth-highest peak, and I was loving every minute of it. This was one of those climbs where everything came together. I was climbing hard on steep ground for hour after hour—fast but not so fast as to exhaust myself—overcoming all obstacles with fluid movements, having the confidence to take on each successive challenge, and watching the mountains drop away below me. I absolutely thrilled in those conditions.

I've experienced similar emotions, although not to the same extent, on long training runs in the Australian bush. It takes me several kilometres to warm up, but once I've found my pace I can run for hours on end, physically and psychologically in the zone. I doubt I'd find the same enjoyment pounding the pavement, though. I suspect it has something to do with the sustained, almost meditative intensity of concentration that's required to keep one's footing in the outdoors, in conjunction with the sustained intense physical activity. It's a feeling of testing myself, stretching myself, but still being in control.

The hours ticked by quickly and soon I was approaching the top of the couloir. I knew I had to climb up a rocky buttress to the left, even though the buttress to the right actually looked higher from below. The final climb up to the summit was tricky because the rock was quite shattered and I picked my way delicately up the loose stone and snow, careful not to slip and also not to dislodge a rock that might fall and hit another climber somewhere on the lower face, with catastrophic results. I reached the top at 9.20 a.m.

I crouched on the top for fifteen minutes and gazed over to the south-east ridge of Everest, where I could see a trail of ant-like people making their way to the top. It was stunning to see Everest from another perspective. On the other side of Lhotse's summit, the face dropped away very steeply. I checked my footing carefully before shooting some photos over towards Makalu and the more distant peaks.

As I looked down at my own route, I could see the top of the rock buttress on the right side of the couloir. There were signs there that climbers had mistakenly climbed to that point, rather than to the true summit. It must have been so frustrating to make that error, and I wondered if they'd satisfied themselves with that peak or whether they'd made the very delicate and exposed traverse over to the real summit. By this time I was getting pretty chilled, so I eased myself back into the couloir and down-climbed to Camp 4.

As the sun was now shining on the Lhotse Face, rocks began to melt out of the snow, and the couloir became a shooting gallery. I'd had a similar experience on Nanga Parbat years before. There was nowhere to hide and rocks whistled past me, but such was my exhaustion that I was forced to stop and recover my breath for minutes at a time, despite the danger. The best I could do was hold my backpack over my head as protection. Forcing myself to carry on, I reached Camp 4 around 2 p.m., quickly packed my equipment and continued down to the safety of Camp 2 that evening.

Once safe, it was down the mountain and a quick trek out to the airstrip at Lukla, where I tried to book a flight back to Kathmandu. Only one plane came that day and there weren't any available seats. I refrained from hijacking it this time, but as I walked back to my lodge, someone called through the airport security fence to say that a helicopter was heading to Kathmandu and had four places available. Along with about ten other people, I raced to get my gear and head for the 'gate'. Victory went to those still supercharged with acclimatisation and summit adrenaline, and I was the first on board! By evening, I was enjoying a cool beer at Sam's Bar in Kathmandu.

The year 2002 was one of the most satisfying I'd had in the mountains. Having decided that I would enjoy the journey to summit the fourteen 8000ers, I'd climbed in my preferred style: in small teams with minimal support. When Alex had become sick on Manaslu, I'd pushed on to achieve the first Australian ascent of the mountain. My solo ascent of Lhotse had been one of the most thrilling climbs I'd ever done—unroped on steep ground on one of the highest peaks in the world, but in the perfect conditions of which every climber dreams.

With those two ascents, for the third time I had climbed two 8000-metre peaks in a year, and it was the second time that I'd climbed two in a single season. I felt that I was now a seasoned high-altitude climber at the top of my game, and I could face any challenge.

*

Christine Boskoff and I had stayed in contact after Everest in 2000. In early 2003 we decided to team up and attempt an ascent of the South Face of Kanchenjunga. At 8586 metres, Kanchenjunga is a monstrous five-headed beast, although its name means 'Five Treasures of Snow'—obviously named by a dreamer, not a climber. It sits in the far east of Nepal, overlooking the Indian city of Darjeeling, and it so dominates the surrounding landscape that it dictates its own weather patterns. Four of Kanchenjunga's five summits reach above 8000 metres. Until 1852 it was thought to be the highest mountain in the world.

While a number of early expeditions trekked and climbed around Kanchenjunga, the first climbing on the actual mountain was done in 1905 by the British explorer Aleister Crowley. A number of valiant but unsuccessful attempts by Norwegians, Germans and Austrians followed, until the British returned to achieve the first successful ascent in 1955. Kanchenjunga has been the scene of many major epics since then, including an extraordinary traverse in 1989 of all four 8000-metre summits by a Russian expedition, which included the late, guitar-playing Anatoli Bukreev.

A highly spiritual peak, Kanchenjunga is worshipped by the inhabitants of the Sikkim region in which it sits, who believe that gods reside on its summit. At the request of the locals, it is traditional for climbers to stop just a few metres short of the very summit, so as not to disturb the inhabitants.

Christine and I found an expedition that was already going to the mountain, comprising Italians Silvio Mondinelli, Mario Merelli and Christian Kuntner, and Spaniard Carlos Pauner. I'd climbed on the Gasherbrum mountains in 1999 with Kuntner—he of the chocolate-bar-on-the-summit incident. My trekking agent managed to get our names onto their permit for our share of the cost, which meant we didn't have to buy a whole permit—costing US$10,000—for just the two of us. Christine and I would share the base-camp kitchen and dining tent with the international team, but we would climb separately.

Christian was even less friendly on this trip than he had been in 1999. His group had brought in some additional sponsored rations of pork and pasta, and various condiments to spice up their meals. We didn't expect to share any of that with them, but Christian made sure by regularly giving the cook strict instructions not to give any of his group's special food to Christine or me. Our cook was a great guy and felt embarrassed by this. He tried his best to imitate for us what he was cooking for the others, so we experienced such culinary delights as Nepali tinned spam with Nepali spaghetti in tomato sauce. Disgusting, but we ate it with appreciative noises anyway so Christian would think we were eating his stuff. Every time he saw us eating what looked like his food, he ran off to his supply tent to check the packets of pasta and meat.

I had two other sources of entertainment on this expedition. Since 1998 I'd been studying a degree in disaster management. It was a distance-education course so that, rather than attending university regularly, I could study and send in my assignments from wherever I happened to be. By this time, I'd submitted them from Antarctica, Pakistan and Nepal, among many other far-flung places. I'd also achieved quite a reputation for unique excuses for late assignments. On this expedition, I was trying to complete an assignment in social research—probably the least interesting of all the subjects on the course. My rest days at Base Camp were spent labouring over my textbooks and writing a draft assignment by hand.

My other distraction was a small radio that I took on all expeditions to try to catch up on news and events via the BBC. I suspect Christine might have been in the employ of my university lecturers, because one day she asked if she could borrow it. Within an hour she returned it, the aerial snapped. There was nothing left for me to do but go back to the books.

Christine couldn't really find her pace on this expedition, and after a couple of weeks she gave up and went home. I'd come to the mountain to climb with someone I respected and liked, hoping that we'd have fun. In her absence, I once again found myself essentially alone in pursuit of an 8000-metre summit. It wasn't my choice, but I was far from being depressed about it. I was even excited and it led me to do some soul-searching, a rare thing:

Why do I climb these things? Why am I here? I'm sharing a base camp with a bunch of climbers whose leader lives in constant fear that I might eat his food. The mountain is high and dangerous. Summit day will involve a lot of steep rock climbing, which worries me more than anything else. Going up is okay but descending will be very tough. The idea scares me seriously. The summit is the third-highest and looks to be my toughest one yet. I get butterflies when I look at it.

Yet here I am. Why? I could be at home, working a good job, working on my house, pursuing a nice relationship. Base camp has people but I am lonely and virtually alone against this mountain. What inner force drives me to it? I haven't finished this one; indeed, I am apprehensive about it, yet already I am thinking of the next one and the one after that. The summit is a relief, at best, no major high. An inner euphoria to be celebrated, in my case alone, if, and only if, I succeed. And yet I feel a nervous excitement, an inner tension at the thought of pushing through the barriers of fear. The pain and exhaustion I am prepared for. It is the fear that has to be overcome, and perhaps with that, the greatest sense of achievement.

Yet at the same time I long for the fear to be gone, to be over and finished with. I feel that I must finish the fourteen to vanquish the fear and earn the peace. I long for simplicity on the one hand, yet adventure on the other. The two do not go hand in hand. Is there a middle ground or am I destined to jump from one to the other in the search for myself? I want this summit, and then I want good friends and family, social contact, warmth, simplicity. The mountains are simple but they do not bring simplicity.

My relationship with everyone except Christian was actually pretty good, and they invited me to join them on their summit attempt. We climbed to Camp 3, which we placed at about 7500 metres. I proposed that we put in a Camp 4 the following day at 7800 metres to give us a reasonable climb on the summit day; however, the others wanted to make the summit push the next morning, making a massive day of it by climbing directly from Camp 3 to the top at 8600 metres. I thought this was a mistake and that we'd be exposing ourselves to too many risks, but the others were adamant. I agreed to join them but only for as long as it felt right.

We got away at 2.30 a.m. Although the weather forecast had been good, the thin line of cloud on the horizon was ominous. Within a couple of hours it was upon us and the weather was deteriorating significantly. I also found that I was suffering some warning signs of altitude sickness—double vision, nausea and headaches—a sure sign that I wasn't sufficiently acclimatised. Going higher would only worsen the symptoms.

Since 1997 I'd been climbing with a firm commitment to continue, unless the risks became absolutely too great. I had succeeded on every expedition since then. However, I had no intention of climbing into a blizzard at such extreme altitude, particularly as I was becoming ill. The risk on this occasion was too great. It was unacceptable to me, so I turned around and descended. The others kept on for the top.

The storm completely hid the mountain, and the other climbers soon became lost. They kept going for the top over unknown ground. With great determination, they reached the summit, probably achieving a new route along the way. When they started to descend they were soon separated, and it became every man for himself. All of them fell at different times, and all suffered frostbite. Eventually, the three Italians made it back down to base camp. Carlos Pauner, however, had disappeared.

The weather didn't improve and the season was drawing to an end. Without the prospect of another summit attempt, I trekked out. The Italians rested for a while after their climb, but as they were packing up Base Camp and preparing to leave, they saw a faint light at Camp 1. Climbing up quickly, they found Pauner, barely alive. He was exhausted and badly frostbitten but had somehow crawled down the mountain on his own, an amazing story of survival.

I was happy for the guys who had summitted but was absolutely content in my decision not to have continued with them. They were lucky to have survived, and the frostbite they'd incurred during the storm was a terribly high price to have paid. It would impact on their lives forever, and would henceforth impede their ability to tolerate cold. My goal was to climb all the 8000ers, not just this one. Injuring myself in a way that would affect my main aim was unacceptable.

In Kathmandu I found that the city was celebrating the fiftieth anniversary of the first ascent of Mount Everest. Hundreds of Everest summiteers were in town, and for three days we were treated to banquets and parades, and I had an opportunity to catch up with old friends as well as meet some famous Everest celebrities. I was invited to the final function, which showcased this royalty, including Sir Edmund Hillary, the first person to climb Everest; Junko Tabei, the first woman to climb Everest; and Reinhold Messner, the first, with Austrian Peter Habeler, to climb Everest without supplementary oxygen, and the first to climb Everest solo without oxygen. The function concluded with a medal ceremony.

Nepal's Prime Minister Lokendra Bahadur Chand presented the Nepal Mount Everest medal to a number of climbers. I wasn't really paying attention and was caught very much by surprise when mine was the first name read out. I wasn't first for any special reason but simply because Australia and Andrew both started with the first letter of the alphabet, which dictated the order of presentations.

I was honoured to receive the award, but as I stood on the stage with the prime minister while the media's cameras clicked madly, I rather wished I'd read the invitation a little more closely. It had requested that attendees wear either a suit or their national dress. I guess that in some parts of Australia my grubby shorts and T-shirt probably did meet that criteria.

*

Kanchenjunga in 2003 was my first unsuccessful expedition since 1996, so I was keen to get another summit under my belt. I'd been putting off going to two particular mountains, Cho Oyu and Shishapangma, because I'd read that they were the easiest 8000ers. I was planning to knock them off at the end. But big hills like these are quite adept at putting you in your place, and I was about to be put in mine. A friend was running a commercial group to Shishapangma, so I joined his team for base-camp services. Once on the mountain, I would climb on my own.

Shishapangma is the only 8000er that sits entirely within the so-called Autonomous Region of Tibet—better known these days as China. It's an unusual mountain. At 8027 metres, it stands alone on the Tibetan plateau, a beautiful white monolith presiding over the plains below. The origin of its name is the subject of several theories. Some believe it means 'Crest above the Grassy Plains', which sounds about right to me, but I prefer the more interesting interpretation from its literal meaning in the Tibetan language. In Tibetan, *shisha* means 'meat of an animal that died of natural causes', and *shangma* 'malt dregs left over from brewing beer'. Legend has it that, years ago, a blizzard killed all the livestock in the fields below Shishapangma, leaving as the villagers' only food the dead animals and some malt dregs left over from making beer. Who can pass by that interpretation?

I was planning a quick expedition. What I didn't know at this time was that the true summit of Shishapangma is very rarely climbed. Most expeditions climb to a point on the north ridge where it turns towards the summit. They refer to this as the Central Summit, but in fact it isn't a summit at all. It has been assigned various heights over the years—many records indicate that the height of the central summit is about 8012 metres, while the real summit is 8027 metres; others say that the Central Summit is less than 8000 metres and the true summit is 8013 metres. Either way, Shishapangma is still the lowest 8000er, so it's ironic that it was the last 8000er to be climbed. The Chinese achieved that glory with a risky climb across the avalanche-prone North Face in May of 1964.

For some reason, the Chinese Mountaineering Association provides summit certificates to people who've only been to the Central Summit. Thus, the mountain is attractive to commercial expeditions and less-experienced climbers, who can then claim an 8000-metre summit without actually getting there. While the real summit is only about 15 metres higher than the false summit, it is a much more difficult place to reach. The original ascent route up the mountain by the Chinese has been repeated several times, but the significant avalanche danger on the traverse across the North Face above Camp 3 to the top puts a lot of climbers off. A number of other ascents have been achieved via the steep and technical South Face, first climbed by a British expedition led by Doug Scott, with whom I climbed on the Mazeno Ridge of Nanga Parbat in 1995.

Somewhat lazily, I had done no research whatsoever into Shishapangma before heading there. I'd heard that it was an easy climb, and therefore I assumed it wouldn't pose too much trouble. I didn't realise that most climbers' claims to have summitted the mountain were actually falsely based on having reached the Central Summit. Perhaps my years of successes also caused me to be a little blasé about the challenge.

From Kathmandu we bounced and jostled our way by road in a dilapidated Indian-built Tata bus to the border town of Khodari, stopping on numerous occasions at checkpoints en route. The Nepali Army and police force gave us the once-over each time, satisfying themselves that we weren't Maoist desperados intent on overthrowing the government, posing as western climbers—or, given the direction we were travelling, returning home from having done so. We were duly ushered through.

Khodari is a squalid township of rickety timber and brick shacks. It's etched into the side of a gorge, alongside a raging torrent that descends from the Tibetan plateau. Water runs everywhere from the cloud-enshrouded hills above, and there's a constant stream of people ferrying loads of goods along the muddy road that leads to the bridge that is the border crossing. This bridge and others on the Nepali road that leads from Kathmandu up to the border were apparently built courtesy of the largesse of the Chinese government, so I'm sure there couldn't be any truth to cynics' claims that they were built strongly enough to support Chinese tanks, particularly since the main bridge is called the Friendship Bridge, while the road that runs all the way from the bridge to Lhasa, the capital of the Autonomous Region of Tibet, is the Friendship Highway.

Once across that bridge, and before reaching the customs post, I was obliged to stop at a little booth. An official pointed a small, black, gun-shaped object at my forehead, and for a brief moment I thought that my irreverence was not appreciated. The gun was in fact a thermometer, and my forehead's temperature was apparently able to indicate whether or not I was a carrier of the latest mutation of a nasty influenza virus. I wondered whether it wouldn't have been more appropriate to do that test on my way back, and I wasn't overly surprised when given the all clear. Once through the bureaucracy, we piled into a minivan for a zigzagging ride up the steep Chinese—sorry, Autonomous Region of Tibet—side of the gorge, to the first town, known as Zhangmu, a concrete version of Khodari.

Mountaineering in Tibet is strictly controlled by the government through the Chinese Mountaineering Association and the 'autonomous' China Tibet Mountaineering Association. All transport, hotels, meals and expedition permits are organised by these associations, and one is essentially ushered to the mountain by vehicle—no wistful meanderings along alpine trails on these trips. After a night in Zhangmu, during which we were introduced to the mandatory meals of monosodium glutamate with a garnish of unidentified vegetables, and which would be repeated for lunch and dinner for the next six days, we drove up the Friendship Highway in chauffeured Land Cruisers to the Tibetan town of Nyalam.

The drive was quite incredible. Reminiscent of the infamous Bolivian Yungas road from La Paz to Coroico, known as the most dangerous road in the world, the Friendship Highway had been blasted from near-vertical cliffs. At times it tunnels right through them, and at others it snakes its way up the precipitous gorge to the plateau above. Landslips from above and from the road itself were common. Teams of workers constantly maintained it, repairing the damage caused by legions of trucks that carted goods between the two neighbours.

Nyalam is cold, windswept and barren, and its inhabitants are as tough as the packs of marauding dogs that patrol the streets looking for unsuspecting tourists. Part of the Tsang Province in the old Tibet, you can still see Tibetans wearing traditional garb, including densely woven woollen shoes, but these days it is the administrative capital of the local county in Shigatse Prefecture, with a strong Chinese presence to help guide its autonomy.

The attempted food poisoning continued in Nyalam's dining room; however, due to Nyalam's significant altitude (3750 metres), we were obliged to spend two nights there to acclimatise. When not seeking enlightenment through abstinence, I spent my time pushing my acclimatisation by climbing the nearby hills, which provided up to a thousand metres' height gain for those with the energy.

After Nyalam and another couple of nights in the next town, we drove to the official Chinese base camp of Shishapangma, which, at an altitude of 5000 metres, is well and truly up on the Tibetan plateau. Using yaks to ferry our loads 20 kilometres across the plateau to Advance Base Camp, we strolled across gently undulating grassy hills populated by large flocks of Himalayan blue sheep, which look like goats. The lucky few caught a glimpse of a Himalayan snow leopard or a wild ass. Impossibly deep blue skies above distant shimmering lakes surrounded by white-capped Himalayan peaks make this trek an absolute delight, albeit a cold and constantly windy one.

My plan was to commence climbing from Advance Base Camp on 20 September, a Saturday, but one of the Sherpas there told me that Saturday is an inauspicious day on which to begin. I'm not sure if my superstition has increased since surviving various accidents over the years or if I've really come to embrace the belief systems of the locals, but I saw no sense in challenging the gods. I could wait for one more day.

The route up the north ridge to Camp 3 is very easy, and I quickly reached this point. From there, I hoped to follow the original Chinese line, a rising traverse across the North Face for several hundred metres, which would bring me to a saddle on the summit ridge between the central and the true summit. The face was heavily loaded with snow, however, and I wasn't prepared to risk setting off an avalanche, so I kept climbing up the ridge.

My repeated attempts to traverse across the face as I gained altitude were thwarted by the loose snow, so I continued upwards until I found myself at the Central Summit. There I looked out across a steeply sided, heavily corniced ridge. I could see why most expeditions stopped at this point. The mountain's South Face dropped precipitously away to the right, and the precarious and top-heavy cornices that perched above the North Face were impassable. Frustratingly, I was halted just a couple of hundred metres horizontally and only about 20 metres below the real summit. I could see it clearly just beyond my reach, but I couldn't get to it. There would be no summit of a mountain by me that year, and so I returned home.

The year 2003 was a disappointing one for me. For the first time since 1996 I'd failed to achieve my objective—and on not one but two expeditions. I hadn't been too worried about not reaching the summit of Kanchenjunga earlier in the year, because that had been a sound risk-management decision, but I knew that my approach to Shishapangma had been far too lax. More than anything, it was a wasted opportunity. My goal to climb all the 8000ers was delayed, and I'd wasted a fair amount of money. Worse, I'd have to return to this mountain in another season, which might have been better used to climb a different mountain.

It was a timely reminder for me that big mountains are not impressed by résumés. I was only ever a visitor, and I still had a tough road ahead if I was to succeed in, and survive, this project.

Postscript

Carlos Pauner is still alive and continues to climb but must be one of the luckiest—or unluckiest—climbers in the Himalaya. In 2009 he was evacuated from Shishapangma after falling and breaking two ribs. He was rescued in 2010 from Annapurna—the highest helicopter rescue in history—and again in 2011 from Lhotse in Nepal.

Christine Boskoff died in 2006 in an avalanche while climbing in China with her partner, Charlie Fowler.

Another team on Kanchenjunga in 2003 included Australian Mick Parker. Mick was to become a regular in the Himalaya, and we frequently met up for a beer in Kathmandu before or after our expeditions. In 2009 Mick died in Kathmandu shortly after climbing Makalu.

9

HIGH-ALTITUDE HOLLYWOOD

Most of us exist for most of the time in worlds which are humanly arranged, themed and controlled. One forgets that there are environments which do not respond to the flick of a switch or the twist of a dial, and which have their own rhythms and orders of existence. Mountains correct this amnesia.

Robert Macfarlane

L ATE IN 2003, I received an invitation from Ben Webster, a Canadian Everest summiteer, to join a documentary team that would be climbing Mount Everest in the pre-monsoon season of 2004. Ben's plan was for four climbers to comprehensively record an Everest expedition from its inception to the summit, in all its gory detail and—for the first time—in high definition. We would be filming 'daily diaries' to add behind-the-scenes substance to the film, and at every point during the expedition we'd capture as much drama as possible.

Financed by the Discovery Channel Canada, this was a big-budget affair with a full-time director-editor and cinematographer.

We'd use professional video equipment and have full Sherpa support throughout the climb. The climbing team was made up of Ben, who was both the producer and expedition leader; Shaunna Burke, his Canadian girlfriend, who was an accomplished competition skier but a relatively inexperienced climber; the Mexican Hector Ponce de Leon, a two-time Everest summiteer and mountain guide, and me. We four would be both the subjects and the high-altitude cameramen, filming each other as we climbed.

The invitation came as a total surprise, as there were plenty of other highly experienced climbers whom Ben could have asked. I suspect Hector and I might have been invited not only because we had the right high-altitude experience and were a good chance to get the cameras to the summit, but also because we were unknown personalities from completely different corners of the world. I guess Ben was thinking that there might be some tension, which would have added drama to the documentary. But that's just a hunch.

Although I'd already climbed Everest, and joining this trip would further delay the rest of my project, it seemed like a very good opportunity to get back to the mountain. My strongest desire was to climb all the 8000ers without oxygen, but my Everest ascent in 2000 had been with auxiliary oxygen, as I'd been guiding clients at the time. This expedition offered a really interesting experience, and one that I might be able to leverage in the future, as well as a chance to climb Everest without 'gas'. Ben required that we use oxygen while doing the filming, both for safety and to assist us to carry the additional high-definition video equipment. If we succeeded in that task and if there was still time left in the climbing season, however, I could potentially climb the mountain again without oxygen and achieve my own goal as well as that of the expedition. I decided it was worth the risk of being a pawn in the 'drama' and accepted the invitation.

In February 2004, Ben brought us all to Canada for a bit of preliminary filming and training in the use of the equipment.

He had put together a very professional expedition. The support crew—director and editor David McIlvride and cinematographer Frank Vilaca, who would climb as far as Camp 2—were terrific team members and highly accomplished in their fields. For two weeks we climbed, filmed, did some preliminary physical and cognitive testing and got to know each other. The highlight was an ascent of the 600-metre ice face known as the Pomme d'Or in Quebec, a classic Canadian ice climb. While Hector and I climbed the face, Ben and the camera crew hovered nearby in a helicopter, capturing the climb on film.

Two weeks after returning home, I boarded another flight, this time to Nepal. After filming in Kathmandu and meeting the rest of the team, including our doctor, Matt, communications guru Mike, and three young women from Brown University who were there to conduct cognitive tests assessing the impact of high altitude on our memories, we started the trek. Unlike most of my expeditions, where I'd been on a mission to get to the mountain quickly, we took several extra days along the way so we could capture the necessary footage. This made for a very relaxing and enjoyable journey, and provided numerous opportunities to wander off and explore side valleys and nearby mountains.

At the village of Tengboche, the spiritual capital of the Sherpas, Ben arranged for a private puja ceremony to be conducted for the expedition inside the renowned Tengboche Monastery. Originally constructed in 1916, it was rebuilt after an earthquake in 1934, and again after a devastating fire in 1989. Such is the spiritual importance of the monastery that its inauguration in 1993, following its latest reconstruction, was attended by the country's prime minister, many ambassadors to Nepal and Sir Edmund Hillary.

For over an hour we sat cross-legged on colourful Tibetan rugs in the main prayer room, sipping sweet, milky tea, while nearly twenty lamas chanted prayers, blew horns and bashed cymbals to scare away evil demons and seek safe passage for us from the gods. The dimly lit room was stained dark by smoke from charcoal heaters and incense, while its walls were adorned with beautifully embroidered curtains of red, blue and gold. Barely-seen alcoves held ancient prayer books from which the monks recited their nonstop chants. At the front of the room, a huge sculpture of Buddha looked down upon the ceremony. I've always engaged fully in puja ceremonies at base camp, but to take part in a traditional ceremony in that monastery was very spiritual. I could literally feel the benevolence of the gods being bestowed upon us.

As it turned out, our expedition group didn't have any conflicts and it was a great trip. In fact, about halfway through the expedition, Ben called a meeting and declared that there wasn't sufficient drama happening in our own team. Several of the more 'interesting' members of other expeditions on the mountain were approached and asked if they were willing to be filmed. We soon found three volunteers.

The first was Annabelle Bond, a British socialite who, although so inexperienced that she'd crawl rather than walk over the ladders we used for crossing crevasses, had every intention of reaching the summit. Despite the occasional outbreak of tears, and her insistence on putting on a little makeup before I filmed her, even at 8000 metres, she was plucky and determined. To her credit, she overcame her fears and self-doubt to successfully reach the top. The second subject was Will Cross, an American who was trying to become the first diabetic to climb Everest. Despite making a strong attempt, he was unable to summit on this occasion, although he did successfully scale Everest during a later expedition. The final subject was an entirely dysfunctional joint Mexican-Canadian team, which I'm sure provided all the drama Ben was hoping for, and then some!

With the help of the Sherpa team, we established our camps on the mountain. As we moved up from camp to camp, we filmed ourselves, each other and our new subjects constantly. To get the best results possible, Frank would reshoot various sequences from multiple angles—at one point, he had us traversing the same serac in the Western Cwm between Camp 1 and Camp 2 for hours. I sure hoped that bit of footage would make it into the documentary and not end up on the cutting-room floor.

Throughout the climb I focused on keeping strong for the summit push. I knew that carrying the video equipment and capturing footage along the way would make it a much harder and slower climb. On several occasions, when the group decided to rest for a day at Camp 2, I dashed down the mountain in the evening, rested at Base Camp and then climbed back up to Camp 2 the following morning to join the team. Even with the effort of down-climbing and reascending the mountain, that one night's rest at lower altitude was exponentially more beneficial to me than spending the day lying in a tent higher on the mountain.

On one rest day, though, I suffered a bout of a really virulent gastric bug that was going through all the expeditions. It hit me so hard that I was unable even to drink a sip of water without immediately reacting. I was flat on my back for five days. On the third day, our expedition doctor, Matt, came to check on me in my tent. He declared that I was becoming so dehydrated that he'd have to give me an intravenous drip, and told me he'd be back with it in a few minutes. That was the last I saw of him. As he went off to get my drip, he was struck by the same bug.

Another doctor put him on an intravenous drip, while I lay semi-comatose in my tent for another three days, waiting for the treatment that never arrived. I lost so much weight that I seriously doubted I'd have the strength to finish the climb, but in due course I overcame it naturally. After a couple of runs—pardon the pun—up the nearby trekking peak of Kala Pattar, I felt fit enough to rejoin the expedition.

A window of good weather opened up in May, and we prepared for a summit push. As we now had three extra subjects to follow, though, we no longer had sufficient cameras to film the four original team members. Ben decided that Hector and I would climb in the first summit team, each accompanied by a Sherpa who would assist with the filming, while the remaining cameras would be used to film Annabelle, Will and the Mexican-Canadian team. Shaunna and Ben would go for the summit during the second window of good weather—assuming a second one came.

At 10 p.m. on 15 May, I set out from Camp 4 for the top with Mingma Tsiri Sherpa. To protect our high-definition video cameras, which were about 30 centimetres long, from the extreme cold, we'd made little insulated covers into which we inserted small chemical heat packs. We shot some great footage on the way up, but by dawn the heat packs were failing and at times we had to shove the camera inside my down suit to coax the batteries and operating mechanism into life. Hector set out several hours later with his Sherpa, Lhakpa Gelu, who at the time held the speed record for climbing Everest. Hector would carry a light load and go as fast as possible, as he found climbing through the night to be too cold. I preferred the slow and steady approach, trying to walk the fine line between pushing myself hard enough and pushing too hard.

In a relatively straightforward climb, Mingma Tsiri Sherpa and I summitted Everest at 7 a.m. on 16 May, my second successful ascent of the 'Big E'. On the summit, we filmed our radio call to Ben, who'd waited anxiously through the night for news. The relief in his voice was palpable. He had invested a huge amount of himself in the project, and numerous financial and media stakeholders were awaiting news of our success. I confess to feeling a little emotional myself. Despite its ever-increasing popularity, Everest remained an enormous physical and psychological challenge, and I felt truly blessed to have been able to visit that beautiful, spiritual peak a second time.

Hector and Lhakpa Gelu arrived about thirty minutes later, and we enjoyed a fabulously clear and still summit, with crystal-clear views to the horizon in every direction. It was a far cry from the storm-battered summit I'd been on four years earlier. We were so high above the brown Tibetan plains to the north and Nepal's green forests to the south that the curvature of the earth was quite distinct. I found it almost overwhelmingly enriching to soak up the energy of that very special place. I'm not one to jump and shout with joy, but the inner glow I felt was certainly burning brightly.

After staying on top for nearly two hours, filming and photographing, it was time to descend. Our bottles of oxygen were running low. I'd changed to my second bottle some hours before, and had cached my third bottle at the South Summit, ready for use as we descended. With about an hour's oxygen left in my second bottle, I had ample time to get down to my third, and then six or more hours' worth of oxygen to enable my safe descent. More than enough.

Enter the human element.

*

We quickly backtracked to the Hillary Step, but as I moved away from the bottom of that cliff I came across a British climber, Ted Atkins, whom I'd seen on the summit earlier. He was now slumped against the rock face. When I asked if he was okay, he rambled on without really answering my question, so I checked his oxygen supply. It was empty.

To run out of oxygen at extreme altitude is a disaster. In fact, it's worse than not using auxiliary oxygen in the first place, because the body has become used to the enriched air supply. When the supplementary oxygen is cut off, the result can be severe hypoxia, leading to clumsiness—not recommended near the summit of the world's highest mountain—as well as altitude-induced cerebral oedema, which can cause collapse and death, if you haven't already fallen off the mountain. I'd seen first-hand the results when

Lobsang Tshering had run out of oxygen during my 1993 Everest expedition and had shortly afterwards fallen to his death.

I told Ted to keep climbing down to the South Summit, which was only about 80 metres away. He could use my third bottle of oxygen when he got there. I would go ahead to find it for him, but I needed him to keep down-climbing to save time. He understood and slowly started moving.

I took off quickly but had only descended another 40 metres when I came across Luis, a climber from the Mexican-Canadian team we were filming. He'd collapsed onto the snow and was barely able to talk. His mittens and other equipment were scattered on the steep slope below him. Luis, too, had run out of oxygen and clearly had already fallen victim to cerebral oedema. Without supplementary oxygen, he would quickly die. He needed my third oxygen bottle even more than Ted.

Lhakpa Gelu went to the South Summit and collected my oxygen bottle while I put Luis' mittens onto his hands and shook him back to consciousness. I met Lhakpa halfway, took the bottle back to Luis and exchanged my full bottle with his empty one. It was incredible how quickly he recovered when I turned on a full flow of oxygen. Within a few minutes he was conscious, sitting up and talking to me. By the time I'd collected his camera and reattached him to the rope, he was able to stand.

While the extra oxygen enabled him to walk, he was still unsteady on his feet and very likely to fall, so I tied a 'short rope' between us, which would allow me to hold him if he slipped. It would have been a challenge to actually stop him from falling, though, as he was very solidly built and much heavier than me. And he was using my last bottle of oxygen—the very oxygen which might have afforded me the strength to hold him if he did fall. But there was little choice, so we climbed on.

I was in a dilemma. Ted still needed a bottle of oxygen, and I'd just given away my last bottle, putting me at risk of suffering exactly the same effects as Ted and Luis. I needed to find oxygen for both Ted and me if we were to get off the hill alive.

I shouted at Ted to keep moving, then traversed to the South Summit with Luis, in the hope of finding an abandoned bottle, or even a half-empty one that might have been left behind. No luck, so we kept descending. On the way, I radioed Ben at Camp 2 to have him ask the other teams if they had a hidden stash of oxygen somewhere on the mountain. This set off a quite a communication chain. Ben radioed our base camp and asked the Sherpas, who then went to the other expeditions and asked them to radio their own climbers to find out if they had spare oxygen somewhere up above Camp 4. The answers would have to be recommunicated back along the same chain to me.

There wasn't a quick response from below, so I kept looking. The next most likely spot to find a bottle, I guessed, was around 250 metres lower, at The Balcony. Many climbers changed bottles there, I knew, rather than at the South Summit. I descended with Luis as quickly as I could but was briefly delayed when we came across a Greek climber who'd caught his foot in the rope on a short rock cliff. He was hanging upside down, unable to free himself. I freed him from the tangle and kept on with Luis, but within another hundred metres we came across two more members of the Mexican-Canadian expedition who were also in trouble. Both were trying to summit without oxygen and were suffering badly as a result.

The leader of that expedition, Andres Delgado, was in agony, battling to regain warmth in his hands and feet. He was moaning aloud from the pain, willing himself to continue despite the very serious risk of frostbite. More serious, though, was his teammate Tom, who was lying face-first in the snow, flailing, with one crampon hanging loosely from his boot. He was calling out that he'd lost his jumar, an essential piece of climbing equipment. When I rolled him over, I saw immediately that his jumar was in place and correctly attached to the rope. Tom was clearly also suffering from cerebral oedema. He needed oxygen immediately and, I suspected, a shot of dexamethasone to reduce the oedema's pressure on his brain. I radioed base camp to confirm with our doctor, Matt, that this was appropriate, and he agreed.

Things were getting desperately serious. Both these guys needed help, as did Luis, who was still tied to me, and Ted, who was still way above us, near the South Summit. Thankfully, Hector and our two Sherpas arrived. Hector handed his third oxygen bottle to Andres, an act that undoubtedly saved Andres' fingers and toes from the ravages of frostbite. Andres agreed to descend.

Tom was another story. He refused to allow me to give him the injection and literally fought me off. I was hanging on to the needle with one hand and the mountain with the other. I was already feeling quite groggy from lack of oxygen myself, and didn't need this idiot to kill me before the altitude did. I tried to talk him into having the injection and taking some oxygen, but he refused. He actually told us that he was going to continue for the summit. At that late time in the afternoon, and in the state he was in, he'd have died within the hour.

Luckily, Andres, with the aid of Hector's oxygen, was considerably more alert than he had been when I arrived, and he convinced Tom to at least take some oxygen. One of the Discovery Team's Sherpas passed over his final bottle, receiving a wholly ungrateful response—'I don't need this! You people have ruined my expedition!' I wondered whether that was the altitude or the character talking. With the aid of the oxygen, though, he too decided that the summit was no longer an option and agreed to descend.

The whole group, including Andres and Tom, then made its way down the slopes towards The Balcony, still a couple of hundred metres lower. Even with the aid of oxygen, Tom was very slow and shaky and had to be supervised by the Sherpas, lest he have some relapse en route to Camp 4. Luis and I continued our own descent more slowly than the others. I had to keep him on the short rope to safeguard him, and I was starting to suffer, having now run out of my own oxygen. Already I was feeling light-headed and unsteady on my feet.

I still had an obligation to Ted, but the hopeful suggestions that Ben had radioed through failed to materialise. Luis and I arrived at The Balcony without finding a single bottle along the way. Luckily, a Sherpa from another team, who was resting at The Balcony, still had a full bottle in his pack. I asked him for it, to give to Ted. Luis had improved significantly by that time, so I handed him over to the Sherpa, who escorted him down to Camp 4.

I'd been out of oxygen for a couple of hours by now, so I hunted around The Balcony for an extra bottle. I could feel the effects of hypoxia starting to grow—my vision was becoming blurry, it was an effort to think clearly, and I had to literally force myself to focus on what to do next. I hoped that my state wouldn't deteriorate into cerebral oedema before I reached Ted with the oxygen he needed. Unfortunately, there weren't any oxygen bottles to be found for me.

The idea of climbing back up to Ted seemed as hard as ... well, as climbing Mount Everest. Again. I barely had the strength to continue descending. I waited at The Balcony as the last few climbers came down from the top, hoping Ted would be one of them, but he wasn't. After half an hour I had no option but to start back up the ridge.

This was probably the most exhausting climb I had ever had to do. Every step was a mountain in itself, and I felt as though I was in a trance. I desperately wanted to lie down and sleep but knew that it would be fatal. In any case, Ted needed the full oxygen bottle I had in my backpack. From somewhere deep within my memory, I recalled the mantra sung by the lama who'd conducted the puja ceremony at base camp. It gave me something to focus on and actually eased the stress I was feeling a little. I continued up the mountain. The ridge and the valleys so far below swirled and moved in my vision, almost in time with the chant.

Finally, Ted came into view, slowly and unsteadily making his way down from the South Summit. He was the last person on the mountain. We must have been like two drunks staggering towards each other. When we linked up, he didn't recognise me or remember that I'd gone to fetch oxygen for him. He could barely speak. I connected the bottle to his regulator and turned the valve to 4 litres per minute, double the normal flow rate, to ensure it acted quickly. As with the others, the effect was almost immediate and Ted suddenly had a new lease of life.

The descent to Camp 4 was dreamlike as the effects of altitude took control. I could lurch only a few steps before sinking into the snow to regain my breath and my balance. Ted became the fast one, while I tottered behind. I knew that the hypoxia was developing into cerebral oedema, just as it had for the others, but there was no one left to help me. Shaking my head to clear the fuzz allowed me to keep going for another few steps. It was like a strange race as I moved a couple of metres at a time, aiming for Camp 4's lower altitude and renewed oxygen supply.

When Ted and I made it there, Hector was waiting for us. He tried to interview me for the documentary, but it was eight hours since I'd given up my oxygen and twenty since I'd set out for the top the night before. I was beyond exhaustion and couldn't speak. With a fresh oxygen bottle, however, I too came back to life, warm and secure in the confines of our high-altitude nylon home.

Altitude is a funny business. For some reason, my body had held out without oxygen where others had failed. No matter what your experience, you never actually know how you will cope with extreme altitude. I'm glad that, on this day, I did.

Ted Atkins later drew upon his near-death experience on Everest, designing a new oxygen mask that he called the TopOut mask. More efficient than the older Russian masks that had been used for many years, Ted's mask has since become the preferred choice in the Himalaya.

*

The next day, Hector and I descended from the mountain, our jobs complete. We stopped at Camp 3 to rest and found both Andres and Tom packing up their equipment. Andres was humble and grateful for our assistance the day before, but Tom was still hostile. He was also demanding that Andres source a Sherpa to carry his equipment down the mountain. Andres kept telling Tom that they didn't have any Sherpas, so how then could he provide one?

This went on for half an hour or so, until Andres snapped. He picked up Tom's duffle bag of equipment and threw it off the side of the mountain. It bounced down the steep Lhotse Face and dropped neatly into a crevasse, not to appear for another thousand years or so. He then turned and yelled at Tom: 'Is there anything else you want a Sherpa to carry?' Hector and I laughed so hard that we nearly followed Tom's bag into the same crevasse.

A week or so later, a second window of good weather appeared, and Ben and Shaunna launched their own summit bid. By this time I'd recovered, so I asked Ben if I could attempt to climb to the summit without oxygen and he agreed. Despite the earlier epic I'd been through, I was feeling incredibly strong. I climbed direct to Camp 2 on the first day, and the next day continued straight to Camp 4. These were big jumps, each of around 1500 metres in altitude. In fact, I was feeling so strong that I overtook a couple of teams climbing from Camp 3 to Camp 4, and they were using oxygen!

A short distance before Camp 4, a strange feeling came over me. The hairs went up on the back of my neck and I experienced a real feeling of dread. I didn't know what the problem was, but I knew that something was wrong. I'd had this feeling before.

My inner voice was telling me to get out of there. Without hesitation, despite being just a day away from an oxygen-less summit of Everest, I turned around and descended. It seemed a crazy decision, even to me, because everybody else was continuing up, but the feeling was so strong that I couldn't ignore it.

That night a storm blew in high on the mountain, although none had been forecast. Those who'd climbed to Camp 4 on the South Col that afternoon were trapped in their tents for several days while the blizzard raged. As the storm wore on, they used the vital supplies of oxygen, which they'd hoped to use during their summit push, but at least they were able to stay alive. Had I, with no oxygen, gone to Camp 4 at 8000 metres and then become trapped in that blizzard, I probably would not have survived. I'd always listened to my inner voice, but that experience was extremely powerful and reinforced for me the value of being open to my 'sixth sense'. I've not ignored it since.

Neither Ben nor Shaunna was able to reach the summit that year, but the rescues in which we were involved provided all the action that the documentary needed. Our footage was eventually produced into a six-part mini-series of one hour each. Called *Ultimate Survival: Everest*, it was shown across North America and further afield numerous times, but it didn't come to Australia, which was a pity, since it was a good one.

More importantly, those rescues demonstrated that the right ethic of helping those in trouble on the steep slopes of Everest was still alive among climbers and Sherpas. Too often, stories have been told of climbers turning their backs on those in trouble. In this case, climbers and Sherpas had come together to assist not just one but many others. I like to think that that is still the norm.

Summitting Everest for a second time was a good confidence booster after the disappointments I'd had in 2003. I'd been strong on the mountain, probably stronger than in 2000, and, importantly, I'd had a really fun time with the team. Over the last few years I'd been starting to feel more at home in the mountains than back in the 'real world', and this trip only strengthened that emotion. Expedition life, for all its remoteness and hardships, felt more normal to me than civilisation. I needed my expeditions, because they filled the dissatisfying void that the pettiness of regular society created in me. I was becoming addicted to the thrill, the fear and the intense clarity of life that the mountains provided.

I was happy, too, to have been able to continue to perform at extreme altitude after giving up my oxygen. Although I'd been affected to a degree by the sudden loss of oxygen saturation, it hadn't knocked me down as quickly as the others. I knew that I'd been lucky, but the experience reinforced to me that I have a physiology that copes well with extreme altitude. This wasn't something to be blasé about, but it boosted my confidence to continue my project and finish the fourteen 8000ers, particularly as I still had some of the toughest peaks ahead of me.

My only disappointment from the expedition was that I hadn't realised my dream of climbing Everest without gas. That would remain a thorn in my side.

Postscript

In 2006 Andres Delgado disappeared on Mount Changabang in India. Hector, hoping once again to rescue his old friend, flew to India to search for him, but no trace was ever found.

10

GOOD DAYS AND BAD

Climbing and soloing aren't worth dying for but they are worth risking dying for.

Todd Skinner

CHO OYU IS the easiest of all the 8000ers, despite being the sixth highest at 8201 metres. Its shape allows climbers to access its summit via a face that isn't too steep, although it can be prone to avalanches. The face has actually been skied a number of times. Many commercial expedition companies use Cho Oyu as a preliminary 'training' 8000er for their clients in the post-monsoon season of one year, before taking the same clients to Everest in the pre-monsoon season of the following year.

I wanted to go back to Shishapangma but thought that I could quite reasonably climb two mountains in the post-monsoon of 2004. Cho Oyu is just down the road from 'Shisha', so it seemed appropriate to climb it first. I'd summit it and acclimatise at the same time, before heading back to my main objective, Shishapangma.

Taking the same death-defying highway from Nepal up and onto the Tibetan plateau, I endured the culinary delights of Nyalam again before continuing another four hours along the Friendship Highway to spend a couple more acclimatisation days in the small town of Tingri. The highway passed through numerous little villages interspersed among fields sown with corn and wheat, and dotted with almost identical Tibetan houses. All were made from mud brick and were flat-roofed with whitewashed walls, and painted simply but colourfully. Every house had a winter's worth of cut timber on the roof. These villages would have been quite beautiful in their simplicity but for the ugly concrete compound each of them had, to house an 'administration office' that bore a Chinese flag and was staffed by uniformed military administrators. Clearly, my understanding of 'autonomy' needs revision.

The windswept outpost of Tingri has been the last point of civilisation for expeditions heading to Everest since the earliest exploration of her northern flanks. George Mallory and his parties, like many other great explorers before and since, experienced the dogs, the dust and a last beverage before turning towards the dominating presence of Everest and Cho Oyu in the distance.

Meaning 'Turquoise Goddess' in Tibetan, Cho Oyu is a striking peak that stands alone from its neighbours and astride the Tibet–Nepal border. As the sun sets across the barren Tibetan plateau, Cho Oyu lights up in brilliant hues, a luminescent beacon in an otherwise cold and oppressive land.

Less than 50 kilometres from Mount Everest, Cho Oyu was the fifth 8000er to be climbed. And it was done in fine style. An Austrian team of Joseph Jöchler and Herbert Tichy, together with Sherpa Pasang Dawa Lama, completed a daring alpine-style ascent. To reach the mountain, the group trekked into Tibet from Nepal over a remote border pass, the Nangpa La. Without the Chinese authorities' permission, they made a lightning-fast climb, reaching the summit on 19 October 1954. Like its peers, Cho Oyu has taken a reasonable toll of would-be summiteers. More than forty-five climbers have died on its slopes since that first ascent. It has an even darker political history.

The Nangpa La is not just an access point to the mountain for unauthorised climbers. Located just below Cho Oyu's Base Camp, it has for many centuries provided a trading and pilgrimage route between the two countries. Several times we saw Tibetans with their yaks heading over the crossing with loads of salt. A few days later, having traded the salt at the weekly market at Namche Bazaar in Nepal, they'd return with fresh vegetables and other necessities. The route has also been used by Tibetans to flee Chinese rule. In 2006 the Chinese border police from a military base close by (in the Autonomous Region of Tibet) opened fire on an unarmed group of Tibetans as they crossed the pass, killing a 17-year-old girl and injuring many others. The incident was denied by Chinese authorities initially, but numerous climbers gave eyewitness accounts and video footage of the shooting was broadcast around the world. A documentary about the incident was released in 2008 called *Tibet: Murder in the Snow*.

I climbed solo but shared the permit and the base camp with an Australian Army expedition run by Zac Zaharias, the leader of the 1997 Dhaulagiri army expedition. Zac's army team had varied levels of experience and progressed more slowly than me. I found myself socialising with other climbers, including Marty Schmidt, an American climbing guide who was then living in New Zealand. He was strong and fast at altitude, and I shared his preference for small, lightweight teams. He was also an excellent skier and planned to ski down from the summit. Marty had previously teamed up with my friend Hector Ponce de Leon on an attempt of the difficult North Ridge of K2. We were soon plotting adventures and lightweight climbs for the future.

I also met some of the who's who of New Zealand mountaineering. A commercial expedition was supported by New Zealand guides Mark Whetu and Lydia Bradey. Mark had numerous ascents of Everest and other big peaks under his belt; indeed, he was the guide who'd assisted Australian Mike Rheinberger to the summit of Everest in 1994 on his eighth attempt. Lydia Bradey, an extreme alpinist in her own right, is credited with being the first woman in the world to have summitted Everest without oxygen, a feat she achieved solo in 1988. The world of dedicated high-altitude climbers is a small one, and I was gradually coming to know most of them.

The climbing was very easy, and I relished being on my own on the mountain, unencumbered by others or competing egos. I made my summit bid from Camp 2, rather than Camp 3, to save having to carry the whole camp another 600 metres up the mountain. The extra distance wasn't too much of a chore, and I soon found myself on the massive summit plateau, facing a long and gently rising traverse to reach the mountain's highest point. That effort was well rewarded, with a sensational view of Mount Everest's north face, as well as Lhotse, Makalu, Pumori and Ama Dablam. I had summitted my tenth 8000er.

Brimming with confidence, I sauntered down the hill and collected my equipment, my mind already on the next goal: Shishapangma. I should perhaps have kept my focus on Cho Oyu, however, because as I descended on loose rock below Camp 1, I slipped and landed heavily on my backside, breaking my coccyx. I was able to climb down to Base Camp, but the injury was so painful that I couldn't continue on to Shishapangma. Game over.

*

I was a little disappointed at not having summitted Shishapangma because it meant returning to Tibet yet again. I had expected to be done and dusted with that mountain by now, and there would be no further opportunities to climb it until the pre-monsoon of 2005. Winter gradually moved over the Himalaya, bringing furious jetstream winds and bitter ambient temperatures of minus 40 degrees Celsius—minus 100 degrees with the wind chill. The Nepali Sherpas and the nomadic Tibetan yak herders retreated to lower valleys and the warmth of their fires. Life slowed, tourists stayed home, rivers froze and snow fell. Only the mountains, ever dominant, stood unmoved by the change, patient beneath their winter shrouds, as the locals and we so-called conquerors fled to the safety and shelter of the lowlands.

At home, I nursed my injured spine back to health and enjoyed the Australian summer. I divided my time between the beach and the Blue Mountains, a mecca for rock climbing, mountain-biking and canyoning. My girlfriend Julie, whom I'd been seeing for about a year, was a very strong rock climber and was eager to hit the cliffs as often as possible.

When I wasn't adventuring, I gave some thought to which of the four peaks that remained on my list I would go to next. Among them was Annapurna. Although its name translates from Sanskrit as 'Goddess of the Harvest', Annapurna is anything but godly. It is the most dangerous mountain in the world. More climbers have been killed per successful ascent of Annapurna than on any other mountain. The main reason for all the carnage is avalanches. There just isn't a safe route on the mountain.

Ironically, Annapurna was the first 8000-metre peak ever climbed. This milestone was achieved by the French in 1950, three years before the British ascent of Everest. The French explored both Dhaulagiri and Annapurna in their reconnaissance but missed an easy way up Dhaulagiri and so chose to climb Annapurna. They were successful, but both men who summitted—leader Maurice Herzog and Luis Lachenal—lost fingers and toes to frostbite. Herzog's account of the expedition in his book *Annapurna*—essential reading for climbers and armchair mountaineers alike—describes in the most graphically chilling detail the agony of the primitive treatment, and the subsequent amputations, that both men endured. If ever there was a story to counter any glamorous or romantic notions of high-altitude climbing, that is it.

The French experience on Annapurna was just the first of many epic expeditions. Among them was the 1970 British expedition, which made the first ascent of Annapurna's brutally steep and avalanche-prone South Face. Its members included three greats of Himalayan climbing—Don Whillans, Dougal Haston and leader Chris Bonington. Their teammate, Ian Clough, was killed by a falling serac during the descent. In 1978 an American all-women's expedition, led by Arlene Blum and supported by a strong Sherpa team, attempted to place both the first Americans and the first women on Annapurna's summit. It was successful, but two died during the climb. The list of similar tragedies on Annapurna is long. By the time I turned my attention to it, there'd been approximately sixty deaths for just 120 successful ascents. Among the casualties was my old climbing friend Anatoli Bukreev, leaving me as the last surviving summiteer of our K2 expedition.

I was intimidated by Annapurna. How could I not be? But I knew that if I wanted to climb all the 8000ers, I had to climb Annapurna. I would just have to accept a much higher level of risk. In April 2005 I bit the bullet and decided to take my chances. I felt that by then I'd accumulated enough skills and experience to have the best prospect of success and, more importantly, survival. Also, I didn't want to leave it until last, as some climbers did, because I could see that putting myself in that position might bring on summit fever, a desperation to keep going for the summit, no matter what the risk, in order to complete the project. Annapurna demanded the very highest level of risk management. Summit fever would be a virtual death sentence on this mountain.

I knew that Ed Viesturs, the United States' most prolific 8000-metre climber, was heading there, so I asked if I could join his permit. He agreed but was heading first to Cho Oyu to acclimatise.

I didn't have the time or the money for Cho Oyu as well as Annapurna, so Ed put me in touch with two American friends, Charley Mace and Brendan Cusick, who were also keen to climb Annapurna. They'd both climbed in the Himalaya previously, so we agreed to form our own expedition.

In Kathmandu I caught up with my friends Ben and Shaunna, who, together with the communications guru from our Discovery expedition, Mike Swarbrick, were back in Nepal to finish off Everest after their unsuccessful summit push the year before. They'd actually been back on the mountain for a couple of weeks before I met them, but Ben's knee had shattered in an accident in the Khumbu Icefall and he'd been evacuated. He was heading home with Mike, while Shaunna planned to return to Everest the next day to complete her climb. It was great to catch up with them again, and together we consumed more than a few liquid painkillers—for Ben's sake, of course.

Charley, Brendan and I trekked into Annapura base camp along one of the best routes in Nepal. We first flew to the tourist town of Pokhara, beside the picturesque Phewa Lake, whose still waters provide glorious mirror images of the mighty Annapurna mountain range to the north. Then we took a small plane to the mountain airstrip of Jomsom, out of which I'd flown after the epic Dhaulagiri post-expedition trek. This is one of the most spectacular flights in the Himalaya. It cuts its way up the Kali Gandaki valley between the Annapurna Himal and Dhaulagiri, the deepest gorge in the world. I craned my neck in a hopeless attempt to look up to the tops of the monstrously high, sheer mountain walls on either side of our flight path. One of those walls was our destination, Annapurna 1.

Most trekkers who visit Annapurna walk to the Base Camp on its south side, which is a beautiful but relatively benign trek. We would be climbing from the north side, however, and so we followed a route that very few visitors to Nepal have travelled. And with good reason. Almost immediately we encountered a problem. A police checkpoint identified that several of our porters' names had been misspelt on our trekking permit. No amount of pleading convinced them to let the porters through, despite the fact that our expedition effectively came to a halt right there. We were left with ten porters for twenty-three loads. Some hurried repacking allowed us to prioritise the loads we needed immediately and those that could be carried in later during the expedition.

Torrential rain dampened our spirits a little but not as much as the news that another expedition heading to our same Base Camp had helicoptered in, due to impassable snow on the approach. After spending a night in an impoverished village in the gorge between Dhaulagiri and Annapurna, we trekked across some sparse corn-fields, then ascended a series of hills and ridges towards a high pass that was still well out of sight. We spent the entire day going uphill, gaining 1500 vertical metres' altitude, and even then our campsite at 3750 metres wasn't on the top. The only available water was a 1½-hour round trip away, so we had a dry dinner, moistened only by a puddle on the track that the local birds had used for their daily ablutions.

The following day we finally reached the top of the pass. The earlier news that we'd be stopped by deep snow proved to be incorrect, and we crossed a meadow-like plateau before descending to the side of a fearfully steep gorge called the Hum Khola. There it did snow heavily, disguising the track and making every step a potentially fatal slip. Indeed, a number of porters and even climbers have been killed in this area since it was accessed by Herzog's team in 1950. As if to prove the point, one of our porters suddenly back-flipped off the track and tumbled 10 metres towards the precipice before somehow coming to a stop.

Herzog wasn't the first to pioneer this route. As we edged our way around the cliffs, we came across a small cave with hand-painted figures on the wall. One of the porters told us that it had been painted a generation earlier, when a shepherd and his son had brought a few livestock this way in the hope of finding some pasture. They'd become trapped by the winter snows and, after eating their livestock, began to starve. Close to the end, the father told the son to kill and eat him, with which order the dutiful son complied. His fidelity to duty didn't save him, though, and he too eventually perished, but not before documenting the events by way of the rock paintings. A sad story, but pretty good paintings.

*

After crossing several more gorges and taking numerous more falls, we descended into the Miristi Khola gorge, which would take us to Base Camp. I handed my ice axe to a porter who was struggling on the slippery track and kept my fingers crossed that it would survive longer than the axe I'd lent to our porter on Nanga Parbat, as I needed it for the climb ahead. The following day we arrived at Base Camp and paid our porters, rewarding them for their efforts with a fat tip. They were a tough bunch and deserved every rupee. In a perfect world they wouldn't have had to labour in this way to earn their living, but it isn't a perfect world and they needed the employment. The least we could do was pay them top dollar.

Ed Viesturs was already at Base Camp, having arrived a couple of days earlier from Cho Oyu. Annapurna was the final peak in his own quest to climb all the 8000ers. To summit it, he had partnered with his long-time climbing buddy, Veikka Gustafsson of Finland. Climbing the big peaks is such a tense and dangerous game that few people wish to expose themselves to the risks year after year. Those who do frequently end up dead. Finding a like-minded climbing partner in this game is a rare gift, but Ed and Veikka had established just that rapport.

Annapurna is a peak whose deadly reputation sees seasons come and go without a single expedition daring to test her temper, so it was unusual that we found a couple of Italian expeditions there as well. One included the two Italians with whom I'd climbed on the Gasherbrums in 1999, Abele Blanc and Christian Kuntner. The other comprised the outstanding mountaineer Silvio Mondinelli, probably the strongest mountaineer I've seen after Anatoli Bukreev. His teammates included Mario Merrelli, whom I'd met with Silvio on Kanchenjunga and Shishapangma in 2003.

Silvio, the elite alpinist, was a picture of health, while Mario had a permanent cigarette hanging from his lips. He'd look me in the eye and, with a wry smile, mutter, 'Oxygen, Andre'. Both were incredibly friendly, and I spent many a meal at their Base Camp tucking into their drums of cryovacked pork knuckles and other delicacies that, unlike their countryman Kuntner, they were more than happy to share. They were great people to spend time with.

Charley, Brendan and I were the last team to arrive at the mountain, but the hard pass-crossing trek had aided our acclimatisation and we were able to start climbing after a couple of days' rest and preparation. The route up to Camp 1 followed an easy grassy trail from Base Camp before dropping over a 40-metre wall of lateral moraine that had been exposed by the slowly advancing glacier below. After crossing that same glacier, we picked our way up a headwall of ice and rock. This brought us to a steep and crumbling rock ridge interspersed with loose scree slopes and snow patches, the top of which led out to a broad glacier, surrounded on all sides by threatening, avalanche-prone mountain faces. Our first attempt up the ridge was thwarted by ice seracs, which collapsed around and in front of us, so close as to cover us in ice dust, followed by constant rockfall on the ridge. We returned to Base Camp, determined to make an earlier start on our next attempt. This proved more successful and we reached Camp 1 after a solid push of five and a half hours' constant climbing.

To reach Camp 2, we crossed the glacier roped together for safety against hidden crevasses, then slogged our way up easy but deep snow slopes for several hours. We placed our tent underneath some ice cliffs that we hoped would protect us from miscreant avalanches above. Although we'd already had to overcome rockfall, crevasses, avalanche danger and altitude, the hazards to this point had been no greater than those on most other high mountains. Above Camp 2, however, the game changed considerably.

To assist with our acclimatisation and to get a better look at the route, we climbed up from Camp 2, crossed the plateau above the tent site and approached the bottom of the north face. Just to access the face we had to cross terrain that was threatened by some of the biggest seracs I'd ever seen, which clearly avalanched every day. I wrote at the time:

> This part of the route is absolutely deadly. There are huge
> seracs that overhang the plateau on the left as you head up,
> not to mention the sickle serac above. Our track crossed some
> avalanche debris but it is quite clear that any big serac avalanche
> would sweep the entire plateau clean. There would be no hope.

We climbed a ramp of snow and ice that was hundreds of metres wide, hundreds more long and whose depth could only be imagined. The ramp was completely out of place until we realised that it had been formed by the debris of the continual avalanches that crashed down from the hundreds of seracs on the face above, which itself was crowned by an astonishingly enormous ice cliff known as The Sickle. The Sickle's exposed bluff was easily a hundred metres of sheer, crumbling ice. It curved right across the top of the face in the manner of its namesake for more than a kilometre. Just standing on the debris below the face was enough to make my palms clammy. The route we planned to take to Camp 3 climbed over that avalanche debris, up through the entire serac-filled north face, and through that deadly ice cliff at the top. Gulp!

Having intimidated ourselves sufficiently, we retreated to Base Camp to fortify our courage with a few nights' sleep and proper food. In the interim, Ed and Veikka launched their summit bid, as did the Italian team with Silvio and Mario. They were all a couple of weeks ahead of us on the mountain. They climbed through the dangers to Camp 3, their highest camp, but were caught there for three nights in strong wind. Silvio descended to Base Camp, having suffered very cold feet and not wanting to incur more frostbite on top of his Kanchenjunga injury. The others made a desperate lunge for the top in a lull in the conditions.

That break in the weather was short-lived, though, and the ascent became a battle against strong winds and deep snow. While they successfully summitted, they were separated on descent. Two of the Italians spent the night after the summit sheltering in a crevasse, unable to find their way back to the tents. Thankfully, they all survived, and a couple of days later we greeted them back at Base Camp. With that ascent, Ed had completed his project to climb all the 8000ers, becoming the first American to do so. After a grand party, he was helicoptered out to great acclaim back in the United States.

A week later it was our turn. For the first time, I'd taken a satellite phone to Base Camp, which had allowed me to ring Julie every few days. It was great having contact with her, particularly given that I was climbing with people I didn't know well. Julie was also able to give me regular weather information, and told me that a good spell was forecast. My team and the second Italian team, which included Blanc and Kuntner, were joined by Silvio Mondinelli, whose feet were feeling better and who'd stayed on at Base Camp to try again. We agreed to climb as a single group and share the work of breaking trail in fresh snow. We would also provide each other with support on this most dangerous of mountains.

We were delayed at Camp 2 for a day due to high winds, but the next morning we faced our fears and set off for the shooting gallery that was the climb up to Camp 3. Kuntner and his team were a little slow off the mark, but Brendan, Charley, Silvio and I crossed the plateau and ascended the field of avalanche 'runout' at the base of the face. Above us was a gully that clearly channelled much of the avalanche debris that came down the face. It was only a 50-metre climb until it fanned out above and we could move to the side out of the firing line, but for those 50 metres our hearts were in our mouths. We knew with absolute certainty that an avalanche at that moment would be fed straight on top of us, and we'd have little hope of survival. I climbed rather quickly.

As I went, I scanned continuously for a safe place to hide should an avalanche fall. Sure enough, as I emerged from the couloir about 7.25 a.m. there was a massive roar from above and the ground beneath my feet shook. A serac had collapsed somewhere on the face above and was sweeping down towards us. Simultaneously, we all yelled, 'Avalanche!' and sprang for cover.

I'd spotted some large seracs about 20 metres away that would provide excellent shelter, but I hadn't time to reach them. The only possible protection at that moment was a small serac of ice about 1.5 metres high and 2 metres long. I dived onto the slope below it. I could hear the avalanche thundering down the face, and wondered whether my backpack might be sticking out above the top of the block. If so, it would be hit by the avalanche and I would be dragged off the mountain. I considered ripping it off, but that would mean rolling away from the block for a few seconds, exposing myself even further. I decided not to risk it but forced myself as flat as possible into the snow.

Time passes rather slowly in this situation, perhaps because your every sense is heightened with the expectation of instant oblivion. There was time to ponder my fate. It seemed likely that I was about to die, and for a brief second my stomach tightened. But it felt hypocritical to panic about dying, given that I'd known and rather carelessly accepted that risk on all these mountains over so many years. I put my head down and accepted my fate, whatever it was going to be, writing later:

It's an eerie feeling lying helplessly, waiting for such a powerful natural force to run its course. If my serac didn't offer enough protection, or if the debris or wind blast caught me, I'd be pulled in an instant from my hiding place and literally thrown down the mountain, with about 1000 tonnes of ice and snow following.

If that happened, I would probably only have a few seconds of terror and would then be killed. How to describe the expectation of death within a few seconds, but not knowing for sure? A feeling of dread, an acceptance that this was always possible; not so much regret, but certainly a question: 'Is this how it all ends?'

As I lay there, I couldn't tell if it was going over me or not, but the sound was deafening and the ground shook. It seemed to last a long while—my guess would be around twenty seconds—before it passed.

Gradually, the deluge lessened and the noise faded. I raised my head. The gods had been kind and I had survived. My teammates above me were also okay. But Kuntner and three of his team—Stephan, Marco and Abele Blanc—had been below me, right in the neck of the couloir, when the ice hit. The four of them had been swept back down the couloir and about 300 metres out onto the football field of debris.

We raced back down the slope, our hearts full of dread at what we'd find. Overall, the injuries were surprisingly light. Stephan had a broken arm, cuts and bruises, while Marco, battered and bloody, had a face wound that was open to the bone. Blanc was in total shock and not aware of his surroundings, but physically he was relatively unharmed. Kuntner, however, was badly injured.

He had a massive wound to his head and a dislocated shoulder. Most troubling of all, though, was that he preferred to lie on his injured shoulder rather than on his other side, which he clutched constantly, moaning, 'Malo, malo.' He had obviously sustained a significant internal injury.

After some emergency first aid, the walking wounded descended to Camp 2. We bandaged Christian's gaping head wound and gave him a shot of dexamethasone for his concussion, but we then had to consider our next move. He'd been lucid when we first reached him but had deteriorated quickly. Now he was writhing on the snow, unable to walk. He needed urgent hospitalisation.

Ideally we'd have stabilised him and organised a Nepali helicopter to evacuate him, but we were at too high an altitude for one to land. In any case, we couldn't stay in that location because it was beneath another massive ice serac, nearly a thousand metres above us, that avalanched daily. We were standing right on its debris. We used our sleeping pads and a sleeping bag to make a sledge, into which we zipped Christian. Silvio, Brendan and I then dragged him down the mountain.

At Camp 2 Silvio tried to contact the Nepali authorities with his satellite phone but couldn't get a connection. It actually proved easier to ring his wife in Italy and have her ring Nepal, and she successfully organised the chopper. Brendan, a trained medic, attended to the walking wounded while I stayed with Christian. He was in extreme pain from the internal injury—so much so that he was waving both arms around, including the one with the dislocated shoulder. My attempts to calm and reassure him achieved nothing. It was frustrating beyond words not to be able to do anything more.

Gradually, he stopped writhing and lay still. I hoped his pain was starting to ease. His tight grip on my hands slackened, though, and when I looked into his eyes I could see the life in them literally disappearing. Brendan did a quick check of his vital signs and immediately commenced cardio pulmonary resuscitation for some minutes, but it didn't help. Christian was dead.

I turned my head away and looked up to the mountain's summit. Another life lost. *Are mountains really worth this price?* As I looked up, both to avert my eyes from a team member who'd died in my arms and also to seek some divine reasoning for this loss, the most incredible thing happened. At 5600 metres, on the side of one of the highest mountains in the world, a butterfly flew past me. Right in front of me. Amid the tragedy of Christian's death, this beautiful, gentle life form fluttered by.

It sounds crazy, and perhaps I was desperately clutching at some kind of spiritual hope, but my first thought was that it was Christian's soul. I was moved and inspired beyond words. It was uplifting. I felt almost joyful. Here was life, completely out of place, in the midst of death. I shall never forget that feeling.

*

There were still three other injured climbers who needed to be evacuated, so we covered Christian with a sleeping bag and escorted them down to the glacier. The helicopter arrived soon after. With the walking wounded on board, the pilot also managed quite a daring flight up to Camp 2 to retrieve Christian's body.

The rest of us descended to Base Camp. All the others decided to cancel their expeditions and return home; the only dissenter was me. While I was saddened by Christian's death, and all the more aware of my own mortality as a result of it, I wasn't traumatised by it. He was another victim in an ever-growing list of climbers who'd paid the price for their passion, but he'd known the risks, particularly on this brutally savage peak. I'm also sure that I was feeling more settled than the others because of my encounter with the butterfly. More than anything, though, I was still committed to my goal and wanted to continue.

I pointed out that nothing would be gained from quitting. Christian's death would seem all the more pointless if we just gave up. I also argued that there was now one less avalanche that would come down the mountain. Some might see my attitude as callous, but for me it was practical, given that we were there to climb the mountain. To quit at that point would just mean we'd have to return another time and face all those risks again, not to mention the expense and the time commitment. But the others were too depressed to continue.

I rang Julie and told her about the accident before it hit the press. She wanted me to come home with the others, but I couldn't get over the feeling that I'd be throwing away a perfectly good chance to climb this mountain. Sure, it was dangerous, but it would always be dangerous. I just couldn't see any reason to give up when so much work had already been done. I decided to make an attempt by myself.

After one day's rest, I set off alone back up to Camp 1 and continued climbing up to Camp 2. In the short time since we'd been there, though, there'd been a heavy dump of fresh snow and I needed help to break through it. By the time I reached Camp 2, I was wading in deep, wet snow. Without the physical support of the others, I couldn't continue in those conditions. Reluctantly, I accepted that the expedition was over, ending my first attempt on Annapurna. The experience made me think extremely hard about how I would attempt the mountain again—who I would climb with and which route I would choose. The French route on which we'd been avalanched had truly been death's bowling alley, and I had no desire to experience that again. But I knew I would return to Annapurna.

The positive lesson I took away from this expedition was in relation to butterflies. I have never deliberately hurt animals, but ever since my experience when Christian died, I have taken the utmost care not to harm butterflies, even when driving. I wonder what the Police will say if I one day have to tell them that I ran off the road to avoid a butterfly?

*

By 2005, having long since left full-time employment, I had quite a varied existence. I was consulting in risk and crisis management, leading treks to remote areas around the world, lecturing and guiding on small Antarctic tourist vessels, and taking on interesting mountaineering projects. I was also delivering keynote leader-ship and motivational presentations around the country, which I really enjoyed. In the post-monsoon season of 2005, I took a job to guide a Spanish climber, Inigo de Pineda, on both Cho Oyu and Shishapangma.

There were several other climbers in our team at Cho Oyu. They climbed independently, but all were under my oversight. One of the climbers was Billi Bierling, a public-relations profes-sional who has worked for many Himalayan climbing seasons in Kathmandu as an assistant to Elizabeth Hawley, the 8000-metre expedition chronicler. Ms Hawley has long been revered by climbers for her almost mystic ability to know exactly when they have arrived in Kathmandu both before and at the end of their expeditions, and in which hotel they're staying. She then ambushes them in the foyer, requiring them to fill out her information sheets. Billi has now taken on that role with gusto and is regularly seen cycling around Kathmandu, preparing her own ambushes of unsuspecting climbers to elicit the expedition details.

On the mountain that season, although on a different expedi-tion, was one of world's leading 8000-metre climbers, Iñaki Ochoa de Olza from the Basque country in the western Pyrenees of Europe. I'd met Iñaki in Pakistan in the 1990s and had bumped into him from time to time since then. He had a reputation as a very strong and capable climber, and a man with an easygoing, relaxed nature. Over several conversations we agreed to look for opportunities to climb together in the future.

Silvio Mondinelli and Mario Merelli were also there. This was the third time I'd shared a mountain with them. My circle of friends and social scene were becoming more and more populated with high-altitude mountaineers. It seemed perfectly natural, though, and reinforced my feeling that the mountains had become my real home.

At Cho Oyu's Base Camp our food was the usual fare—buffalo meat, local vegetables, dahl and rice—but to our delight Inigo produced a great quantity of beautifully cured, ever so finely sliced, melt-in-your-mouth Spanish *jamón*. He worked as a salesman for a company that produced the cured ham. I doubt he achieved significant sales in the backblocks of Tibet, but he certainly won our appreciation. Reinforced by our diet of wafer-thin pork slivers, and inspired to get up the mountain and back to Base Camp as quickly as possible so we could enjoy more carnivorous delights, Inigo and I soon summitted Cho Oyu and moved on to Shishapangma.

While the two base camps were only 50 or so kilometres from each other, they were worlds apart. Cho Oyu's is on a glacier with rocks, ice and dust everywhere, whereas Shishapangma's is on grass with a bubbling brook nearby. The psychological revitalisation we experienced from this link to life and warmth was tangible, and it made the expedition infinitely more enjoyable.

Shortly after we arrived, however, a sad procession passed us by. Two Tibetans were leading a donkey with a body strapped over its back to the road head, followed by the dead climber's teammates, their expedition over in tragic circumstances. We were told that the climber had developed pulmonary oedema but that his inexperienced friends had failed to recognise the symptoms. He'd died alone in his tent during the night. They were a small team with limited experience and had engaged a company to deliver base-camp logistics only—meaning they had no guide or expedition manager. While I'm an ardent supporter of learning to climb and developing altitude skills over many years rather than being guided, I also think that, if you choose to shortcut that process and go with a commercial group, you should spend the money that will buy the leadership and experience you lack. A body wrapped in rice bags and trussed with rope was a high price to pay to save a few dollars.

It was a timely reminder for me, also, not to be tempted to push Inigo too hard in pursuit of Shishapangma's true summit, despite my personal ambition to reach it. Inigo was very keen to reach the real summit, but I knew I had to balance his enthusiasm with sound leadership. Small and softly spoken but surprisingly strong at altitude, he intended to take up climbing as a profession after this expedition. At the time, however, he lacked significant experience, so I wasn't prepared to lead him up anything other than the normal route on Shisha's north side. Guiding a client is quite different from climbing with an experienced partner, and I took very seriously my responsibility to keep him as safe as possible. It would not have been appropriate to put him into a technical climbing situation where we had to rely on each other.

We hoped that the snow on the North Face would be firm enough that we could traverse from the north ridge over to the main summit but, as in most seasons, it was dangerously unstable. As we climbed, I stepped out onto the face several times to assess whether a traverse to the true summit was feasible, only for the slope to crack and threaten to avalanche. Inigo had to be satisfied with the lower Central Summit, the usual end point for guided clients on that mountain.

During our walk out to the road head, we spoke at length about the risks inherent in mountaineering. Inigo had performed strongly on both peaks and had gained a good understanding of the skills and experience he'd need to take on other 8000ers, but I impressed upon him that he was entering what I considered to be the most dangerous game in town. Already I'd lost many friends over the years, either on my own expeditions or on others, and we'd seen the tragic end to another climber's dreams on this expedition. I encouraged Inigo to consolidate his experience on less technical peaks, and at lower altitude, in order to develop his climbing and risk-management skills. Sure, you need luck in the hills, but without sound skills you are a dead man climbing. With them, you just might survive. And the mountains only reveal their incredible secrets to survivors.

*

Back in Kathmandu, I caught up with my many mountaineering friends in downtown Thamel, the tourist region of 'K-town'. Some had been successful in their projects, others not. We congratulated, commiserated, laughed, mourned, ate and drank. Hard. More than anything, we bonded, as only comrades who've shared adversity can bond. I was happy to be in their company.

I'd just as happily have stayed there, but I'd planned a climbing holiday with Julie to the Wadi Rum in Jordan and needed to get back to reality. As much as the mountains felt like home, I had another, semi-normal, life back in Australia. But as the plane climbed steeply out of the Kathmandu valley and the distant Himalayan giants stood above the clouds, as though to bid me farewell, or perhaps taunt me, I was already planning my return. I had four peaks left before I would be finished with the project: Shishapangma, Makalu, Kanchenjunga and Annapurna.

It seemed Shishapangma was becoming my nemesis. I'd been unsuccessful on my first attempt, broke my bum before I even reached the mountain on my second go, and was unsuccessful with Inigo on this last expedition. I needed to finish it off, to find an achievable route and do it.

Makalu, the fifth-highest mountain in the world, and Kanchenjunga, the third-highest, would both be tough. But the real thorn was Annapurna. I had unfinished business there. While my teammates had been perfectly within their rights to abandon the mountain, I felt that the effort, the expense and the risks we'd taken on that expedition had been wasted when we were so close to summiting.. As much as my stomach tightened and my jaw clenched when I thought of the almost unjustifiable dangers there, I would return. It was the jewel in the crown and I had to climb it. I would find the strongest, most motivated climbing partners, and I would return.

Postscript

Christian Kuntner died after having summitted thirteen of the world's fourteen 8000-metre peaks. Annapurna was to have been his last 8000er.

Mario Merelli, having successfully reached the summit of the world's most dangerous mountain, continued expeditioning to other 8000ers but died in a rock-climbing accident in Italy in 2012.

Inigo de Pineda, having achieved his first 8000-metre summit on Cho Oyu and having had a near miss on Shishapangma, was inspired to climb more of the world's highest mountains. Despite my strongest advice to consolidate his experience, in 2007 Inigo joined a Spanish team to Kanchenjunga, one of the toughest peaks in the world. He was killed in a fall during the expedition.

Despite meeting Marty Schmidt many times in the mountains over the years, I didn't ever get to climb with him. In 2013, having been unsuccessful in an earlier attempt on K2 with Hector Ponce de Leon, Marty returned to the mountain with his son, Denali. They were both killed by an avalanche at Camp 3.

Rick Allen, climbing unroped during our attempt on the unclimbed south ridge of Broad Peak in 1997.

Self portrait on the summit of Broad Peak after my solo ascent. Within hours of taking this shot I would endure my first bivouac, at 8000 metres, without equipment.

A long line of porters carries our expedition equipment up the Baltoro Glacier to Gasherbrum Base Camp in 1999.

My first summit of Mount Everest on 24 May 2000 with one of my clients, Paul Giorgio (in blue). (Photo courtesy of Christine Boskoff)

Trajce Aleksov (Alex) reducing our excess baggage before returning home from Mount Manaslu in 2002.

Sherpas throw rice into the air as an offering to the gods during a Puja ceremony at Everest base camp. The colourful Tibetan prayer flags are an important part of the ritual.

Dragging the mortally injured Christian Kuntner to Camp 2 on Annapurna, in a make-shift sled with Silvio Mondinelli (centre) and Brendan Cusack (at left).

Colourfully dressed female porters carrying full loads towards Kanchenjunga.

Lucky to be alive after descending alone from Kanchenjunga's summit in a wild storm.

Forcing a route up the huge, unstable ice cliff at the top of Annapurna's German Rib. This was the technical crux of the ascent and one of the most dangerous parts of the climb.

Tiptoeing up the perilous wind slab of Annapurna's vast summit slopes.

One side of the mountaineers' memorial at Annapurna base camp.
Annapurna had claimed more than sixty lives by the time I climbed it.

Dawa holds the rope to Neil who is 10 metres down a crevasse. The dark patch ahead of Dawa is the hole Neil made when he broke through.

Bivouacking with Neil (in yellow) on descent from Shishapangma's summit in 2009. We spent the night in minus 25 to minus 30 degrees Celsius, praying that the forecast blizzard would hold off.

At home and happiest in the mountains.

11

A BIG DAY OUT

... by bringing myself over the edge and back, I discovered a passion to live my days fully, a conviction that will sustain me like sweet water, on the periodically barren plain of our short lives.

Jonathan Waterman

In October 2005 I started planning for the following year, and contacted my 8000-metre friends from around the world. By early 2006 I'd organised to join with a very strong team of high-altitude specialists for another attempt on Kanchenjunga. My 2003 experience had taught me that this mountain deserved enormous respect, in particular because of its savage storms close to the summit. I wanted to climb with similarly experienced people, but this time I wanted conservative, careful teammates.

I could not have chosen a better group than Gerlinde Kaltenbrunner, the Austrian woman I'd fallen for on Manaslu in 2002; her new husband, Ralf Dujmovits, whom she'd fallen for on Manaslu in 2002; Veikka Gustafsson from Finland, whom I'd met on Annapurna in 2005; and Hirotaka Takeuchi from Japan. While they would climb as a team of four, I joined with two

Portugese climbers, João Garcia and his friend Tose Antonio. I'd climbed on Nanga Parbat ten years earlier with Garcia, although he'd since suffered extreme frostbite on Mount Everest in 1999, resulting in the loss of most of his fingers, part of his nose and much of the skin from his forehead. Although independent groups, we would share the base camp and the work on the mountain.

We trekked in through very mountainous countryside in the far east of Nepal, an area that at the time was heavily controlled by the Maoists. At one point on the trek, a Maoist 'representative' came to demand a fee of 5000 Nepali rupees per person (about $100) for permission to trek through their region. The reasoning was quite simple and understandable. Expeditions like ours paid significant permit and visa fees to the Nepali government, but very little if any of those funds found their way to the impoverished villages in the areas where we climbed. The Maoists therefore imposed their own levies, backed up by significant firearms.

Apparently our employment of about 100 local villagers as porters and the purchase of numerous supplies along the trek didn't satisfy the Maoists' tax department. Their representative was about seventy years old. Hunched over, he could barely have hurt a fly, but it was absolutely clear to us that if we didn't pay up, we'd be visited by an armed group of Maoists and, at the very least, robbed of all our equipment. There was a palpable threat in his words. We paid up and were efficiently provided with a Maoist receipt, lest we encounter another group of the bandits. It seemed they only taxed you once.

Leaving the Maoist threat in the lowlands, we trekked over numerous mountain passes that connected ever more remote valleys. These were inhabited by hardy rural folk who farmed rice and corn and grazed their livestock, and whose one link to civilisation was their battery-powered radios, from which Nepali music blared incessantly. Up on the passes, though, we were treated to silent forests of blossoming rhododendrons with flaming red, pink and yellow flowers that overhung the track, creating a magical tunnel of colour. Gradually, we left the dense forests behind and emerged onto open hills of alpine grasses dotted with grazing yaks and intersected by bubbling mountain streams. It's at this stage of most treks that I really come to life, when the views open up and the air takes on a chill, crisp feel. My heart beats faster, my walking pace increases and my eyes strain at each bend in the trail to catch my first glimpse of our objective.

The final two days of our trek to Base Camp traversed a long and convoluted glacier, at the head of which towered Kanchenjunga, her massive five-headed summit shrouded in wind-whipped fury some 3500 metres above us. It was cold and difficult walking, so we equipped the porters with warm clothing and good footwear. Nevertheless, only a few porters were prepared to carry the loads over this tougher terrain, which meant that it would take us a week or more to get all our equipment to Base Camp, delaying our start on the mountain. This is one of the inherent risks of climbing in the Himalaya. Many expeditions have failed to reach the mountain they were there to climb when porters have refused to continue or demanded additional wages that the expeditions couldn't afford. Now that a number of old Soviet helicopters have found their way to Nepal, climbers' reliance on porters has been partly relieved, but these helicopters crash relatively frequently, and those that don't are in such demand that delays can still occur.

In order to progress our acclimatisation while we waited for our gear, we trekked ahead to Base Camp, arriving on 16 April. A Swiss expedition led by Norbert Joos, a highly experienced mountaineer with twelve 8000-metre summits to his credit, was already there, as well as an Ecuadorian climber, Ivan Vallejo, who was well on the way to finishing his own quest to climb all fourteen 8000ers.

On 23 April we carried our first load to Camp 1. João, Tose and I left Base Camp together, but we soon found that Tose was unable to maintain the same climbing pace as João and me, and he fell behind until he was out of sight. João and I continued to Camp 1, deposited our loads and descended, expecting to find Tose still climbing up. Instead we found him lying on the ridge below us, pretty much where we'd last seen him. When we reached him, he said he was experiencing great pain in his abdomen and had felt something rupture inside.

We took his backpack and escorted him down to Base Camp, where Gerlinde, who had nursing training, examined him. All of us had completed various wilderness and first-aid medical courses over the years, but it was a great advantage to have someone professionally skilled. Gerlinde suspected Tose had a burst appendix, which, given our location, was a serious state of affairs. Tose had to be evacuated, but at such altitude and in such rough terrain, no helicopter could land. After we dosed him up on antibiotics, João and one of our base-camp cooks walked him through the night to a grassy paddock about a thousand metres lower. Back in Kathmandu, Gerlinde's diagnosis was confirmed and Tose was operated upon immediately.

This left me in a difficult situation, since both my climbing partners had now departed. Ralf and the rest of his team invited me to climb with them, which I gratefully accepted. I still had to carry my own gear and operate slightly independently, but I could rope up with them on dangerous ground. It was fun to share the climb with a strong, like-minded team. Ralf and Gerlinde used one tent, and Veikka and Hiro another. To save me the effort of carrying the three-person tent that I would have shared with João and Tose, Ralf lent me a lightweight 'summit' tent; a squeeze for two people, but ideal for one.

The lightweight tent allowed me to carry a little extra clothing, which was a good thing, because this was a particularly cold season, with strong winds most days, considerable snowfall and really bitter nights. I was trialling a new sleeping bag on the trip but found it wasn't appropriate. After shivering my way through a couple of nights at Camp 1, longing for the faint warmth of the morning, I brought up my down suit to wear inside the sleeping bag. Toasty.

We established the usual camps up the mountain. On our first climb to Camp 2, though, we ran out of daylight and were obliged to camp on the steep mountain face in the middle of a highly unstable field of ice cliffs. Sometime in the night there was the sound of massive blocks of ice crashing. Although our ledge shook, it stayed firm, so we stayed where we were, albeit rather hyper-alert in case the whole thing suddenly collapsed underneath us—not that we could have helped ourselves if it did. The next morning we found that the inside of the ice cliff on which we were camped had collapsed in on itself, so we were sitting on a hollow tower of ice. We packed up and climbed out of there pronto.

At a safer camp a few hundred metres higher, we were pinned by bad weather for two nights. As I was on my own in my tent, I was quite bored, so Veikka tore out a couple of chapters of a book he was reading and gave them to me. I quickly devoured them and asked for more, but he was still reading. So I re-read the first two chapters, then re-read them again. And, again. I also occupied myself by drawing out my meals for as long as possible.

Over the years, I'd refined my high-altitude food to provide maximum energy for minimum effort. I particularly favoured food that didn't require cooking and the use of my scarce supply of gas. Most days started with a couple of cups of lukewarm tea—the low pressure at high altitude means that water boils at much less than 100 degrees Celsius—and a muesli bar. Not much, but that's about all I can stomach anyway, because the altitude seriously affects my appetite. Lunch would be another snack bar, if I had the appetite. Dinner was the cordon bleu meal and usually comprised a cup of powdered soup mixed with powdered potato and some slices of salami. I sometimes supplemented this with a bit of cheese, tinned fish or pate on a biscuit. Chocolate was a rarity because, unlike at sea level, I really can't stand it at altitude. Not surprisingly, I lose a fair bit of weight while climbing, but I tend to make up for that by eating huge amounts while I'm at Base Camp.

After two days, by which time I could recite those two chapters verbatim, the storm eased a little, so we packed up the camp, buried our equipment to prevent it from being blown away and, having acclimatised sufficiently for a summit attempt, descended to Base Camp to await a spell of good weather. By this time João had returned from Kathmandu, but we were stuck at Base Camp in a prolonged period of bad weather. Finally, on 10 May, after eight interminable days, we received a promising forecast with indications for a good summit day on Sunday 14 May. João's acclimatisation was dubious since he'd spent so little time on the mountain, but he decided to try to summit with us if he could.

At Camp 1 the next night I ate something that didn't agree with me and suffered terrible stomach cramps, which left me weak and nauseated. Continuing on to camps 2 and 3 became an exhausting battle as I tried to ignore the cramps and my lack of energy to push myself up the hill.

We placed our Camp 3 on the mountain face at 7700 metres. Although that was 500 metres higher than our high camp in 2003, it still left us with about 800 vertical metres of climbing on summit day. We could have placed it a couple of hundred metres higher still, but that would have meant lugging our heavy loads for several more hours and then resting at such a high altitude that it would have been less beneficial. We shared the camp with the Swiss expedition, which was also going for the summit the next morning, so there was quite a group of us.

My friends in 2003 had been caught out when bad weather hit the upper slopes of this peak, burying their tracks and shrouding the mountain in complete whiteout. To avoid a repeat of that epic, I had brought up a bunch of bamboo wands to mark our route to the summit, so we could find our way back in the event of any such storm. However, in my fatigue, not having slept or eaten for the previous several days, I couldn't face carrying them. I could justify leaving them behind, though, because I'd also brought my GPS, which João agreed to carry.

Our plan was to set out for the top at midnight, but a snowstorm kept us pinned in the tents until dawn, around 4 a.m. Within the first few steps, I knew I was in for a very hard day. My stomach cramps were severe, and I was half-starved and absolutely listless. The only thing that kept me going was that I wanted this summit badly. It wasn't the weather or the dangerous conditions preventing my success, it was my own physical weakness. I couldn't and wouldn't accept that as an excuse to fail, so I forced myself onwards.

The route from our camp to the summit was a complex one. It angled up and to the right, to reach a rock band, then it zigzagged through that and emerged left, leading us up a long and very exposed snow and ice ramp that seemed to stretch to the heavens. I knew that leaving the bamboo wands behind would make it harder for us to find our way down if there was a storm, but I had faith that the GPS would keep us safe. After about an hour's climbing, though, I looked down to see that João had turned around and was heading back to camp. Clearly, he wasn't sufficiently acclimatised to make the climb that day. With him went the GPS and our navigational safety net.

The rest of us pushed up the mountain, praying that the forecast was correct and that we wouldn't need the GPS to find our way back to camp. Hour after hour we ground up the steep ramp. The day seemed interminable. I didn't have my usual climbing stamina and kept falling behind the group. Each time they reached a rest point, I would keep climbing until I caught up with them. By the time I arrived they'd have finished their rest and would be ready to resume, leaving me gasping for breath in their wake. It was soul-destroying. Worse, the predicted good weather had morphed into cloud, snow and ever-increasing wind. Our forecast, which had been so accurate throughout the expedition, was wrong on the day when we needed it the most.

As the sun crossed the sky, our height gain seemed imperceptible on that never-ending ramp. The only breaks were a series of short, steep sections that would have made great ski jumps in the right location. Finally, we turned off the ramp to thread our way up steep rock and ice across the exposed upper slopes of the mighty South Face. Miserable in my exhaustion and desperately hoping that we were nearly at the top, I searched through the patchy cloud for the summit. Through the fog of my high-altitude awareness, forgetting the image I'd studied at Base Camp, I saw what I thought was the top, not too far away. Hope gave me a burst of energy, and I forced myself to continue, panting for oxygen, hands clutching at the rock. The climbing became technical as we clambered delicately over and around small granite outcrops that overhung the face up which we'd just ascended. This was not the place to fall.

At 1.30 p.m. I reached that hoped-for highest point, but cruel humour was the gods' pleasure that day. A hidden section of the mountain face was then revealed, stretching at least another 100 metres above and well into the distance. A hundred metres might not sound much, but it meant at least another two hours' climbing into yet more extreme altitude, in ever-deteriorating weather. Worse, I did not have a single calorie of energy to draw upon.

I was in hell. I knelt on the snow, my head in my hands, desperate for oxygen and feeling completely crushed. Over the past few hours my stomach cramps had worsened and I was now vomiting frequently. I was nearly at the end of my tether. The sensible option was to go down. But what is 'sensible', anyway? Resting when you are tired or feeling sick? Turning back because of pain or a lack of motivation? Is that sensible? Comfortable, maybe. But I wanted this summit. If I didn't get to Kanchenjunga's summit this time, I'd just have to come back and overcome all the dangers and hardship again. In that context, what was 'sensible'?

Don't give up. I pulled myself to my feet and, somewhat unsteadily, climbed on. To save weight, I shoved my backpack, water bottle, headtorch and one of my two ice axes into the snow. At least the angle had eased and the climbing was straightforward, so I didn't have to concentrate as hard. You lose track of time in those situations and enter a kind of trance, placing one weary step after another, attentive enough simply to hold on to the mountain. Lost in that blankness of mind, I maintained a good climbing rhythm, actually overtaking two of the Swiss climbers to catch the rest of my team.

As we neared the top, the face steepened. We traversed beneath the summit pinnacle to avoid a rock chimney that looked too exhausting. Tricky and exposed rock scrambling on the far side required every speck of what limited focus we could muster at almost 8600 metres without oxygen. After a final short, steep pitch, we emerged onto the summit at 5 p.m., four hours after climbing over that false peak just a short way below. Out of respect for the local religious beliefs, we stopped just a few metres short of the very top. Not all climbers follow this request to leave the mountain's gods undisturbed, but I did and would later be glad of it.

Too tired to join in the celebratory backslapping, I sat and filmed the others, then enjoyed the vista for a few brief minutes. Cloud was all around us, like the view from a jet airliner. Except we were outside the plane. The wind had picked up to near gale force and darkness was fast approaching. It was time to get down to safety. The trickiest part of the route on the way up had been the steep rock and ice just above where we'd turned off the long ramp, so it was vital that we get below that section and onto the ramp in the last of the day's fast-fading light.

My reserves of energy were gone. Knowing that I'd be slowest, I started down first, but the others soon caught up and overtook me. Norbert, the leader of the Swiss team, paused as he caught me.

'Andy, do you want me to climb down with you?' he asked.

I couldn't accept. I had climbed myself into this situation, made my choices and accepted the risk.

'No, you go ahead, Norbert,' I replied.

He quickly descended ahead of me into the encroaching gloom, and with him went a tangible link to my own survival. Even amid that gale, the desire to lie in the snow and sleep was overwhelming and I shouted at myself to keep going, the words whipped away as I voiced them. I had to find the ramp before dark or I'd be stuck high on the mountain in an increasingly fierce blizzard. That could only be fatal.

With raw lungs rasping in the freezing wind so that I tasted blood and my heart thumping so hard that I thought I'd simply faint and fall off the mountain, I pushed down past the hump that had deceived me as a summit on the way up, through the steep rock and onto the snow slopes below:

> We'd left the summit about 5.30 pm and then began a race
> against the oncoming dark. It was relief to reach the cache at
> the overhanging rock where I'd left my headtorch, as I thought
> I'd be okay to go down by myself. However, as the darkness
> came on, so the wind increased; by the time I reached the ramp
> in almost total darkness, the wind was a genuine gale and I had
> to hide my face from its furious lashing.

It was 7 p.m. and right on dark when I reached the top of the ramp. In the whipping snow and utter blackness I could see nothing. I turned on my headlamp, but the cloud was so thick that it reflected back to me, like car headlights in a fog. It was better to be in darkness than have that blinding light in my eyes.

The situation was more than a little serious. I crouched on the snow, buffeted by the storm, and considered my options. I'd bivouacked twice before on descents from 8000er summits, but those had been at least 500 metres lower than I was now, and in quite calm conditions. Although I'd survived, it had been marginal on both occasions. In my already weakened state, in this raging storm and at this higher altitude, I would not last the night.

My team was well below and would never find me, even if they had the energy to look. I was too tired to stand up and climb down the ramp. The only option was to glissade. This meant sitting in the snow and sliding forward, like on a slippery dip, using my ice axe as a brake by my side. It was fraught with danger because I could easily lose control, gain too much speed and rocket off the side of the ramp, out into the void. I recalled that David Hume, my teammate on the 1993 Everest expedition, had been killed on Makalu in 1995 doing exactly what I was proposing, glissading. And he'd tried it in daylight, in good conditions.

The ramp was not straightforward. From my position, it angled steeply down and to the left, but it also tilted sideways towards the massive abyss a few metres to the right. If I slid too far to the right, I'd shoot off the ramp and drop a thousand metres down the face. Not a good option. As well, there were those ski-jump steps that I would have to locate and down-climb, as they were way too steep to glissade. I'd be launched into eternity if I tried. Most importantly, all this had to be done in total darkness. There was no moon and my headlamp was worse than nothing. All in all, glissading was the worst possible way to descend the mountain.

I sat in the snow, put my ice axe by my side and started sliding down the slope. I could only guess at my speed. I could see nothing at all but was vaguely aware, more by sense than anything tangible, of the massive face of the mountain to my left, so I kept my direction parallel with it. I had no perception of the right-hand edge of the ramp or the abyss below it, but that was probably just as well. My biggest worry was the steep steps that I'd climbed earlier in the day. I recollected that they existed but had no idea of where I was in relation to them. I had to stop sliding before I reached them or I would be killed.

As I bounced and skidded my way down the slope, trying desperately to conjure up a picture of the ramp in my mind, I was suddenly overcome by the strongest awareness that I should stop right at that point. This was the same type of feeling that had saved me from a storm at 8000 metres on Everest in 2004. I stopped immediately and rolled onto my front. I tentatively felt my way down the slope and, sure enough, found the first steep step beneath my feet. After carefully climbing down it for a few metres to the ramp below, I sat down and continued glissading. Somehow I was able to do this at each step—never able to see them, but always sensing them just in time.

I cannot explain how this worked but can only think that my inner voice was working overtime, or that the gods were giving me a helping hand for having respected their summit earlier that day. It was almost an out-of-body experience with my guide hovering over me—not another person so much as my own self guiding me down. It was an incredible but very real experience.

*

The risk I'd taken paid off. Within an hour I caught up with the others near the bottom of the ramp. They'd stopped because they were unable to find the exit point from the ramp that was the start of the zigzag through the rock buttress and the traverse back to our tents. It was imperative that we turn off at the right point—if we crossed the slope too high, we'd never see the tents below the ice cliffs, and if we descended too low, we'd fall off the bottom of the ramp. Had we planted the bamboo wands, or had any of us been carrying the GPS, we'd have found the way easily. As I wrote:

> We were in pretty bad shape. No moon, the wind howling and freezing, lost, and exhausted. I was sick and had only drunk

200 millilitres of water since twelve midnight, twenty-one hours before.

As it was, we were 700 metres down from the summit but were still stuck in a wild gale at around 7900 metres. We had at least descended out of the cloud and so could use our headlamps to see our immediate surrounds, but without moonlight we couldn't identify our position on the mountain face.

Suddenly, in the distance, down and to our right, was the flash of a headlamp. It was João. The light lasted only for a few seconds, but it was enough to save our lives. We frantically set the bearing on our compasses and staggered desperately towards that point.

In my haste and absolute exhaustion, however, my concentration lapsed and I fell over a small ice cliff, about three metres high. The feeling of falling through space in the darkness, albeit only for an instant, was not particularly comforting. In the blackness I didn't know if I'd started a long plunge to my death or if I would hit the ground immediately below. Luckily for me, it was the latter, and with my reflexes back on high alert I instantly rolled onto my front and plunged my ice axe into the snow to stop from falling any further.

It took us another thirty minutes to reach the tents. We arrived about 9.30 p.m., seventeen and a half hours after setting out that morning. The storm had raged in our absence and left only carnage. One of the tents had been blown away and the remaining few were bent and broken in the wind. But, still, they seemed like paradise. I collapsed inside, covered in ice, my down suit and mittens full of snow. I was frozen solid, and was lucky to get back in one piece!

My and João's tent had been so buried by the snow that there was only room for one person inside, but I crammed in anyway. We were forced to sit back to back with our knees hunched up, our heads slapped constantly by the whipping tent walls. We couldn't light the stove to melt snow, which was particularly terrible for me, because I'd drunk almost nothing since midnight the night before. But just being out of the storm and knowing that I'd somehow survived was absolute heaven.

When finally I could speak, I thanked João for shining his headlamp for us, as it had saved us. He didn't know what I was talking about, and told me that he'd simply gone out of the tent to try to shovel away some of the snow. Our lives had been saved by pure luck! We'd been in the right spot and looking in the right direction at precisely the right time to see his headlamp flash. Was it luck, or were we given a helping hand? I can't say, but I know what I'd like to think. Either way, we'd lived through a brutal event and survived by the skin of our teeth. And we'd achieved the summit of the world's third-highest mountain, in a storm and without oxygen. It was a big day out.

By morning the storm had eased. We emerged from our shattered tents like the shell-shocked victims of war. I had never been so physically wrecked. Nor had the others and our faces showed it. We spent the day in a near stupor, packing whatever we could recover and then descending painfully to base camp, which we reached at dusk. We were alive.

It's difficult to describe the physical impact of an epic like this. Rather than the gradual wearing down of the body's reserves that occurs on a long overland or polar trek, to which the body has some time to adjust, high altitude ravages the body so savagely that it is common to lose kilograms of weight in just a few days. You put yourself through extreme cold, starvation, dehydration and lack of oxygen, not to mention endless hours of maximum effort, with your heart racing continuously. All this nonstop for days. The body has no time to adjust, so it strips itself. The line between life and death in those circumstances is as fine as silk.

I have no doubt that our survival that night was largely a result of our years of experience, which gave us the mental strength to

cope with the extreme challenges. We took our chances to succeed, and fought to survive. But still we were lucky. Ironically, so
great was my mental exhaustion that when I retrieved my thermos
from Camp 1 on the way down to base camp, I didn't notice it
was full. Although dying of thirst, I carried a litre of water back to
Base Camp!

For the next couple of days we rested at Base Camp, happy
to lie for hours in our sleeping bags and enjoy endless hot drinks.
Ralph, Gerlinde and Hirotaka had plans to climb another mountain,
though, and needed to travel there quickly, before the season ended
and the monsoon arrived. None of us was keen to make the long
and tiring trek back out to civilisation, so we contracted a large
Russian-built Mi-17 helicopter to pick up us and all our equipment
from a point one day's walk below Base Camp—the same place
from which Tose had been evacuated nearly two months earlier.
We flew parallel to major Himalaya mountains for nearly a hundred
kilometres, passing peak after peak, including several 8000ers—
Kanchenjunga, Makalu, Lhotse and Everest. We were transfixed
by the incredible vista. The callous savagery we'd encountered just
days before had transformed into serene splendour, those majestic
giants now slumbering peacefully in the sun. That vision alone was
worth every hardship.

The chopper dropped Ralf, Gerlinde and Hiro at Lhotse's Base
Camp, and then took Veikka and me to Kathmandu. Ultimately,
the others were unsuccessful on Lhotse due to their exhaustion,
which was hardly a surprise. In Kathmandu I barely had the energy
to catch up with friends and enjoy a celebratory beer.

I experienced on that expedition something I haven't felt with
such intensity on any other trip. I don't know exactly what it was,
but I had a heightened sense of the mountain spirit, a oneness with
nature, a deeper understanding of my 'self' and my inner voice.
I came away a far richer person for the experience, and whenever I reflect on it, I feel a more powerful sense of spirituality and

inner calmness. I wonder also if that solo cross-country skiing trip all those years earlier, back in the mid 1980s, during which I'd virtually sensed my way through an eight-day blizzard, had been an introduction to this amplified, subconscious perception of the environment around me.

While I endured most of that epic descent on my own, I had shared an incredible journey with the whole summit team. There were no false agendas and there was no self-aggrandising after the event. We were all humbled by it, and once again I felt charged by the camaraderie that was wrought through great adversity. A post-summit photo at base camp with Ralf, Gerlinde, Hirotaka and Veikka remains one of my favourites.

Kanchenjunga was my eleventh 8000er. I knew that I'd pushed the limits of my physical endurance on this climb, and that I would probably have died had I not escaped the storm. Far from being scared off the mountains, though, I actually felt psychologically stronger and fully committed to continue my 8000er project. Indeed, I was on a high for months. While it took me a few weeks to regain my physical fitness, I'd never felt more capable of enduring what the mountains could throw at me. That is not to say that I'd become arrogant about the dangers or dismissive of the hardships, but I relished the challenges ahead and was anxious to face them. I was focused, motivated and confident.

That was just as well, as I would soon need every scrap of that mental strength. It was time to return to Annapurna.

Postscript

Norbert Joos, the leader of the Norwegian team who'd summitted on the same day as us, and who'd generously offered to help me descend, suffered a stroke shortly after reaching Base Camp and had to be evacuated by rescue helicopter. Kanchenjunga was his thirteenth summit of the fourteen 8000-metre peaks. Everest was to be number fourteen and he'd deliberately left it until last. He survived the stroke but never climbed at high altitude again.

In 2007 Hirotaka Takeuchi broke his back in an avalanche on Gasherbrum 2. He was evacuated and survived but spent years in recuperation. He returned to the high mountains in 2012 to complete his own quest to climb the fourteen 8000ers.

12

THE MOST DANGEROUS
MOUNTAIN IN THE WORLD

In order to climb properly on big peaks one must free oneself of fear.
This means you must write yourself off before any big climb. You must
say to yourself, 'I may die here.'

Doug Scott

AFTER THE DISASTROUS attempt on Annapurna in 2005, I
felt the safest way to ascend it would be to acclimatise on
a different mountain, then climb Annapurna as rapidly as possible, thus limiting my exposure to its dangers. With this plan in
mind, I arranged to join an international team on Annapurna for
the pre-monsoon season of 2007. First, however, I would acclimatise on Shishapangma. Ideally, I would summit it too, making the
season a double success if all went well. To fit in both expeditions,
I needed to start climbing ahead of when most expeditions begin,
so I would be in the Himalaya for almost three months. However,
after returning home from Kanchenjunga in 2006, I'd taken a
job with the Australian Public Service in Canberra. I had been

honest at the interview about my climbing passion and the amount of time off I'd need for my expeditions. While they'd agreed at the time, I think my boss was a little taken back when, after just nine months' employment, I asked for three months' holiday! Thankfully, he agreed.

I organised with a trekking agent in Kathmandu to provide me with transport to Shishapangma and base-camp support early in the season. Another climber, Neil Ward from Wales, was also on the permit. I hadn't met him previously and had planned to climb by myself, but it would be good to have someone to talk to at base camp.

For several years I'd been trekking in the Everest region of Nepal for a couple of weeks before each expedition to initiate my acclimatisation, and I did that again this time. I then travelled back to Kathmandu to commence the journey to Shishapangma, and arrived at Base Camp on 15 April. To keep in touch with home during the expedition, I'd equipped myself with a satellite-linked mini laptop so I could send and receive short emails, but the cold kept causing the device to fail. At one point, while connected to the internet, it crashed and the clock reverted to 2005. When I got it running again, I reset the date to 2007, only to find that, when I signed off, it had recorded two years' worth of internet usage! At a dollar a minute for satellite access, that was rather pricey. I wondered if I'd have to live in hiding in Tibet for the rest of my life.

Neil was a good bloke, but this was his first Himalayan expedition. We agreed to climb together, at least on the lower, crevasse-prone slopes, where it was wise to rope together for safety. Neil had hired a Sherpa, Dawa, to climb with him. Despite having a business card that proudly proclaimed him to be a mountain guide, he was completely inexperienced and it soon showed.

Early in the expedition, the three of us climbed to Camp 1 and stayed the night there, with the intention of climbing to Camp 2 the next day. Just beyond Camp 1 there were several very large crevasses. As we prepared to leave, we roped up, with Neil and I tying into opposite ends of the rope and Dawa in the middle. Dawa took a bunch of coils of loose rope in his hands. When I told him that he should drop the loops and keep the rope tight between him and Neil, he laughed and said that he could hold anyone's fall, because he was a Sherpa. I pushed the point but he refused to drop the loops, and Neil said not to worry. I did worry, though, so I put myself at the back end of the rope, with Neil at the front.

We started walking and had gone no more than 25 metres when Neil broke through the surface and plunged into a crevasse. Immediately, the 10 metres of loosely coiled rope was ripped from Dawa's hand, adding a major distance to Neil's fall as he plummeted downwards. Expecting exactly this scenario, I had backed up so that the rope between Dawa and me was very tight. As soon as Neil broke through the crevasse, I threw myself down, buried my ice axe to the hilt in the snow, and then hung on for all I was worth.

When Neil hit the end of the rope, the full force of his fall came against Dawa, who was ripped off his feet and jerked towards the crevasse. Immediately, however, the rope between him and me snapped taut, and he was slammed down into the snow, the rope stretched tight in both directions. My anchor held and I quickly placed two snow stakes as backup. Dawa was white as a ghost, so I told him to anchor his ice axe and stay where he was, while I crawled forward to the edge of the crevasse.

I yelled down to Neil. He was okay, but his foot was caught in the rope and he was hanging upside down and couldn't climb back up the rope. One of the benefits of tying correctly into your climbing rope is that you have about 10 metres of spare rope at each end to set up a pulley system, so you can get someone out of a crevasse if they are injured or incapacitated, as Neil was. This was one of the lessons I'd learned all those years ago on my technical mountaineering course in New Zealand, and I'd used it a number of times since then.

I set up a three-to-one 'Z pulley', and Dawa and I tried to pull Neil up. Even with the two of us hauling, the rope didn't budge. I re-rigged the system to give us a six-to-one mechanical advantage and, straining ourselves to the maximum, we managed to pull in the rope about an inch. The friction was incredible. There was nothing for it but to bust our guts and heave.

Slowly, inch-by-inch, we pulled. It took us a good hour but, finally, we saw a foot, then a leg and soon he was out. Dawa and I collapsed onto the snow, exhausted. Neil wasn't in any better state, having been hanging upside down for an hour in a bottomless, frozen abyss, his very survival dependent on our ability to get him out. I asked if he was okay and if I could get him something, to which he replied, 'Gosh, I could really do with a cup of tea.' That was it—no 'Thank god!' or 'I thought I was going to die!' or anything dramatic. He just wanted a cup of tea. Our thermos was full, so his wish was easily catered for.

Neil was happy to continue climbing straight afterward, so we pushed on up the mountain. Dawa chose to keep the rope tight between him and Neil thereafter and we agreed to keep climbing as a team of three. I enjoyed the company and it was a good opportunity for Neil to pick up some pointers on climbing the 8000ers, as he was keen to take on other big ones. And it was safer for all of us.

As we'd started the expedition so early in the season, we didn't see anyone else on the climb. What a joy to have a great Himalayan peak to ourselves. The downside, of course, was that we had no one to share the work of breaking trail in the deep snow. On our push for the summit a couple of weeks later, the snow above Camp 2 was particularly deep, so the going was exhausting and very slow. In the end, we didn't get to where we'd hoped to place Camp 3, on a ridge at 7400 metres, so we set up a Camp 2.5 on the glacier at 7050 metres, some 350 metres below the ridge.

About 1 a.m. Neil and I set out for the top, Dawa electing to remain behind. When we were three-quarters of the way to the ridge above us, a storm unleashed itself. It was so brutal that we were blinded and frozen and could neither ascend nor descend. Without shelter, we hunkered down near some rocks for about an hour. The storm eased around dawn, by which time we were too frozen to continue, so we descended back to our tent, great icicles hanging from our faces.

Still motivated, we tried again the next night, and this time we made it to the ridge at dawn, but Neil was too exhausted to continue so I had to proceed alone. I'd been planning to climb a new route across the bottom of the North Face, potentially avoiding the avalanche danger higher up, but I needed a climbing partner with whom to rope up because of the dangerous hidden crevasses. Without Neil, I was obliged to follow the normal route up the ridge towards the mythical Central Summit.

I tested the snow and tried to traverse the upper North Face towards the real summit a number of times. Crack—like a lightening bolt, a jagged line zigzagged across the hard-packed snow. The surface had fractured and the whole slope threatened to avalanche. I froze.

Careful, now, I thought to myself. I knew of too many climbers who'd been swept away by avalanches. My life depended on no sudden movement. Ever so lightly, I tiptoed—as much as one can in heavily insulated, knee-high mountain boots—back along my tracks. The same thing happened each time I tried to traverse. Eventually, I conceded that it was useless. I wouldn't be getting to the summit via the North Face that season. It was my third unsuccessful attempt on the true summit of Shishapangma, and I was really disappointed, as I felt fit and strong. If I'd had a climbing partner to rope up to, I was confident that I'd have made the summit easily. But it wasn't Neil's fault; he was simply too exhausted to continue.

I descended to find him waiting for me at the top of the face above our Camp 2.5, when he could have descended to comfort and safety. That sort of fortitude or mateship—staying at altitude even when exhausted, just so he could provide support for a team-mate—was by 2007 a rare thing in the Himalaya, and I was touched. Neil is one of the good guys.

We dropped down to the tent and packed it up. Once we reached Base Camp I departed quickly—I had an appointment with Annapurna.

*

I caught a lift in a jeep across the border into Nepal, then spent a night in Kathmandu before chartering a small helicopter to fly me directly to Annapurna's Base Camp, avoiding the time-consuming, albeit spectacular, trek. As my helicopter came in to land, I saw that there were two base camps set up. I didn't know which was mine, but as we touched down a man came running from one, a duffel bag across his shoulder. He sprinted for the chopper and, as I unloaded my own duffels, threw his bag across me and onto the backseat. He dived in after it, yelling out, 'Annapurna crazy!' He was buckling himself in even as the helicopter pulled away. It wasn't the most inspiring start to an expedition.

The team I'd arranged to join was an international group and included some very strong climbers: the Russian Sergey Bogomolov and two of his friends—although, as it turned out, one had just departed in my helicopter!—the Spaniard Iñaki Ochoa de Olza, and his Romanian friend Horia Colibassanu. The Russians had trekked in while I was on Shishapangma and had been climbing on Annapurna for a couple of weeks. They'd already established Camp 2. Indeed, Sergey had captured some incredible video of an avalanche coming down the face above Camp 2, precisely where my 2005 expedition had been hit. Iñaki and Horia were still on their way to Annapurna, having also first gone to another mountain to acclimatise.

After settling in, I learned that the other base camp belonged to a Spanish-speaking team led by the Basque climber Edurne Pasaban. She was on a mission to climb all fourteen 8000ers too, although she still had a few to go at that time. Her group included several climbers from Spain, as well as Fernando Gonzalez from Colombia and Ivan Vallejo from Ecuador, whom I'd met on Kanchenjunga the year before. He'd succeeded on Kanchenjunga after I'd left and, with thirteen 8000ers in the bag, he had just Annapurna to go. Like Christian Kuntner and Ed Viesturs in 2005, he'd left the most dangerous to last.

Remembering the disaster on the French Route in 2005, both my team and the Spanish-speaking team decided to attempt an alternative route known as the German Rib. It followed the same line as the French Route as far as Camp 2 but then branched off up a different face, before making a long traverse above the dangerous North Face back towards the summit. While it was longer, this route avoided the main avalanche-prone area of the North Face, and we hoped it would be safer.

On 7 May I climbed to Camp 2, where Sergey and his remaining teammate, Emil, were camped, but they descended to Base Camp after Emil twisted his knee, leaving me on my own. Dangerous avalanche conditions delayed me there for two days, but I was keen to continue the climb. Ivan and Fernando from the Spanish-speaking team were in their own Camp 2, so we agreed to climb together.

It soon became obvious that this route was just as dangerous as the French line on the North Face. To access the German Rib, we had first to cross the plateau over which we'd sledged the dying Christian Kuntner two years before. Next, we crossed several hundred metres of avalanche debris and scaled a short but vertical ice cliff. Then we climbed 100 metres up and out of the way of the cause of all that debris: an absolutely massive ice serac, which hung 1000 metres above our route and avalanched several times a day.

There was no way of telling when it would release, but if you were anywhere underneath it when it let go, you were dead. No ifs, no buts. It was massive.

It took about thirty minutes of speed climbing, if you can call it that at 6000 metres, to get through death's bowling alley. The key was to not stop. That sounds obvious, I know, but when you are in an environment where you are obliged to stop every minute or so to get your breath, climbing as fast as you can for thirty minutes feels like it will bring on a heart attack. When we reached safety, we slumped over our ice axes, screaming for breath for fifteen minutes as we recovered. I wanted to throw up, faint, collapse— you name it. But the route could not be avoided.

Once we were on the rib, the ground was more stable, although it too was littered with seracs that forced us to edge up the side of the rib rather than on top of it. As we ascended, the snow became less and less secure. We could feel that it was tight and avalanche-prone, and with every metre it became more so.

Conditions like these are as dangerous as can be found. Constant storms had created a great depth of snow, the top metre of which had been compacted by the ever-present wind. Below that crust, though, the snow was soft and had lost its strength. A little too much weight on the upper layer would cause it to sheer away from the snow below. Anyone on that top layer would be carried down the mountain.

As we advanced, we constantly discussed the conditions, aware that we were pushing the limits of safe climbing but knowing too that there was no other choice if we were to succeed on Annapurna. Although the threat of danger was psychologically exhausting, the climbing itself was fun, with twists and turns, steep steps and tiny ledges. We spent a night on one of those ledges before climbing the next morning up even less stable snow. Finally, we reached the obvious crux of the route, a 200-metre cliff of crumbling, rotten ice. A teetering mass, it was overdue for collapse.

It was clear that this would take us more than a day to over-come. With a blizzard building, we cached our loads, then abseiled for 1000 metres over several hours down the rib, through the avalanche chute and trekked back across the plateau to Camp 2. In the mood for some warm food and a good sleep, we continued all the way down to Base Camp, where we rested for some days while the weather raged above.

I love my rest days at Base Camp, and on Annapurna they were even more enjoyable than usual. At 4000 metres we could sleep soundly, eat well and relax for a short time without feeling the constant dread of an imminent avalanche. I hung out with the Spanish group quite a bit. Their base-camp manager, Ferran, produced a golf club, and we spent an inordinate number of hours in pursuit of golf balls that ricocheted off jagged rocks as we devel-oped our skills in 'glacier golf'. It distracted us from the knowledge that we would soon have to re-enter the battle above.

Unfortunately, though, we received word that an avalanche on nearby Mount Dhaulagiri, which I'd climbed in 1997, had killed two Spanish climbers, friends of many of the Spanish team on Annapurna. Given the dangerous conditions on our hill, the mood was dark, and there was considerable discussion about abandon-ing the expedition. I willed them not to give up and was greatly relieved when they agreed to continue.

*

One morning I was stretching my legs on a hill above Base Camp when puffs of dust started exploding on the ground around me. I realised that rocks were falling from the cliffs several hundred metres above me. They were absolutely silent through the air but hit the ground with a great whack and then ricocheted in every direction. To be struck would be fatal, but there was no protection available, so I bolted downhill to escape the onslaught. Somehow I avoided being hit, but it was pure luck. *Even on our rest days at Base Camp*, I thought, *this bloody mountain is trying to kill us!*

It was a very windy and wet season, and for eight days we awaited a forecast that would give us the good news we needed. Finally, it was predicted that the wind, which for weeks had been at gale force near the summit, would drop to 30 knots on 24 May. That is still a very strong wind, but it was the best forecast we were going to get, so that would have to be our summit day. In the meantime, we had to reclimb the rib and overcome the 200-metre ice cliff.

Iñaki and Horia had by now arrived at the mountain, but rather than climb with us they planned to start up a day or two later and make a fast dash to the summit. For that plan to succeed, they would rely on the rest of us to find a way through the ice cliff.

Over the next few days, most members of the two teams reascended the route to Camp 2, then raced through death's bowling alley and continued up the rib. Retrieving the cache, we advanced right up under the ice cliff, where we were forced to place Camp 3 for two nights, while we took turns to climb on the cliff and fix a safety rope up its forbidding yet hopelessly fragile face.

On our second day at the cliff, Iñaki and Horia arrived, disappointed to find the route still not open. Sergey, Ivan, Fernando and I spent most of the day fixing rope up the face, while the others waited below. Exhausted and stressed, we were blocked at 6500 metres, near the very top, by an ice overhang. Iñaki came up to have a go. He attacked the obstacle with fresh vigour, overcoming it with some very delicate climbing. Sergey and I climbed through and fixed another 100 metres of rope, before Ivan and Fernando took over and fixed the last length.

We'd hoped to drop down to Camp 3, pack everything up and climb back up the cliff that evening to put a safer camp on the ramp above, but there wasn't time before dark. There was still more rope to be fixed to reach the snow ramp, so we were forced to spend a second night in the lower Camp 3 before climbing the ice face the next day to finish the job. No one was happy about this. The night before had been sleepless and nerve-wracking. The cliff above us had creaked and groaned, and chunks of ice the size of fridges had broken off the face, crashing down onto the ridge on which we were camped. We'd placed the tents in the safest spot we could find, but there was still a strong possibility that we'd be hit by one of those blocks of ice. Worse, the whole cliff might collapse on top of us. *At least that would be quick*, I thought.

With the understanding that there was still more of the cliff to be fixed next day, the team debated the wisdom of continuing. Everyone except Ivan, Fernando, Sergey and me declared that the climb, the campsite and the whole mountain were just too dangerous. They were calling their expeditions off and quitting the mountain. It was interesting that those of us who had been opening the route and assessing the risks posed by the conditions thought it was still appropriate to continue. This was not because of any crazy summit fever but because we were more intimately engaged with the mountain, I believe, and had a better understanding of the risk. Those who had been following and perhaps not embracing the challenge to the same extent decided to go down.

Risk management doesn't mean removing all risk; it means managing it. At every step we'd assessed the potential for avalanches—the depth of the snow, the angle of the slope, the time of day and the strength of the sun, even the shape of the snow crystals. While I agreed that the conditions were extremely dangerous, I also knew that to climb Annapurna meant accepting a higher level of risk, as there simply wasn't a safe route. Giving up then would mean I'd have to come back and go through all that danger yet again. I did not want to come back a third time. I wanted to summit. It was better to own the challenge and manage it than run from it.

Despite that rationalisation, the four of us settled into our tents fearfully, knowing that we had another sleepless, stressful night ahead while the others descended to safety. Every noise had our stomachs knotted, our nerves on edge, lest it be the last thing we ever heard:

> Plenty of serac debris came down in the night, and every noise was a matter of waiting to see if it was coming down on us. A long night and very tense. By morning we were still alive, though, and the weather was clear although a little windy up high.

The morning light brought hope and relief, but it was short-lived. Sergey was snowblind, having spent too much of the previous day with his sunglasses off. His eyes were red and swollen and he was clearly in agony. Snowblindness, while not permanent, feels like having sand or dirt in your eyes. The only cure is to cover them for several days. He could not continue. I administered some antibiotic cream to his eyes and thought about what this development meant.

I cursed the gods, because it had seemed we were past the main difficulties of the route. Sergey couldn't descend without help. I could not leave him, which meant I would not summit Annapurna. I could think of nothing worse than coming back to this terrifying killer mountain. This potentially meant the end of my project to climb all the 8000ers, as there'd be no point continuing with the project if I wasn't coming back to Annapurna. Project over—and all because of a pair of sunglasses!

I was devastated, and Ivan and Fernando were equally upset. We'd made a good team and needed each other's support. I started packing Sergey's gear, but he stopped me. His eyes were bad, he said, but they would recover. He couldn't continue going up, but with a day's rest he felt he could descend on his own. I asked him again and again if he was sure. I told him that it wasn't his fault and he didn't need to stay. But he was adamant. A reprieve.

Ivan, Fernando and I needed to adjust our approach to the climb since our logistical support had changed. We no longer had the backup of the group following us with extra rope and tents; in fact, we could no longer even take the two small summit tents we'd been using on this push, as we needed to leave one for Sergey. My tent was slightly larger, so we took it for the three of us and moved Sergey into the other one. With three of us in my tiny two-person summit tent, we wouldn't be able to lie down, so sleeping bags were now no longer worth their weight and bulk. We took one between the three of us as a blanket. One stove, a tiny amount of food and the minimum of rope and other climbing equipment, and we were away.

We hoped to climb another 800 metres up the ramp to the upper slopes of the North Face, where we would site Camp 4 at 7400 metres. Thankfully, the last bit of climbing out of the big ice cliff was less technical than the previous day, and to our relief we were soon over the crux and on the ramp.

Like the slopes below, the ramp was terribly avalanche-prone. Great slabs of it echoed like a drum underfoot as we battled our way up through the blasting wind. As often as we assessed the avalanche danger and agreed to continue, we knew in our hearts that we were pushing safe limits beyond normal boundaries. But every step forward was a step closer to the summit, and by the end of that exhausting day we were at the top of the ramp, about 7200 metres in altitude. We hadn't reached the site where we'd hoped to camp, but night had caught us.

We hacked at the ice under a serac for an hour and a half to produce a tiny sloping ice ledge, the best refuge we could manage in the freezing blackness. With the three of us crushed inside our tent, sleep was impossible but irrelevant. We were at least protected from avalanches for the night—the first time in nearly a week. We nibbled some morsels and fought the buffeting tent to prepare a few tepid drinks, all the while waiting for the wind to drop to the forecast 30 knots. That was the very maximum into which we could climb, so if the forecast was even slightly off, we'd either have to give up or accept the reality that we'd be donating some body parts to the frostbite god. That prospect did not excite me.

The sins of all weather forecasters were forgiven, though, when the wind did indeed ease, and at dawn we emerged into minus 20 degrees Celsius and a strong but manageable breeze. Having camped a little lower than planned, our climb was longer than we'd hoped for. It was also considerably steeper than we'd anticipated. We edged carefully around the serac from our tent and onto the face, where we took turns to lead, plugging steps in what is probably one of the biggest slabs of snow in the Himalaya.

The gods had deigned to grant only one wish that morning, because the solid snow we'd prayed for overnight was nowhere on the mountain. It was the very worst possible slab and it echoed with every step. For the entire day we climbed with the constant expectation that it would suddenly break free and slip like a massive toboggan to the edge of the North Face, a free ticket to a decidedly deadly finish for the expedition. It was heart-in-the-mouth stuff, and not a fun way to spend a day out:

Hardened by strong wind, the slab varies from a few centimetres to half a metre thick. Like the crust of a pavlova, it is firm but brittle and bonded to the layer below by little more than its own weight. You tell yourself that another 70 or 80 kilograms won't make any difference to the tonnes of weight in the slab itself. You step up and hear the hollow reverberations echo through the entire slab. A few steps on and it feels like you are walking on air. If it slides you are finished. The slab will break up, swallow you and drag you to the inevitable precipice and a cold, crushing death below. You tell yourself that this is risk management, that the conditions are okay, that this slab will hold. Rubbish. You have no idea, really. It is blind luck if it holds and bad luck if it doesn't. It is a game of chance where the winner's reward for staking his life is a temporarily sated ego. The loser dies, as so many have. What drives this madness?

Mad or not, we continued, hour after anxious hour. An avalanche thundered elsewhere on the mountain and we stopped, fearful that the vibration would trigger our own slope's release. Ever so gradually, we progressed.

The snow was worst near the top, and the three of us chose different paths. None was better than the others, but each provided us with hope. Eventually, we found ourselves under a small cornice. The summit ridge is reasonably level and dreadfully long—I'd read of climbers traversing the entire ridge to ensure they'd actually stood on the correct summit—but we could see from this point that the rest of the ridge was lower than us. It was knife-edged, so we took turns to belay each other up to the top, where we balanced precariously and looked 4000 metres down each side to the valleys below.

For the fifth time, I'd become the first Australian summiteer of a particular 8000-metre mountain. I pulled out my Aussie flag and held it aloft for the others to photograph me. In the inebriation of the high altitude, though, I couldn't work out which way to hold it for the camera. I made a choice and now have a photograph with the flag in reverse. It didn't matter. In the end, I'd made it to the summit of my twelfth 8000er. Now my only worry was getting down safely to enjoy the success.

We quickly debated which route to descend. Ivan and Fernando were keen to follow the ridgeline back across the top of the face to avoid the slab danger below, but I felt very strongly that the ridgeline was an unknown quantity and that it would be quicker and possibly also safer to return the way we'd come. They relented, and soon we were battling our way back to the tent. Darkness caught us and we struggled to find our safe shelter:

As it got dark, we raced down and I pulled out the GPS to try and track our way to the tent but it struggled in the cold and the steep descent, and gave wildly varying readings.

Fernando went high as Ivan kept heading down, and I slowed to look behind each significant serac band. It seemed as though we must have dropped below the tent. By eight pm it was pitch-black, getting cold and the wind picked up significantly.

This was not the place to bivouac and the situation was getting desperate because the forecast had told us that the winds would become almost cyclonic tonight. I was getting ready to turn back and climb up to search higher when Ivan yelled out that he'd found the tent.

There followed a most miserable night, as the tent was gradually but inexorably buried by the blowing spindrift. Ivan made a cup of water for each of us, but eventually gave up. We settled in for a long, cold, sleepless night.

*

By morning, spindrift had frozen the tent into the mountain face. We tried half-heartedly to retrieve it but were too exhausted, so we abandoned it and began descending. At Camp 3, where we'd left Sergey, we found that he'd packed up and descended, his eyes having recovered sufficiently. We also saw that the place from which we'd taken my tent had a fridge-sized piece of ice sitting on it. Had we not moved Sergey into the other tent, he'd very likely still be there, somewhat flatter. The gods had been granting wishes after all.

Water became our overriding focus, and the thought of it drove us down the mountain. At Camp 1 there were streams, and we collapsed onto the rocks and drank and drank. It was only at this point that I could fully relax, being off the glacier and out of the avalanche danger. Brilliant! We walked back to Base Camp.

Ivan and Fernando were talking wildly, still high on adrenalin, but I became sombre as we neared the camp. After what I'd experienced in 2005, I felt humbled and simply grateful to have climbed the mountain and survived.

At Base Camp I returned to a quiet dining tent. The cook brought me a cup of tea as my teammates went off to their tents. That was okay with me, as I wanted some time to reflect on the climb and its significance. I slept poorly that night but that was normal after a summit, as the adrenaline continued to course through my veins and I relived the climb. The bond that the three of us had formed was the strongest. We'd overcome the most dangerous mountain in the world and it was incredible.

I knew even then that this was the climb of my career. It wasn't the most technical, although it was tough. But it was far and away the most dangerous. We'd spent the entire climb, the entire expedition, on edge and expecting disaster at any moment. It had been as much a supreme psychological battle as a physical challenge, and mental exhaustion stalked us constantly. Success brought intense feelings of relief, as much as of victory, and I still regard my survival as an achievement equal to summitting. I shall never set foot on that mountain again.

Postscript

Iñaki Ochoa de Olza, whom I'd first met on Broad Peak in 1997, was one of the most experienced high-altitude climbers in the world. As well as having achieved some great climbs and put up new routes, he was well known to most of the veteran high-altitude community in the Himalaya, and to many of the ladies, as a really nice guy. He returned to Annapurna in 2008 to reattempt the mountain from its south side. While making his summit bid, he developed pulmonary oedema. Despite a strong and coordinated rescue attempt, he died in his tent.

13

GETTING CLOSE

*There are two kinds of climbers; those who climb because their heart
sings when they're in the mountains, and all the rest.*

Alex Lowe

W HEN I RETURNED to Kathmandu after the Annapurna
climb, I was emotionally tired. Exhausted, actually. I found
it difficult to celebrate with my friends in the usual bars and had
no interest in socialising with the eclectic mix of climbers and
international characters that Kathmandu attracts. I wasn't quite sure
why, but I felt distanced from others. I wanted to be on my own.

Although that feeling diminished a little over time, Annapurna
had been such an intense experience that it made my 'normal' life
back at home seem wasteful and self-indulgent. This wasn't exactly
a new emotion. As I'd spent more and more time in the Himalaya,
I'd felt ever more strongly that that was where I was most comfortable. But while adopting this simple, albeit dangerous, life was
attractive, I knew that it wasn't 'real'. It simply wasn't possible for

me to climb all the time, if only because I had to work to fund each expedition. So a return to normality was unavoidable.

For the first time in many years, though, returning home was a bit of a culture shock. I found it difficult to engage with my girlfriend Julie, despite her strong support throughout my expeditions. I found work in the public service far less interesting than I had previously. More than anything, I had no time whatsoever for the mundane concerns of people whose lives revolved around gossip and office politics. In truth, I'd never really afforded those people much attention, but now I gave them very short shrift. I just couldn't be bothered with their pettiness and irrelevance.

I knew that my experience on Annapurna had had an effect on me—if not in changing my values, then at least in clarifying them. It had reinforced for me what a valuable gift life is, and that it should be lived absolutely to the full. A number of times over the years, I'd found myself in lonely base camps for weeks on end, even months, wondering if I was wasting my life, my money and my opportunities in order to chase a foolish dream which, in the end, meant nothing, and would bring me nothing more than personal satisfaction, *if* I survived. There was no pot of gold at the end of this particular rainbow. I'd never been very adept at selling myself or my story at home. Even after all these years and successes, I was predominately self-funded, although my ever-growing keynote-speaking business did at least support the habit.

It was ironic, really. I had quite a profile in international mountaineering circles, but at home I was barely known. This made it difficult for me to attract sponsorship. My peers around the world were heavily sponsored and able to live as professional climbers, whereas I had to work a normal job to fund my climbing passion. This was partly my fault for not promoting myself and partly because I came from the flattest country on Earth. Mountaineering has never rated too highly in Australia compared to cricket, or our other national sports.

I wondered if perhaps I'd run my course in the mountains. Was I burnt out? I'd been luckier than all those who'd paid the ultimate price while chasing the Himalayan grand slam, but was climbing these big peaks really worth such risk? By this time, I'd been climbing on the 8000ers for sixteen years, and had spent more than three years of my life actually clinging to the sides of these hills. Three years! Surely I could find better ways to spend my time. Surely life was worth more than a few brief moments on the top of some big chunks of rock and ice. Was it time to hang up my ice axe?

I'd taken the job in the public service to consolidate my finances and to create a new career opportunity—if I actually wanted to have one. But to pursue that career, I would have to devote myself to it and spend less time in the mountains. It was decision time: mountains or money?

I'd never considered giving up. I wasn't quite sure I was actually considering it now, but I was definitely asking myself whether I should consider it. That was about as far as I'd ever taken the question before, even in those lonely base camps. I'd never forced myself to answer, because on each of those expeditions my self-doubt had evaporated the moment I was back on the mountain. The dark thoughts stayed at Base Camp, and as soon as I'd started climbing again, I was exuberant and fulfilled. I was re-energised and refocused.

While I tried to assess the value of my project—indeed, of my whole lifestyle—back in Australia I relived in my mind many of the expeditions. As soon as I started reflecting on my high-altitude experiences, my pulse beat more strongly, my breathing quickened and I felt a surge of happiness. I wasn't stressed by the memories; I was excited by them.

The more I questioned myself about the point of these climbs, the more worthwhile they appeared—and the less relevant 'normality' seemed. My frustration was not that the mountains were impeding my life, I realised; it was that my 'normal' life was impeding my mountain experiences! I came to clearly understand what I'd always suspected. While the summit of any mountain was the sweetest prize, for me it was not the main game. Indeed the summit could almost be an anti-climax. The thrill was in the fight to get there. The camaraderie of shared adversity, the exuberance of overcoming seemingly impossible challenges, the thrill of life after escaping death's clutching fingers—these were the real rewards. And only the high mountains could provide the intensity of that experience.

To hell with my career, I decided. I didn't just *want* to climb; I *needed* to.

*

Maurice Herzog, the leader of the French expedition that had made the first ascent of Annapurna in 1950, said afterwards that Annapurna was a treasure on which he should live the rest of his days. It was a treasure for me also, but I knew I could not live out the rest of my days on that experience alone. Or even on all the experiences I'd had to that point. I had moved beyond being an amateur enthusiast. I was addicted. To the beauty, the thrill and the savagery, even to the pain. I wanted more.

I didn't want to die—indeed, I was more focused on managing risk than ever—but that just added to the game. For an objective to be worthwhile, it had to have risk. Without it, I might as well have quit climbing and become one of those I pitied in the office. There was no question that I wanted to finish my 8000er project; it had been hanging around my neck for long enough. But over and above everything else, I just wanted to get back to high altitude. I threw myself into planning the next climb.

With twelve 8000ers under my belt, only Makalu and Shishapangma remained. Shishapangma I knew well, but Makalu, the fifth-highest mountain in the world, had quite a tough reputation. It was also the mountain that had seen the demise of my friend David Hume in 1995.

Before I could get too far into planning, I needed to repair my relationship with Julie. For several years she'd wanted to join me on an expedition. I'd always resisted, firstly because I didn't want the distraction from my goal of summitting the mountain, and secondly because I felt that it would be an awful thing for my partner to have to walk out from a base camp on her own if I was killed on the climb. I decided to compromise on my principles, though, and agreed to take Julie to Shishapangma for the 2007 post-monsoon season. I didn't really anticipate summitting with her but thought that she might enjoy the expedition experience. I still hoped to summit but expected it would be on my own.

The trip did not start well. In Nyalam, Tibet, we shared a hotel with several other climbers who were also heading to Shishapangma. One of them had developed a nasty hacking cough a couple of days earlier. When Julie and I returned from an acclimatisation walk, we learned that he'd literally coughed himself to death, having ruptured an internal organ. I could not think of a more depressing and lonely death than dying like that in a squalid hotel room on your own without even having seen the mountain that had brought you to your end.

At Shishapangma the weather was woeful and we didn't get too far up the mountain. Constant heavy snow prevented any real climbing. Julie and I spent more time in our base-camp tent than on the mountain, but it was a fun, although very expensive way to relax and spend some time together. The most exciting part of the expedition came when Julie insisted on trying to rescue a Tibetan mastiff that had somehow become trapped in an ice gully on the glacier.

After hearing its yelps and going to investigate, we saw the poor mutt running back and forth, having no way to climb out. With a savage mauling on the cards from the panicked pooch, not to mention the very real threat of rabies, I was happy to let our Tibetan yak herders take care of it, given that it belonged to them. Julie, however, insisted that I lower her into the gully so she could tie a rope around the monster and I could haul it to the surface— What could go wrong? 'Lower me down, lower me down!' I lowered.

Naturally, as soon as Julie was at the bottom, the dog, which was one and a half times her size, started snarling and gnashing its teeth as it advanced towards her. With new instructions issued instantly—'Pull me out, pull me out!'—I then had to heave and haul her up the ice slope before the mastiff made a meal of her. It was duly rescued by our Tibetan yak herders.

We also provided a bit of assistance to a climber who had descended from the mountain confused and slurring his words— clear signs of cerebral oedema. I administered dexamethasone and within a few hours he was back to normal. Our own climb, however, ended with me going no higher than Camp 1. Shishapangma 4, Andrew 0.

*

While the trip with Julie had been good for our relationship, it hadn't been a serious attempt on the mountain. By the beginning of 2008 I was ready to hit the hills again with a vengeance. After the stress of Annapurna the year before, I wanted to go on an expedition with a small and skilled team of friends, rather than a large and unwieldy group. More than anything, I wanted to enjoy the climb. I invited Neil Ward and Hector Ponce de Leon to join me, and both accepted.

Although Shishapangma remained an elusive summit for me, it was still the lowest of the 8000ers and I felt that it could be climbed as preparation for a higher, tougher mountain. We therefore decided to climb Shisha in April 2008, before travelling to Nepal for a quick, well-acclimatised ascent of Makalu in May. It would be a similar approach to my Shishapangma-Annapurna expedition of the previous year.

Before meeting the guys in Kathmandu, I set out on my usual two-week acclimatisation and fitness trek. I planned to push myself over long distances and as many high passes for as many hours a day as possible. I wanted my body to hurt and to respond to the altitude. Julie joined me for the acclimatisation trek. She was fit and motivated, and her passion for adventure travel and the Himalaya hadn't been diminished by our unsuccessful expedition the previous year. Trekking was a much less intense way to spend some time together, although the relationship nearly came to an end on one particularly hard day.

We had trekked from the remote and beautiful village of Gokyo, over a high snow-covered pass known as the Cho La. Most parties making the crossing stop at a little outpost a couple of kilometres below the pass. Julie knew that I wanted to walk hard and agreed to keep going to the next village, Lobuche, which was several hours further on. That meant a long day, perhaps 20 kilometres, most of it at 4000 to 5000 metres in altitude. I knew that we should stop, because I could see that Julie was tired, but I really wanted to push myself.

About an hour before we reached Lobuche, poor Jules hit the wall. She'd used every last ounce of her energy and just sagged to the ground. It was my fault, and I knew it. Luckily, I had a small chocolate bar. The sugar revived her and she was able to continue, although I paid the price by having to carry both of our heavy rucksacks for the final kilometres. Oh well, it was good training!

In Kathmandu a week later, I met Hector and Neil while Julie flew home to Australia. We organised our equipment and bought food and fuel for the two mountains. However, the world of international politics was about to conspire against us. It was 2008, the year of the Beijing Olympics, and the Chinese authorities wanted the Olympic torch to be carried to the summit of Mount

Everest. Not only did they refuse permission to foreign expeditions to Everest, in order to allow their own expedition to proceed uninhibited, they closed all the mountains in Tibet, including Shishapangma. I suppose they didn't want any pesky foreigners waving 'Free Tibet' flags around on Tibetan mountaintops.

Rather than actually declining applications for Tibet permits that season, the Chinese Mountaineering Association simply 'delayed' the issue of permits. After a week in Kathmandu, during which we were repeatedly told 'maybe tomorrow', we decided to stop wasting our time and get some acclimatisation. We went trekking for a week in the Langtang Valley, close to the Kathmandu Valley.

This is a beautiful trek and provides quite a range of environments. A jarring 12-hour jeep ride over deeply potholed and rutted dirt roads was followed by a steep and steamy walk uphill through thick forest, heavy with humidity. We were soon drenched in perspiration. Monkeys screeched overhead, and the impenetrable foliage above us blocked any relief from the cooler air above.

The next morning, after a dawn start, we pushed ourselves hard to climb out of the valley before the heat caught us again. The vegetation thinned and soon we were walking on alpine trails, the jagged peaks of the Langtang Himal looming ahead, with crisp, cool skies above and stunning mountain vistas all around.

At the head of the valley we reached the village of Langtang, a collection of twenty or more teahouses. We selected one without other trekkers and were soon ordering food and hot drinks. Teahouses had evolved considerably since tourism came to Nepal. Originally, they were just rudimentary rural houses from which porters and other locals could purchase a simple cup of tea and *dhal baht*, and sleep near the fire, as they traversed the country by its myriad trails. With trekkers came money, and soon teahouses in the more popular valleys were being purpose-built with small rooms, bunks, and even tables and chairs. Menus increasingly catered for western tastes, with spaghetti, apple pie and beer replacing the traditional rice, lentils and *rakshi* (a traditional homemade spirit). Having pushed ourselves hard on the walk in, we were happy to enjoy the comforts on offer.

Over the next few days we trekked up nearby hills to gain a little altitude and test our fitness, returning each evening for a hearty meal and a good night's sleep. After three nights we descended to the road head and endured the backbreaking drive back to the city. Upon our return, though, the stalling by the Chinese Mountaineering Association continued: it was soon clear that no permits would be forthcoming that season. We decided to proceed directly to Makalu.

*

At 8481 metres, Makalu stands alone and proud on the border of Nepal and Tibet, just 19 kilometres south-east of Mount Everest. A beautiful four-sided pyramid with impossibly sharp and jagged ridges at each corner, it is one of the most striking of the 8000ers.

Despite (or perhaps because of) its proximity to Everest, it received scant attention as other 8000ers were successfully climbed. A reconnaissance expedition that included Edmund Hillary visited the area in 1952, but the first real attempt on the mountain didn't occur until the pre-monsoon season of 1954. Named the California Himalayan Expedition to Makalu, its members included Willi Unsoeld, who would become a household name among climbers for his first ascent, with Thomas Hornbein, of the very technical West Ridge of Everest in 1963. In 1976 he joined with his daughter, Nanda Devi Unsoeld, and others to climb her namesake mountain, Nanda Devi, in India. Tragically, Nanda Devi Unsoeld perished during that expedition. Willi continued to climb, but he died in an avalanche in 1979 on Mount Rainer in Washington, United States.

Also on Makalu in the spring of 1954 was an expedition led by Hillary, who by then was a household name because of his Everest climb the year before. Hillary's expedition did not fare so well this time. Two members of the team, Jim McFarlane and Brian Wilkins, fell into a crevasse. They both survived, but McFarlane was severely frostbitten and lost part of his feet and fingers. Hillary broke several ribs during the rescue and became so ill that he had to be evacuated.

A French expedition in the pre-monsoon of 1955 saw the first ascents of the mountain. Lionel Terray, already a revered lion of the mountaineering world, reached the summit on 15 May 1955 with his teammate Jean Couzy. Expedition leader Jean Franco and Guido Magnone, along with Gyaltsen Norbu Sherpa, summitted the next day, followed by four other team members a day later. This was the largest number of climbers from a 'first ascent' expedition to go to the summit—a particularly impressive achievement given the technical difficulties, constant wind and altitude.

The trek to Makalu is tough, traversing numerous passes and deep gorges. At some points you can see your day's destination just over the other side of a valley, and you might reasonably think that it looks close. The trek to get there, though, requires a steep, seemingly endless descent into a gorge, followed by a tortuous climb of a thousand metres or more up the far side. By the time you reach your destination, your leg muscles are quivering with exhaustion. After a full ten hours of hard slog, it is demoralising to see that you've only progressed towards Makalu's Base Camp by a few short kilometres. But you are pretty fit by the time you saunter into that camp a couple of weeks later.

The downside of the trek, though, is that it has a reputation for porter strikes and demands for increased wages. Several expeditions have failed even to reach the mountain. To avoid that issue, we booked a large Russian Mi-17 helicopter to fly us and our equipment from Lukla to Base Camp. However this too, carried risks.

A number of these helicopters appeared in Nepal after the breakup of the Soviet Union, but over the years most have been lost through crashes in the treacherous flying conditions of the Himalaya. Indeed, the flight to Makalu Base Camp is one of the most difficult, as the route penetrates a narrow gorge enclosed between the walls of giant mountains. A few years earlier, one of the same helicopters had disappeared there with a full load of Sherpa passengers, never to be found. Still, the flight seemed a better option than the trek, given how much time we'd already lost while trying to get a Shishapangma permit.

We first flew by light plane to Lukla, where we waited for our scheduled helicopter flight. The next morning we were told that our flight had been put back three days because the helicopter was being used by the Nepali government to collect ballot boxes from the recent national election. We used the time to train on the steep mountain tracks that crisscrossed the surrounding hills, which I'd never previously had the time to explore. Three days later, the chopper arrived.

Our flight was to be the second trip of the morning, since another expedition had also booked the helicopter to Base Camp. We filmed the first team take off, then sat back to await the chopper's return in an hour or so. After two hours and four cups of tea, it had not appeared. Three hours and six cups of tea later, it had still not returned and we went in search of answers. It had crash-landed at Makalu Base Camp. While no one had been injured, the helicopter was inoperable, probably for several months. That left just one operating helicopter big enough to ferry us and our equipment in all of Nepal.

Our trekking agent contacted the owners of that last chopper and was told that we'd be able to access it in another four days. We considered whether to give up on the flight and make the long trek, but the advice I'd received from climbers who'd done that was to avoid the porter problems at all costs. So we took the risk and waited for the helicopter. In the meantime, we hiked in the surrounding hills to keep fit and acclimatised, and drank beer to give ourselves more reason to go hiking to keep fit.

The risk and the beer paid off, and after a full week in Lukla, we were finally able to experience one of the most spectacular flights in the world. Because of the unpredictable winds, the high altitude and the tough flying conditions, the helicopter, which could carry 4 tonnes at sea level, would only take a load of 1600 kilograms in total—passengers and equipment combined. Given the recent and previous accidents, we were happy to comply. The helicopter swooped over Himalayan passes, past massive mountain walls that towered thousands of metres above us, and along seemingly bottomless gorges with thundering mountain rivers pounding down below—probably not the place to run out of gas.

We were deposited onto an open rocky plain at the base of a glacier, immediately below the south ridge of Makalu. Known as Hillary Base Camp, the site is still a day's trek below the actual Base Camp for our intended route on the north side of the mountain, but it provided a suitable landing place for the helicopter and a safe altitude for us to spend a few days furthering our acclimatisation.

While there, we took the opportunity to examine the chopper that had crashed a week earlier and now sat forlornly on the cold glacier. It had come in too fast, hit hard and broken the undercarriage. Another climber showed me a video of the accident. It appeared that the helicopter was lucky not to have broken in two, such was the speed at which it hit the ground.

After a few days we trekked to our Base Camp, accompanied by a small team of porters. We couldn't take all our loads with us, so we prioritised them to allow us to start climbing with the bare essentials while the rest of the expedition stores were brought up over the next week.

To save costs, we'd arranged to share camp logistics with a Kazakhstani team. Not finding them at the Hillary Base Camp, we were intrigued to learn that they'd already moved up to the higher Base Camp—they'd been there for over a week. Virtually without food, fuel or equipment, they'd survived on charity from other climbers. Undaunted, they'd already started their climb and established their lower camps on the mountain. I soon came to understand the driving force within the team. Their leader was Denis Urubko, a highly accomplished 8000-metre alpinist who had a bucketload of tough climbs to his credit.

We were also sharing our permit with Portugal's João Garcia, with whom I'd climbed on Nanga Parbat in 1996 and Kanchenjunga in 2006. João had a Belgian climbing partner, Jean-Luc. Initially we considered climbing together as a team of five, but a clash of personalities early in the expedition obliged us to stay separate.

The climbing, at least at first, was easy and we made quick progress. Hector and Neil were good teammates. Hector was a true comedian—no matter how exhausted, he always had a joke to suit the situation. Neil was uncomplaining and quick to take on chores, like setting up the tent or collecting snow. I found it very motivating to share an expedition with like-minded souls who truly enjoyed just being on the mountain—none of us was there for self-aggrandisement or sponsorship endorsements.

The climbing was fantastic. The route was interesting and varied, with steep snow and ice sections, rock steps and lots of exposure. I was in my element and buzzed with adrenaline as we climbed higher and higher, jumping crevasses and forcing our way through the mountain's barriers. My entire focus was on the climb, with the dullness of normal life forgotten. Everest stood just a few kilometres away, and we were treated to extraordinary views of its remote Kanshung Face and the Mother Goddess in all her moods.

Our focus was interrupted one night when we cooked up a packet of tom yum Thai soup. High altitude affects your taste-buds, so that nothing is very appetising and most things taste bland. When we'd shopped for the expedition in Kathmandu, we'd thought the tom yum soup might be tangy enough to have some flavour. But as we ate it, I had no idea whether it had any flavour or not because it simply blew our heads off. At minus 20 degrees Celsius, the sweat ran off us. Snow never tasted so good!

The real problem on this expedition, though, was that we were constantly sick from colds and flus. Hector was the worst affected, but Neil and I were also knocked down at different times. No amount of antibiotics seemed to clear them up. Antibiotics don't work as well at altitude, and they also leave you more susceptible to other infections. Hector lurched from one chest infection to another, never quite getting on top of them. It affected his fitness and, understandably, his morale.

Despite these challenges, we progressed up the mountain until we were ready for a summit push in mid May. While resting at Base Camp, however, Hector and I became sick again. Days ticked by and so did the good weather. Worried that he'd miss his summit chance, Neil set out for the top on his own. I didn't see any need to rush, though. Julie was sending me weather forecasts by SMS from Australia, and I judged that the best weather would come on 21 May.

*

On 17 May Hector and I started out from Base Camp and climbed directly to Camp 2. We continued up to Camp 3 on 18 May, where we stopped for a day while strong winds pounded the upper slopes of the mountain. Several climbers challenged the winds and went for the top the next day. As Hector and I sheltered in our tent, a number of them, including Neil, returned dejectedly to join us, having been defeated by the wind. Some were frostbitten but, thankfully, not Neil.

Hector and I pushed up to Camp 4 on 20 May. The next day, on a brutally cold morning, we set out for the summit at 3.45 a.m.

This was quite a late start, given the long climb ahead of us and the forecast for strong wind around midday, but it was just too cold to leave any earlier. We needed the sun. Even so, I almost instantly lost the feeling in my toes. My high-altitude boots were rated to minus 40 degrees Celsius but seemed to have no effect that morning.

While the slope wasn't too steep, Hector quickly dropped behind. It was obvious that he'd been severely weakened by the perpetual colds and flus he'd suffered. We kept climbing, but when I stopped around 6.30 a.m. to rewarm my frozen feet, I could see that Hector was finished. At 8100 metres he turned back. This was a great disappointment to him; he really wanted to summit. His departure also meant I was on my own for the rest of the climb, and my safety net and the camaraderie of the climb went with him.

Such was the bitter cold that morning that I came close to turning around myself. The usual toe wriggling did nothing to get the blood flowing. For a full thirty minutes I swung my legs back and forth, trying to force some blood down so that I could regain just the slightest feeling in them. Normally I can feel a bit of movement in the joints of my toes even when the toes have lost all sensation, but on this occasion I couldn't feel anything at all. I knew I was on the very precipice of frostbite. The summit wasn't worth a smaller shoe size, I decided, but just when it seemed that I would have to forgo the top and retreat to the warmth of the tent, I felt a slight twinge and knew that my toes would stay attached for a while longer.

The excruciating pain of blood returning to my severely frozen feet was almost crippling, though, and I had to clench my teeth to stop from crying out as I buckled over my ice axe. Wave after painful wave swept over me and I could do nothing except curse. After a few minutes it passed and I could breathe freely again. On with the climb. I started up the steep rock and ice slope, climbing quickly to keep the blood flowing to my feet.

There were two other climbers going for the top that day: a Czech named Radek, whom I soon overtook, and another man who was coming up behind me. He was making very quick progress and was actually catching up. I realised that he was using oxygen, and as he caught me I saw that he had a new type of oxygen mask. It turned out to be Ted Atkins, the British climber for whom I had searched for and eventually sourced an oxygen bottle on Mount Everest in 2004. An engineer, he'd since invented his more efficient mask and regulator system for the oxygen bottles that are used in the Himalaya, and he was testing it out. Clearly, it worked well.

We rested together on a little ledge. To save weight, I left my pack and a water bottle there, then led off and climbed towards the summit ridge. It was fantastic climbing. We scrambled over and around rocky outcrops, linking short snow ramps and tiptoeing up occasional ice patches. The sun shone, the snow sparkled and Everest glittered in the distance. It was great to be alive! This was my environment, climbing hard but smoothly, the whole world dropping below me, my goal just another hour or two's effort away.

My exuberance was interrupted when, about 10 metres from the ridge, my left boot suddenly felt quite light. I looked down and saw that I'd lost my crampon, which had dropped into the snow about 8 metres down the face. The loss of a crampon can be devastatingly dangerous, particularly on steep rock and ice. Without it, I was at great risk of slipping off the face. Luckily, Ted was below me, and was able to recover the crampon. While I refixed it to my boot as securely as possible, he led through and up to the ridge. I joined him there a few minutes later and we sat together, enjoying the sun's life-giving warmth. We couldn't stop too long, though, as we anticipated strong winds around midday.

We started the final traverse along the summit ridge to the top. Ted took off at a great pace, supercharged by his diet of oxygen. It's incredible the difference it makes. He was stronger, warmer and faster than I was, despite the additional weight of the oxygen bottle.

Radek was well behind us, so Ted and I continued along the ridge. We climbed for ten minutes or so, and then there was a short, steep step up a rocky outcrop. The left side of the ridge was corniced, with a very steep drop down. Ted went up the snow and around the rocky outcrop—a false summit. As I followed, I looked back and photographed Radek on the ridge. It was as if he was walking on a strip of snow suspended in the sky, with fluffy clouds all around and below him. Spectacular!

Once over the false summit, I expected to have to down-climb a little before ascending to the true summit, but it was just a delicate snow traverse with a short rise at the end. Ted was approaching the top, so I photographed him and then traversed over. I arrived about 11.15 a.m., seven and a half hours after setting out. That's a day's work in the public service. *Where does the time go*, I wondered, *when you are just putting one foot in front of the other?*

On top, I stood for Ted to take a photo, and then I unfurled two small strings of prayer flags that Julie and I had bought in Namche Bazaar during our trek. They had been blessed by a lama during our puja ceremony.

The summit was steep, snowy and small. There were some other prayer flags there, so I tied mine onto them. I pulled out my Thuraya satellite phone and called Julie. It was hard to talk as I was puffing hard, but it was great to speak to her from the top. I also put in a call from the very summit to Kelly Higgins-Devine, an afternoon radio host from ABC Radio in Queensland. I'd promised to make the call if I could, as Kelly had followed my climbs with interest for a number of years. I think she was more excited than I was and she cut into her normal program to do the interview live.

By this time the wind was whipping me and it was time to get down. It took just two hours to descend to Camp 4, where Hector was waiting. Despite his own disappointment and exhaustion, he kindly started up the stove and made me some drinks before we packed up and dropped down to the greater safety of Camp 3. The following day we descended to Base Camp.

Poor Hector was despondent at not having reached the summit. Normally, he was a very strong and fast climber, but he just couldn't beat the infections on this trip. Neil, too, was disappointed but pragmatic. He had achieved his own altitude record and learned a lot more about climbing at high altitude. We would climb together again.

When we reached Kathmandu, I was a completely different person to the recluse who'd hidden from others after Annapurna the previous year. I was on a massive high. Makalu had been the ideal high-altitude experience: tough conditions, challenging climbing and brutally cold, but achievable, given the motivation. It was one of the most satisfying climbs I'd done. The perfect mountain. I'd felt so alive and happy during the climb that I was almost sorry it was over, despite being 12 kilograms lighter and struggling to climb a flight of stairs for the first couple of weeks back in civilisation.

As well as the summit, I also came away from the mountain with an empty oxygen bottle that was lying on the plateau at Camp 3. It was from the French expedition that had made the first ascent of Makalu in 1955—a real collector's item.

I knew with absolute certainty that I'd made the right decision to continue with my 8000er project. This was where I wanted to be. This was where I was most fulfilled. Bring on the next one, I thought. Shishapangma, of course, because Makalu had been the thirteenth 8000-metre peak I'd climbed.

14

FINISH LINE

Is this the summit, crowning the day? How cool and quiet! We're not exultant; but delighted, joyful; soberly astonished ... Have we vanquished an enemy? None but ourselves. Have we gained success? That word means nothing here.

George Mallory

THIRTEEN DOWN, one to go. In April 2009 Hector and I returned to Kathmandu with the intention of finishing off Shishapangma. Our trekking agent applied for the permit through the Chinese Embassy in Kathmandu but, just as in 2008, we were stuffed around. Every day the response was 'maybe tomorrow'. It was never 'no', although clearly they had no intention of issuing us a permit with no reason given. After two weeks we gave up and went home. Shishapangma 5, Andrew zip.

I later heard that several climbers on the 2008 Chinese Olympic torch expedition had died in the attempt, and that the Chinese were back on the mountain to recover the bodies before any foreigners discovered them. Of course, that was just a rumour.

Julie wasn't with me this time because we'd broken up a few months after the Makalu expedition in 2008. It was a great shame. We'd been together for five years, and she'd always been accepting of my absences for 8000-metre expeditions, and of the dangers they posed. In many of my earlier relationships, including in my marriage, I'd found that my partner had been attracted to the idea of being with a climber but less enamoured with the reality of it, with the regular three-month absences and no guarantee of a safe return. Those relationships had ended rather quickly. Others had ended before they'd even started: 'Mountain climber? Ah, no thanks. I need a father for my children.' Julie had been the exact opposite. She'd wanted to get married but with my increasing desire to keep climbing and adventuring around the world, as well as a previous failed marriage, I wasn't yet ready to make that commitment again. So we'd separated.

*

In September 2009 I was ready to tackle Shishapangma—again. Hector wasn't able to return in the post-monsoon season, but Neil Ward was keen, so we teamed up. I liked climbing with Neil. He wasn't a big man, but he was hardy and dependable. When we'd met on this same mountain in 2007 and agreed to climb together, we'd clicked. And when he'd stopped from exhaustion during our summit attempt, he hadn't run down the mountain to safety but had waited for me, freezing, while I pushed on and had a crack at the top. If I'd needed help to descend, he'd have been there. He was solid.

This time around our team was a little bigger. We were joined by Neil's girlfriend, Louise, and Kinga Baranowska from Poland. Kinga had reached the summit of six of the world's fourteen 8000-metre mountains, but I hadn't climbed with her before. Through bitter experience I was reserved about climbing with people I didn't know, but her boyfriend, Ferran, who'd introduced me to 'glacier golf' on Annapurna in 2007, was a highly experienced climber and asked me take her.

Louise wasn't a climber at all, and I had strong reservations about her coming along. Girlfriends could be a distraction when the going was good, but if the relationship became strained for any reason it could mean the end of an expedition. And that was unacceptable to me, because I was there to climb the mountain and finish what had become a 16-year project. Only the mountain was permitted to stop me. As it turned out, though, Lou was good fun and a great support to Neil. I was relieved and happy to eat humble pie.

On this expedition, we were climbing the 'wrong' side of the mountain. During the post-monsoon season the steep South Face is usually the better side because it is clad with sufficient snow to make it climbable, while the easier-angled North Face often has too much snow on it, making it more avalanche-prone. My own previous attempts on the North Face in the pre-monsoon had been stopped for that very reason. The post-monsoon is even worse. But the South Face is very tough and has killed some of the world's best, so only the strongest teams should attempt it. Although Neil and I had climbed with each other previously, we hadn't done anything really technical together, so we hadn't yet developed a smooth and efficient climbing style. The South Face of Shishapangma wasn't the place to develop that efficiency. With Kinga in the team, the problem was compounded.

There were other considerations too. Work demands at home prevented me from undertaking my usual acclimatisation trek before the expedition, meaning we'd have to acclimatise on the mountain. We'd need to make multiple trips up and down to achieve that. The South Face was too steep to do that safely—really, you had to be fully acclimatised before setting foot on it. Despite the avalanche danger, the North Face seemed a better choice this time.

Lastly, but perhaps most importantly, I obeyed my gut instinct. I had an inexplicable but clear uneasy feeling about the south side that year. Listening to that inner voice had saved my life on several earlier expeditions and I wasn't about to ignore it this time. We would climb the North Face.

There were several other expeditions at Base Camp when we arrived in mid September. While they all planned to climb the usual route to the false Central Summit on the North Ridge, Neil and I wanted to attempt the route we'd planned to climb in 2007, before Neil had become sick. We knew that almost every expedition that had climbed to the Central Summit, including my own previous attempts, had judged the jagged ridge from there to the real summit to be beyond their ability. Our plan was to avoid the Central Summit altogether, by crossing the North Face's lower slopes, away from the ridge that led to the Central Summit, and much lower than the Chinese traverse route on the upper slopes, and then to climb a direct line up the North Face, which would take us straight to the real summit. While this seemed an obvious route, it wasn't that simple.

To get to that direct line, we would have to traverse the broad North Face, at a height of 7500 metres, which was both undercut by crevasses and threatened from above by massive ice cliffs that could collapse on to us at any moment. Above the ice cliffs was an enormous and steep slope, heavily laden with snow, which could also release without warning and avalanche down the face. This was the slope that I'd tried to cross on previous expeditions and which, on each occasion, had fractured and avalanched.

If we survived our traverse without being wiped off the mountain, we'd then have some steep climbing over terrain about which we knew nothing. At the very least, it would be double the distance of the normal summit day, forcing us to spend way more time at extreme altitude than we'd have preferred. Our chances of success were low. Our chances of survival were a lot less than if we were climbing the normal route. But we were there to succeed and if taking additional risk was necessary, then so be it. We just had to ensure the cost of that risk didn't become too high.

*

After our arrival at Base Camp, we spent a few days sorting our equipment and studying the mountain to get a feel for the weather patterns and the snow conditions. The 2009 post-monsoon season was a good one—dry and clear, with snow on the upper slopes that appeared, through our binoculars, to be consolidated. That meant the risk of avalanche was decreased. We were hopeful but not over-confident about our chances.

Over the next week Neil, Kinga and I hauled tents, ropes, food, fuel and all the other essential climbing equipment up the lower slopes of the mountain, establishing our Camp 1 at 6250 metres, then Camp 2 at 6750 metres. Our lack of acclimatisation hurt us and we suffered terrible altitude headaches each time we slept at a higher camp. But we were pushing ourselves up the mountain more quickly than recommended, so headaches such as these, while uncomfortable, were to be expected. Acclimatisation demands time and patience and we had neither, as we'd arrived relatively late in the season.

Most teams had commenced a month or so before ours. We had only three to four weeks, at most, to complete what would normally be a two-month expedition. Early October would see the arrival of such violent high-altitude winds that tents on the mountain would be shredded and unprepared climbers severely frostbitten. Or worse. As if to confirm our concerns, just a few days after our arrival the Spanish climber Juanito Oiarzabal, one of the most experienced high-altitude mountaineers in the world, left for home after a failed summit attempt.

'You are too late,' he told us. 'The weather is finished.'

I disagreed. The conditions to that point had been extraordinarily good for the time of the year, with day after day of low wind and clear skies. Forecasts for the region indicated that we still had a few more good days. My own assessment of the local conditions agreed. But we knew the good weather couldn't last. A strong storm front was due to hit the area on 3 October and it would bring hurricane-force winds, brutal cold and heavy snow. It would likely spell the end of the climbing season. We were keen to have a crack at the summit before the inevitable change.

Mountaineering is a high-risk game, and rarely is it simple. To succeed, or at least to survive, careful risk management is vital. We needed to start our summit attempt as late as possible to ensure the best acclimatisation but not so late as to be caught by the approaching gale. We therefore decided to begin our summit climb from Base Camp on 29 September. If the predicted bad weather came early, we'd abort the attempt and descend. If all went well, we'd reach the top on 2 October, one day before the storm front was forecast to hit. If possible, we'd continue our descent from the summit through Camp 3 and down to Camp 2 on the same day so that, if the blizzard trapped us there, we'd at least be at a safer altitude. After a night of rest at that camp, we could climb down to Base Camp in the storm, with every descending step bringing the benefit of warmer, more oxygen-saturated air. If we had to stay at Camp 3, then so be it, but descent from that altitude would be riskier in a storm.

Weather issues can generally be managed, even if it means abandoning a summit attempt to retreat to safety. The real threat was severe altitude sickness, as we would be beginning our summit push just thirteen days after reaching Base Camp. Normally, I would reel at the thought of going for the top of an 8000-metre mountain so quickly, particularly as my advice to others has always been to spend a minimum of one month above 4000 metres before attempting the summit of one of these giants. But the approaching jet stream forced us to go sooner than we'd have preferred. If any of us succumbed to the effects of the altitude, the others would abandon the climb to get the victim down to safety.

Overall, it was a good plan but not infallible. This was high-altitude mountaineering, after all. And so it began.

Having spent a week on the mountain, we rested for several days at Base Camp, sleeping, eating and fanatically studying our planned route and the climate. I was tense. The next few days could see the conclusion of my 16-year quest to climb all of the world's highest mountains. The night before we began the climb, I started a frank discussion with Kinga about the need for us to better share the work of making the trail and carrying the equipment. It deteriorated into an argument and she withdrew from the summit attempt. That was not my intention, but secretly I was relieved, as I felt our planned route would be too long and difficult for her.

The next morning Neil and I set out from Base Camp, and over three days we climbed the 2.5 vertical kilometres to Camp 3 at 7450 metres. Still feeling strong after setting up our camp, we climbed another hundred metres higher—one hour of climbing at that altitude—so that we could inspect our intended route across the mountain's massive and highly avalanche-prone North Face. We would be climbing 'off the beaten track', and we knew that our best chance for success and survival was to climb fast and light and to be precise with our route finding. We would have to reach the summit by midday if we were to have enough time to race back down to the relative safety of Camp 3 by nightfall, and ideally, continue down to Camp 2.

As we gazed across the face, we spotted a gap in the line of distant ice cliffs that we would have to penetrate, a chink in the mountain's armour that, just conceivably, might allow us access onto the upper slopes and an almost direct line to the summit ridge. It would be steep and highly exposed, but the snow appeared firm. We had great hopes that it would mean fast climbing and reduced avalanche danger.

That night, in our tiny summit tent, it was impossible to sleep. We were crammed together with all our equipment and had room only to lie head to foot. We nibbled biscuits and a little cheese and washed it down with lukewarm tea but had no real appetite. We were nauseated from the altitude and buzzing with nervousness and excitement for the following day's climb.

Occasionally we dozed, but the night passed slowly. From time to time I poked my head out to look at the sky. It remained clear. At 2.30 a.m. I lit the stove and started the laborious process of melting snow for a hot drink and to fill our water bottles. Every movement coated us in a miserable frosting of frozen condensation as it fell from the tent walls.

We dressed in our clumsy, oversized boots, put new batteries into our headlamps and checked our equipment. I took a GPS reading of our location in case we had to return at night or in bad weather. The breeze was light and the temperature surprisingly warm, perhaps minus 10 degrees Celsius.

I debated how much clothing to wear. Too few layers and the extreme cold we might experience near the summit could kill me, but too many and the heat build-up could be debilitating enough to stop me from reaching the summit. That was unacceptable. It would be at least twelve hours of nonstop extreme physical exertion to get to the summit, I knew, so I opted for one less layer.

I would like to have set out for the summit around midnight, but we were attempting an unfamiliar route and didn't know the terrain. We needed the light of dawn to see the way, so we departed at 4 a.m., just as the first hint of colour touched the eastern sky. We started across the mountain face but very quickly found ourselves in depressingly deep and unstable snow. It was impossible to progress, and after thirty minutes we reversed back to our tent.

We decided to try again from higher up the ridge, so we reascended to our viewing point of the evening before. Thankfully, the snow was firmer there. We moved towards an area of crevasses, the rope between us a lifeline. A few years earlier, a Russian had climbed into this area alone, never to be seen again. His memorial plaque now sits at Base Camp.

Once past the crevasses, we edged onto steeper terrain under the main face. The threat here was that the face might avalanche. If it did, we'd be swept down the mountain to certain death, buried beneath tonnes of ice. We climbed fast to get to the far side and out from underneath that hazard. After two hours we were across, and we found the vital weakness through the ice cliffs above, a zigzagging path that opened onto the uppermost slopes of the mountain.

We knew that our survival would depend on finding the same route back through the ice cliffs as we descended from the summit. I attempted to mark the point with my GPS, but the cliffs and the massive mountain face above us interfered with reception. After ten minutes I still couldn't get a reading, so we placed a bamboo marker wand in the snow instead.

The snow was much softer than we'd hoped for, and the climb became an exhausting struggle against gravity. We alternated leads every hour, taking turns to kick, plough and thrash our way up the steep slope until we could go no further, collapsing face forward, gasping for air, dizzy with altitude and faint from fatigue. Hour after hour our trail breaking continued. The ridge above seemed to taunt us but never come closer as we marked our apparently endless trail with bamboo wands every hundred metres or so. We lost track of time and just climbed mechanically, without talk or food or rest, our bodies begging us to stop and end the agony.

We'd hoped to reach the summit by midday, but already it was mid afternoon and we still had hours of climbing ahead of us. At best, we'd have a night-time descent—and that was if we reached the summit at all. Worse, the wind was increasing. Soon our fear of an early deterioration in the weather was realised. Thin cloud whipped over the ridge above us and the sky started to whiten.

Christ, I thought. *If this is tomorrow's storm arrived early, we're finished. It'll blow us off the hill. Another failure on this bastard of a mountain.* I willed the gods to hold back the storm and clawed more desperately at the snow slope above me. *Don't give up.*

Finally, at 4 p.m. we reached the top of the face at 7950 metres, where we rolled exhaustedly onto the ridge. We treated ourselves to an energy gel and a sip of water—my first since leaving the tent twelve hours earlier. Lunch over, we marked the point with another bamboo wand and pressed on.

The broad ridge on which we were standing sharpened as it rose, but it led directly to the top. Howling wind and swirling cloud afforded only glimpses of that elusive summit, just 80 metres above us. We tiptoed our way up the ridge, the mighty South Face sweeping precipitously down into dark cloud on our left.

I'd chosen to climb the North Face this expedition because it allowed us to acclimatise safely, even though the South Face offered a better chance of success in the post-monsoon season. It had been a risky decision because the North Face was more avalanche-prone, but my inner voice had warned me off the South Face this time. In this deteriorating weather, the technical South Face would have been agonisingly slow to descend. Deathly slow. Once again, my inner voice had saved me and, on this occasion, Neil also.

Just 20 metres below the summit, we met an obstacle: a long cornice of windblown ice that stood 2 metres high and ran along the ridge for more than 50 metres. It overhung both sides of the mountain and blocked our path completely. We couldn't climb onto it for fear of it collapsing—cornices are notoriously unstable. There was no way to traverse under it, either, on the vertical South Face. Our only chance was the North Face, which at that spot was almost as steep as the South Face, but at least it wasn't vertical. Neil, who'd adeptly led the way up the ridge, hesitated at this final hazard, quite understandably. But after five expeditions trying for this summit, I wasn't about to stop.

I pushed past, and crept delicately underneath the cornice. With each step the snow cracked and slid, with just the faintest whoosh, into the white void below. Neil followed carefully. If the whole face had slipped, we'd have gone with it. If the cornice above our heads had fractured, it would have buckled over and shoved us off the hill. *Gently, now, gently*, I told myself. We were so close.

I continued slowly, treading as lightly as I could. Then we were out from underneath it, and all that remained before us was the little summit block. I waited for Neil and we climbed onto it together. It was five minutes past five. The mountain dropped away from us on all sides. We'd done it!

What a relief. We knelt down against the wind and shook hands, then snapped a few quick photos and a little video. I wanted a photo of the ridge back to the Central Summit, but the cloud allowed only glimpses, so I took a GPS reading as well. Party over, we started down.

With this summit, I knew that I'd finished my 8000er project. I'd become one of the few people on Earth—just over a dozen—to have climbed each of the fourteen highest peaks in the world. But that was a distant thought and seemed barely relevant at the time. Neil and I were on the summit of a remote 8000-metre mountain. We had a long battle ahead of us to get back to our tent that night. As far as I knew, we were the only people on the hill. All other climbers were at Base Camp, which was days away. I couldn't allow myself to be distracted by egotistical self-congratulations. That could wait. The job was only half-done. With the summit under our belts, the only thing on my mind was survival.

The wind was strong and cold, and the daylight had started to fade. We had to get down fast. No matter what, we knew that we were going to be caught by darkness; it was just a matter of where. Being stuck high on a mountain in good weather was serious enough, but this wasn't good weather. It could have been the start of the next day's predicted blizzard. If we could find that zigzagging path back through the ice cliffs at the bottom of the face, we'd still have a chance of getting back to the tent that night by the light of our headlamps. If not, we'd be trapped above the cliffs without equipment.

In the cloud and the evening gloom, we climbed quickly but delicately down the ridge to the bamboo wand that indicated where we should drop back onto the face. Here the deep snow was forgiving. I knew that I could descend reasonably safely, so I plunged down as quickly as possible. The race was on.

I shoved my way down through the thigh-deep snow, the resistance tiring but manageable. The windblown snow had buried our tracks, and the increasing murkiness made it difficult to identify the mountain's features. Soon I couldn't see which way to go. The bamboo markers we'd placed throughout the climb should have been visible against the white background. We switched on our headlamps but the driving snow reflected the light back, blinding us.

Unlike on Kanchenjunga, where I'd been caught on the descent without any navigational markers, this time I was prepared. If we couldn't see the wands, we still had my GPS. I remembered having used it at the gap in the seracs on the climb up, earlier that day, so I was confident that it would show us the way home. For some reason, though, the GPS pointed sideways, across the face. I couldn't understand it. To get us through the seracs, it should have been pointing towards them.

This is the insidiousness of altitude. I'd forgotten that my attempt to record a position on the GPS on the way up hadn't worked. It was therefore pointing across the face to Camp 3, where I'd taken a reading before we'd set out that morning. The GPS was working fine, but I wasn't thinking clearly. We couldn't traverse to Camp 3 until we found that path down through the ice cliffs onto the snow face below.

We pressed on, pushing ourselves harder, having no time for rest. We searched desperately for some identifiable feature that might indicate the path before darkness sentenced us to a night of hell. Or a lifetime of it. Reeling with exhaustion, dehydrated and altitude-sick, we were fighting for our lives. But it was a fool's game. We'd lost the race.

At 7600 metres, we stopped. We debated the route but couldn't be sure of what we saw below us on the near-vertical slope. I felt we should traverse to the right, while Neil thought the opposite. Normally, I'd follow my instincts, but the GPS confusion caused me to doubt myself. To continue down-climbing now would put us in even greater danger—we'd either fall over the edge of one of the seracs below us or cause it to collapse with us on it. Dead either way. By myself, I might have taken the risk, but I had no right to risk Neil's life. We decided to bivouac.

*

Bivouac! How many was this now? My third? Yet again I would have to survive on the side of an 8000er without a tent, a sleeping bag, a stove, any food or auxiliary oxygen. It meant an extra night at high altitude, where every minute would bring me closer to the fatal onset of oedema. And on my last climb. The alternative was worse, though, so I resigned myself to it. *So be it*, I thought. *Just have to survive again.*

Neil was stoic and accepted the situation. We had no snow shovel, so we scraped a tiny ledge out of the steep snow slope with our ice axes, then sat on our backpacks for a tiny degree of insulation. I didn't expect to sleep, but just in case, I embedded the shaft of my ice axe into the snow and clipped my harness to it. Then I unstrapped my crampons from my boots and clipped them to the ice axe as well. Finally, I checked that all my layers of clothing were fully zipped up, and all pockets closed.

Our wait for the dawn began. This would be my longest bivouac on an 8000-metre peak. As we were on the north side of the mountain, above the bleak Tibetan plateau, we knew it would be fearsomely cold. I cinched my beefy down hood more tightly around my head and glanced at Neil, who was already hunched over, trying to conserve heat, cocooned in his own private world of suffering. With the end of my 8000er project so near, with victory so tantalising close, I was once again huddled, frozen, clinging to life and hope and a desire to end both the expedition and the entire project.

The mountain had played with us, taunting us with opportunity, tempting me with a goal that had consumed me for sixteen years. And now she was demanding her fee. Having summitted late in the day, we'd accepted that we would have to descend in darkness. But getting trapped at nearly 8000 metres with a blizzard forecast for the following day was not part of the plan. I'd experienced it before, and it wasn't fun.

The snow was still falling but the wind had steadied. It was 7.30 p.m.—nine and a half hours to go. It became bitterly cold, at least minus 20 degrees Celsius, and I regretted my decision to leave a layer of clothing in the tent that morning. Already the snow was several inches deep on my legs. But the wind was the real concern. It was forecast to increase to a gale. Until now it had mostly just snowed, but the snow had also been forecast for tomorrow, not tonight.

With my feet dangling over a precipice, for which the darkness was probably a blessing, I settled into my thoughts: *Lost, frozen, at night, at nearly 8000 metres, on near vertical terrain and a blizzard threatening. Chances of survival? Not high, I suppose. Be a shame if the dream ends here, so close to the end. Did I stuff up? No, we did it right, but we made our choice to push on late in the day and this is the result. So accept it and survive. Right.*

I'm lucky that way, I suppose. Once I've made a decision, I'm prepared to live with its consequences. There's no point in regretting it. It actually gives me strength and purpose. As I thought about our situation, it started to feel like a challenge: *Would I have the strength to handle the ramifications of my decisions?* The answer would be known in a few hours' time. In some perverse way, I even began to enjoy it. I didn't just want to win the fight, I wanted to *have* it—not so much for the victory but for the fight itself. I wanted to know if I could cope with it, if I was good enough.

I was cold. So sick of being cold. I wanted to sleep but didn't dare allow myself. I brushed more snow from the opening in the hood of my down suit and considered checking my watch but steeled myself for the inevitable disappointment. Bitter experience had taught me that time slows almost to a stop in bivouacs. The only thing that really continues at full pace is the pain.

I pulled my sleeve back down over the watch without looking and instead glanced up at the sky: still no moon. The snow continued to fall, but the cloud was patchy with an occasional glimpse of a star. Most importantly, the wind had not increased. I was already so frozen that any further deterioration of the weather would finish me. I glanced towards Neil, who was all but indistinguishable under a blanket of fresh snow. I asked if he was alive and received a grunt in reply. Still alive and still no complaints. Solid.

I drifted in and out of lucid thought, so cold that my water bottle froze inside my down suit. I'd carried two half-litre bottles through the day and had hardly touched them. As we'd settled down for the bivouac, Neil told me that he was out of water, so I'd given him one of mine. Now my remaining bottle had frozen, so it was yet another big summit day without a drink. My kidneys hurt. But so did my back and my head and my poor frozen feet. *Nothing you can do about it*, I told myself, *so just put up with it.*

My dehydration was causing me to cough a lot, and I spat out some great lumps. Some were like huge fur balls from deep down in my throat. They were so big and flesh-like that I thought I was actually coughing up bits of my throat.

I wiggled my toes but there was no feeling—I couldn't tell if they were moving or not. By now I'd made twenty-three 8000-metre expeditions without frostbite, and it was a record I wanted to maintain. I wiggled them harder. Come on, guys, just a few more hours. It's the last time, I promise! After ten minutes of flexing toes and swinging legs, I felt a very faint something. The feeling was so distant that I really didn't know if I was just imagining it. It was as though my toes had been wrapped in wool and stuffed inside wooden clogs.

The night seemed interminable. No words can really describe the misery, the endlessness. The wind picked up and then eased off. Icy snow flurries came and went. Stars appeared—and, with them, hope. But the cloud teased us and closed back over, as if it to say, 'Ha, sorry, mate, it isn't that easy. You want this summit? You want to claim all fourteen? Then you have to earn it. You have to pay a little more.'

I became angry. *Fine*, I thought. Anger cleared my head and brought back my focus. *Bring it on!* I would survive this night. I would succeed on this mountain. I would finish this project.

I shuffled around, forcing blood through my aching limbs, brushed yet more snow from my down suit and gazed out across Tibet. I looked for signs of life, of humanity. There were none, but I realised that it was now possible to distinguish a few features of the terrain way below us. It was getting fractionally, imperceptibly lighter, and I knew that we were on the home stretch.

*

When it was finally light enough for us to start down from our high-altitude perch I prodded Neil. We fought the stiffness in our limbs to reaffix our crampons, then donned our packs and began descending. We barely spoke a word but were grateful to be moving.

Very quickly we saw the route through the ice cliffs below us, and I realised that I'd been right after all about which way we should go. *Could have saved ourselves a cold night out*, I thought. *Whatever, we're alive.* The only thing that mattered now was to get back to our tent—to our stove, its fuel and the blissful nectar of freshly melted snow.

We tried to hurry but our exhaustion prevented it. Every few steps we'd stop, pant for breath, fight the urge to collapse and sleep, then push on. Gradually, we traversed back under the big seracs and down-climbed, slowly and painfully, to the camp. I was so tired that several times I just toppled sideways and fell like a tree into the snow.

When we finally staggered to our tent, it was 8.30 a.m., three hours after we'd set out from the bivouac. It had taken us longer to climb down from the bivouac point than to climb up to it the day before. But we were there and we were alive. Neil got the stove going.

I knew that our friends at Base Camp would be worried by our failure to make contact last night, so I dug out the radio and made a hoarse call. Immediately, we were answered and I heard whooping and crying and laughter in the background. I'd like to have done all three of those things myself but hadn't the energy.

Neil passed me a tepid cup of water. There were bits of food in it left over from a previous meal, and some oily film on the surface. I gulped it down—liquid gold. We rested and drank more. Slowly, as imperceptibly as that frozen dawn, we came back to life. More than anything, we wanted to sleep, but we couldn't. The forecast storm would soon be upon us and it had been snowing heavily since we arrived back at camp. We had to descend to a safer altitude where we could wait out any delays. We crammed our equipment haphazardly into our packs, struggled to lift them, and then lurched drunkenly down the mountain.

It took many hours to descend a distance that would normally have taken just a few. We were forced to stop at Camp 1 for another night because we simply couldn't go on. We slept as if in a coma. But we were alive.

The next day, as we trudged along the glacier, we were met by Kinga and Horia, a climber from another expedition, who escorted us back to Base Camp. It was good of them to help us, although I'd prefer to have finished the descent alone. For me, the climb wasn't over until I made that final step into Base Camp. After that I could relax, socialise and share the experience. Still, it was good to have the company and their excitement sparked us up a little. Despite all my expeditions and the previous bivouacs, this one had exhausted me to the core. I was almost asleep on my feet.

At Base Camp there were many backslaps and congratulations for us, but I quickly retired to my tent. I wasn't yet ready to switch off from the intensity of the experience. I was back in my cave, as I had been after Annapurna. But this time it was a good place, a private place, which only those who'd shared the experience, or lived through a similar one, could enter. I felt an indescribably strong inner glow. I felt sated, enriched and worthy. I had not conquered the mountain—or any other mountain, for that matter—but I'd faced the challenges it had thrown at me and overcome them. I'd tested myself to the limit and endured.

I felt simultaneously insignificant and equal with the mountain, although I knew that Shishapangma saw it differently. She had played with me, entertained herself with me, forced me to grovel to discover her secrets. With those dues paid, she had allowed me to know her. She had considered destroying me at the end, only to allow me, at the very last, to live. She had been in control, not me. We were not equals.

But I was alive and my senses were in overdrive. There was a small patch of semi-frozen grass at Base Camp—its fragrance seemed so strong that I could almost taste it. The stream that trickled past my tent was life itself, bubbling and splashing across the rocks. The clouds above me were more beautiful than I could describe, and I was warm. Warm!

Images rolled through my mind as I relived every moment of our summit day. I had a knot in my stomach, not from the hardship or danger but from the thrill of it. I was riding an internal wave of emotion and adrenaline.

I wasn't yet ready to think about the fact that I'd completed the fourteen 8000ers. At that point I was still in the zone on Shishapangma. This was the incredible buzz I'd felt after all my 8000-metre summits. The feeling was so powerful it blocked out all distractions. My whole existence seemed tangibly linked to the mountain, our energies blended.

Gradually, though, the adrenaline surge wore off and I came out of my cave and began re-engaging with the human world. And it was fun. I socialised with the other expeditions and regaled them with the story of our climb. After such a tough experience, to sit at Base Camp and watch other climbers prepare for their own assaults on the peak was immensely peaceful. I was excited for them, knowing the struggle they'd face, but knowing also that my battle was over. It had been a great fight, and I was relieved that I didn't have to re-enter the fray.

I don't think anyone really understood just how significant the summit of Shishapangma was for me—not because it was my fourteenth 8000er but because of the number of times I'd attempted it. Amazingly, it was my sixth attempt, if I counted the trip earlier that year when I hadn't even made it out of Kathmandu. Six! It seemed unbelievable that the lowest of the 8000ers could have caused me so much trouble. But I'd have attempted it sixteen times if I'd had to. Nothing in the world could have stopped me from returning until I finally succeeded.

As it was, Neil and I were the only climbers to reach the true summit of Shishapangma in 2009. Mine was also the first Australian ascent of the mountain, the sixth time that I'd made a first Australian ascent of an 8000-metre peak. That's a record that can never be broken. And I became not only the first Australian but also the first member of the British Commonwealth to have climbed all fourteen of the world's 8000-metre mountains.

Perhaps most satisfying of all, though, was that while Shishapangma was the final ascent in my project to climb all the 8000ers, it was Neil's first summit of an 8000-metre peak. He'd been a great expedition partner on three expeditions and had finally tasted his own success. I was pleased to have been part of his first triumph. It was time for me to hand over the baton to the next generation, and Neil was a perfectly appropriate person to hand it to.

And then it was time to go home.

15
THE NEXT STEP

*If adventure has a final and all-embracing motive, it is surely this: we
go out because it is our nature to go out, to climb mountains, and to
paddle rivers, to fly to the planets and plunge into the depths of the
oceans ... When man ceases to do these things, he is no longer man.*

Wilfred Noyce

LIFE, WHEN I returned to Australia in mid October, was a bit
of a whirlwind. I received hundreds of congratulatory emails
from people around the world, many of whom I'd never met but
who'd followed my climbing career. I was very touched by their
kind words. I was also presented with the Adventurer of the Year
award by the Australian Geographic Society. To be judged by my
peers as having achieved something worthwhile meant a lot to me.

After sixteen years, the wider media finally decided that it,
too, was interested in my 8000er project. I'd had a few genuinely
interested media followers over the years, but suddenly everyone
wanted to know what the view from Everest was like, how many
bodies I'd seen and how many near-death experiences I'd had.
Almost all the interviewers completely missed the point of why

I'd undertaken the climbs. Few asked about my motivation, the psychological challenges and rewards that I'd experienced, or the journey of self-discovery that the mountains had provided me.

One climbing website demanded a photo of Neil and me on the summit of Shishapangma, so that they could 'verify' our ascent—not that they'd have known it from any other summit. This really offended me. The successful ascents of all my other climbs had been well documented and witnessed by others—but now, on this last peak, my claim needed to be proven to some armchair climbers who reported on climbing rather than actually doing it? Were they really suggesting that I was going to lie about a summit when I'd made six separate attempts to achieve it? It just proved that these people didn't get the point of why I, and probably most other serious climbers, took on the big peaks. For me, it was specifically for the *challenge* of getting to the summit, not simply to *claim* that I'd reached it. The whole point was to see if I *could* do it. If I'd lied about this or any other summit, I'd have cheated myself of the answer to my own question.

I suspect the website just wanted our summit photo so they could have an exclusive for their website viewers, but I'd made a commitment to my sponsors to give them first rights to that picture. I had taken a GPS reading on Shishapangma's summit, however, so I downloaded the metadata from the GPS unit and sent it to the website. It wasn't what they wanted but it certainly proved that we'd reached the summit. I didn't hear from them again.

There was also some debate floating around the ether—again among armchair climbing website hosts—about whether or not Neil and I had completed a new route in our ascent of Shishapangma. On my blog I'd reported that I didn't know if we had. I thought we'd probably combined a couple of previously climbed lines at the bottom of the North Face; certainly the summit ridge had previously been climbed. The question revolved around our route on the face itself. The debate raged furiously among non-climbers—and, like those in the media, they missed the point.

Whether it was a new route, a variation of another route or just an old route mattered little to me. What mattered was that the climb and the bivouac had tested Neil and me to our limits. It had been an extraordinary expedition and the most fitting way possible to end my Summit 8000 project. Ultimately, though, the ascent of Shishapangma hadn't only been about completing the project. It had also been about climbing Shishapangma itself—meeting and overcoming that mountain's specific challenges and obstacles.

Each and every one of the 8000-metre giants I had summitted had been a glorious undertaking in itself. Each and every one had provided me with more personal challenge and self-knowledge than I could possibly have gained in any other field of endeavour. I was glad that there were only fourteen, as I was pretty worn out by the end, but the project had been about the challenge that each peak offered, not about the summits.

Time and again I'd put my life on the line to chase the four-teen, and in doing so I'd experienced life at its rawest. I'd tested myself in the most brutal way and survived. To continue when every fibre of your being is telling you to stop, when you are at your most desperate, is to know yourself. And to face extreme fear and the possibility of imminent death is to really know and appreciate life. I had lived. I felt fulfilled, sated and worthy. This was the reward for pushing myself so close to the edge.

After so many years, I'd come to crave this feeling. It was a feeling I'd experienced only when success had been hard fought for. Often it had come only at the very last minute, when all hope seemed lost and when I'd been forced to draw on an unknown inner strength in order to claw my way back from the very precipice of failure and disaster.

That was what motivated me to climb these giants. That was my answer to the perennial question: 'Why?' I climbed because the mountains allowed me to ask, and answer, my own question: 'Am I good enough?' The answer could not be known until I made the final step up to each summit. Each journey to discover that answer was the richest experience I could imagine. But it was an endless quest, because each success was not enough. If I was good enough to complete one challenge, then I had to find another, tougher one that would ask the question of me again. A question for which the answer was not certain. With each success, I had to return to ask again, and yet again, until I received the answer that I didn't want to hear.

*

When climbing Shishapangma, I'd once again managed to escape the humdrum of normality, the irrelevant squabbles of petty people in the workplace, traffic jams, and the financial and emotional stresses of everyday life. I'd journeyed a path that took me both physically and psychologically to another world. It was the world I wanted to be in, where I was most comfortable. But now, back in the 'real world' in Australia, I had to face up to the future—and to the one relevant question regularly asked of me: 'What's next?'

For the last few years I'd spoken of quitting the 8000ers once I had summitted all fourteen. It was simply too dangerous a game to keep playing, and I'd lost too many friends along the way. I knew my own demise was inevitable if I kept returning to high altitude. It had been easy to make that promise while I still had unclimbed peaks to look forward to. Now that I'd finished the project, the future might have looked rather empty. But even as I'd flown home from Shishapangma, I was planning my next climb. I just couldn't help myself.

There was still one thing that I hadn't achieved on the 8000ers: I'd climbed all of them without auxiliary oxygen, except Everest. On both the 1991 and 1993 expeditions, I'd abandoned my oxygenless summit attempts to help or search for teammates in trouble. In 2000 my focus had been on leading my commercial team up and down safely, and I'd insisted that we all use oxygen to achieve that. In 2004 I'd summitted successfully with oxygen but abandoned my attempt without oxygen a few days later, when my sixth sense had warned me of an impending storm. Everest without gas remained an elusive but very real goal for me.

I wanted an appropriate challenge, and climbing Everest without oxygen seemed pretty achievable, given my experience. I decided, therefore, to traverse the mountain. I would climb up one side, then, leaving my equipment behind in the high camp to be collected by a Sherpa, I would climb over the top and down the other side. The question was whether to climb from south to north or vice versa.

The mountain answered that question for me. I knew it would be imperative to descend from the summit as quickly as possible, at least down to 8000 metres and preferably lower, so I could avoid the onset of altitude sickness. The Nepalese side of the mountain is quite direct, affording quick access to, and descent from, the peak. On the Tibetan side, however, you spend much longer at the very highest altitude. The mountain's shape dictates that expeditions on that side must place a Camp 5 at around 8300 metres. This is the highest camp regularly used on any 8000-metre mountain. The effect of spending an extra night at such an extreme altitude on the way down would significantly compound the likelihood of me developing serious altitude illness, even with supplementary oxygen. Without it, oedema was virtually guaranteed. Far better to climb *up* the long Tibetan north ridge, then drop quickly down the south side into Nepal.

Within a week of returning to Australia I had contacted my agent in Kathmandu and asked him to investigate permits for me to traverse Everest from Tibet in 2010. I needed a permit to climb in Tibet and another to allow me to descend into Nepal. The

Nepalese were happy to issue their permit, but once again, the autonomy of the Autonomous Region of Tibet came into question. The permit had to be approved by a number of Chinese agencies, and somewhere along the way the process stalled. No reason was given.

I was disappointed but could do little about it, so I decided to make 2010 a rest year. I'd been climbing regularly on the 8000ers since 1991, with 1992 and 2001 being the only years I hadn't undertaken at least one 8000-metre expedition. Even in those years I'd climbed to reasonable altitudes, 6000 metres or so. When I sat back and looked at it, I'd been alpine climbing since 1985, and on peaks above 6000 metres every single year since 1987. As it turned out, the timing for the break was pretty convenient. I had a big project on at work, and I was also able to pursue several other high-priority goals.

Having grown up in the Scouting movement—all the way from Cubs to Rovers—I was a big fan, and I really appreciated the significant development opportunities it offers our youth. I wanted to give something back to the organisation that had provided me with so many wonderful adventures, as well as building in me the confidence and skills to identify and pursue my dreams. My regular absences from Australia meant that I couldn't take on a leadership role, but I wondered if I could give motivational talks to scouts, at all levels, to encourage them to get out and pursue their own dreams. Importantly, I recognised that the Scouting movement in Australia had become risk-averse in recent years, no doubt due to increasing liability concerns. I wanted to show scouts and leaders alike that risks could be managed, and that risk-taking could be conducted in a responsible manner. Scouting numbers had dropped, too, and I was very keen to help reinvigorate interest in the movement.

By coincidence, I was asked to speak at the Australian Scout Jamboree in early 2010. I agreed, but on the condition that the national headquarters consider my proposal to become involved in a broader capacity. They did, and before the year was out I was appointed as Ambassador for Scouting in Australia. It's a position I still hold with great pride.

They say that things happen in threes, and before I knew it I was asked to be an ambassador for the Australian Himalayan Foundation, which raises funds to support education, health and the environment across the Himalaya. I accepted the position and also took on an ambassadorship for the Sir David Martin Foundation, which works to rebuild the lives of youth in crisis. Each of these organisations is incredibly dedicated to its cause. It has been humbling for me to see the enormous effort contributed by so many dedicated individuals to achieve outstanding community and social outcomes, both in Australia and internationally.

The extra time I spent in Australia through 2010 also meant I could socialise more with my friends, and re-engage in some other adventure activities that I hadn't had the time for in recent years. Canyoning, mountain biking, cross-country skiing, surfing, bushwalking and fishing were all high on my agenda again—and they remain so today.

*

Between the charities, the Scouts, work and a new relationship, I was pretty busy. But the lure of high altitude did not fade away, and my thoughts kept returning to Everest. At the beginning of 2011, I again sought a permit for the Everest traverse. This time the Chinese were more direct: there would be no permit, although they still didn't offer a reason. *So be it*, I thought. Instead of a traverse, I would make an expedition to just one side of the mountain, and my summit attempt would be oxygenless. To make the climb more interesting, I would do it solo.

After the incredible summit day Neil and I had enjoyed on Shishapangma, where we had the mountain to ourselves, I had no desire to join the ever-increasing numbers on the 'normal' route from the Nepalese side of Everest. That limited me to the North Ridge from Tibet. There would be some other expeditions on the north-side route, but only a quarter or so of the numbers on the south side. If I followed that route, however, I would have to forego my plan for a quick descent from the summit, as I'd have to backtrack all the way along the extensive North Ridge. And that would be after I'd already spent more time at high altitude on the way up than I wanted to. Well, I'd been looking for a challenge.

Having made the necessary arrangements, I travelled to Base Camp in May 2011. I was sharing it with a commercial expedition but would climb alone on the mountain. I waited until most of the other groups had completed their summit attempts, so there'd be no congestion on the route. Rather than making my summit attempt from the highest camp, at 8300 metres, I planned to commence my assault from Camp 4, at 7800 metres. This would make for a very long summit day but would expose me to extreme altitude for less time overall.

All was going well, with two days of good weather forecast in late May. As I climbed to Camp 4 on the first of those two good days, a few friends of mine from another expedition reached the summit in almost windless conditions. If the weather held, I would realise this final challenge in less than twenty-four hours. As it turned out, that was too much to ask.

Setting out at 9 p.m. from my tent, I expected to have to climb for fifteen hours to make the top. After three hours, however, at an altitude of about 8100 metres, the wind picked up and blew itself into a gale. I huddled for over an hour with my back to the storm in the hope that it would pass, but it didn't. Chilled to the core, and with no hope of going any further, I retreated to my tent, where I spent the night being shaken by mighty wind blasts.

The gusts were incredible—frequently, my tent, with me in it, was blasted off the ground and tossed towards the edge of the ridge. All that secured it were the few lengths of cord I'd tied to some nearby rocks. The material strained and the poles bent out of shape but it held. By morning the wind had eased sufficiently for me to descend, but not enough for a repeat attempt. The weather continued to deteriorate, so I returned to Australia.

*

In October 2011 I was awarded the Medal of the Order of Australia for services to mountaineering. It was a great honour. The ceremony was conducted at Government House in Sydney, and the governor presented me with the award. My mother, brothers and girlfriend, Alexandra, all attended, but sadly Dad had passed away a few months earlier. I was sorry he missed it, especially since, upon his death, I'd found in one of his cupboards, twenty years' worth of newspaper clippings about my climbs. While we hadn't spoken much about my achievements over the years, he'd obviously been proud of them.

*

In 2012 I returned to Everest with the same plan as I'd had in 2011. The only difference was that I launched my summit attempt from Camp 5, at 8300 metres. I'd decided that the climb from Camp 4 was just too long. This time the weather forecast was more accurate; the problem was me. Without supplementary oxygen, the extra day spent climbing to 8300 metres, and then camping overnight at that altitude, proved too much for me. Even before I set out for the summit I felt myself deteriorating. I vomited several times, but not having eaten anything for a couple of days, produced only bile and suffered gut-wrenching stomach cramps. I was bitterly cold, despite wearing all my normal high-altitude clothing.

I knew that I was suffering acute mountain sickness, although I didn't feel so bad as to give up the summit attempt immediately.

I decided to continue and to monitor myself closely. The major risk was that I might be affected to the point where I could no longer self-assess accurately, or descend if I needed to. But that was a risk worth taking.

Setting out at 10.30 p.m. into a stiff breeze, it was an excruciating effort even to take the first step, and all I could think was, *Well, this will be a long night.* I had struggled early on during summit attempts on other mountains and then found my second wind along the way, so I hoped that the same would occur on this night. It didn't. As I plodded upwards in the blackness, shivering uncontrollably, I noticed that I was becoming unsteady. Soon I was tripping regularly, and realised that I'd lost depth of field in my vision. In the dim light of my headlamp, I couldn't tell exactly where the ground was.

I pressed on, but to compound matters, started seeing double, which made it difficult to place my footing and see the rope. I found myself dropping into little micro-sleeps each time I rested. These are definitely not recommended when you are trying to hang on to the side of a mountain. Then I lost my peripheral vision. It was as if the darkness was closing in around me and I was looking down a tunnel. The darkness actually appeared to rush at me. Later, writing my blog from Base Camp, I described it as 'giant bats flying at me'—no doubt the effect of some high-altitude hallucinations. That was the final straw.

I was lucky that the analytical side of my brain still hadn't been affected by the altitude—only my coordination, balance, consciousness and sight were failing! It was 1.30 a.m. and I was at 8500 metres, just 300 metres below Everest's summit. But that was still many hours of climbing away, and it would have been suicide to continue. I knew that I was well affected by cerebral oedema and on the precipice of succumbing to it completely. Descent was the only cure.

Very carefully, I backtracked to Camp 5, where I rested until daybreak. I wanted to keep down-climbing in the darkness but didn't trust my vision. With the grey light of dawn I started down to Camp 4, continued through to Camp 3 at 7000 metres, and kept on descending all the way down to Camp 2. With every step lower, I could feel my senses and coordination returning.

The next day I walked the 20 kilometres back to Base Camp, glad to be in thicker air and relative warmth. For several days I noticed that my speech, sight and balance were affected by the oedema I'd suffered. I'd been lucky. Too many climbers have suffered similar effects but not made the decision or had the ability to get back down to safety. Lonely, frozen corpses on the mountain are permanent reminders of their misfortune.

At Base Camp I considered whether or not to have another crack at the mountain. I was quite sure that I could summit if I strapped on the oxygen. But what was the point of that? I'd seen the view from the top twice before. My challenge was to summit without oxygen, and I'd been defeated. My question had been answered.

*

I had several days to wait for the jeep that was to take me back to the border. While I was there, a young Australian climber with whom I was sharing the Base Camp reached the summit with his guide and Sherpas, all using oxygen. While I was happy for him, I wondered about his motivation. On the drive to Base Camp some weeks earlier, we'd stood on a hill near the township of Tingri and looked out across the expansive Tibetan plateau towards the Himalayan chain.

'Which one is Everest?' he'd asked.

I was stunned! What motivates someone to climb the world's highest mountain when he doesn't even know what it looks like? Then again, the previous year I'd met a guided client who'd had no climbing experience at all and whose only motivation for ascending Everest was that it would enhance his business resume. As soon as he'd been guided up and back by a strong team of Sherpas, he'd quit climbing.

As I reflected on this at Base Camp, I thought about how radically the Himalayan climbing environment had changed since I'd started. I'd learned to climb and developed my skills over many years. I'd undertaken the majority of my climbs in small teams with very little equipment. We'd usually forged the routes ourselves, carried our own loads and made our own decisions. We'd climbed without oxygen or Sherpa support. We did things that way for the adventure—that was the fun of it. Now most expeditions comprised relatively unskilled clients who relied on guides, oxygen, fixed ropes and substantial Sherpa support to make their decisions and get them up and down.

Of course, guiding had been around since climbing began, and I too had led people with limited experience on a couple of mountains. But now, more and more commercial expeditions were using even greater amounts of oxygen and rope, and more Sherpas, to take people with less and less experience up the big hills. The spirit of adventure was becoming subservient to success at any cost. It demeaned the mountains a little because the challenge was being taken out of the equation. For me, challenge was the whole point! But now the rules had changed and I felt like an outsider in my own game.

I'd started mountaineering in 1985 and taken on my first 8000-metre climb in 1991. My first success on an 8000er had come on K2 in 1993, and my last on Shishapangma in 2009, sixteen years and twenty-three expeditions later. I'd summitted both Everest and Cho Oyu twice, and I'd made six 'first Australian' ascents. With these latest two expeditions to Everest, I'd been mountaineering for twenty-seven years, eighteen of them on the 8000ers.

This last climb was the only time I'd ever been so seriously affected by the altitude as to be almost killed by it. It had been an extremely close call, and a timely reminder that I'd broken my own promise to quit when I'd finished the fourteen.

And I was tired. I was tired of being alone. I was tired of broken relationships. I was tired of the pain. Most of all, though, I was tired of the cold—that aching, bone-chilling cold of high altitude, where there is never enough oxygen to stay warm. I'd managed to keep all my fingers and toes intact over the years, but they were damaged. They ached painfully in only mild cold, and I lost all sensation in my big toes for months after each expedition.

The acclaimed Australian mountaineer and author Greg Child once wrote, 'Maybe Himalayan climbing is just a bad habit, like smoking, of which one says with cavalier abandon, "must give this up some day, before it kills me"'. It's a great line but it contains a very real truth. Himalayan climbing does kill. It is only a matter of time.

I decided to retire from 8000-metre climbing.

It wasn't a difficult decision. I could see there was no point pursuing a goal that wasn't fun anymore. Nothing could justify the danger in those circumstances. I was saddened to realise that I was less passionate about the mountains than I had once been, but I was also at peace once I'd made the call. There were plenty of other adventures to be had—just not above 8000 metres.

Once I made it back to Kathmandu, I threw a big party at Sam's Bar. Climbers came out of the woodwork for free beer and pizza—a well-developed skill among the mountaineering fraternity. It was a fun night, and particularly meaningful for me to celebrate my retirement with my international peers. These people, more than most, understood the joy of climbing at high altitude, and what it really meant for me to hang up my ice axes.

It felt surreal to be speaking of not returning to 8000 metres, like I was ending the longest relationship of my life, which in fact it was. But it was comforting to think that I could put the fear, the pain and the hardship behind me. From here on, life would be warm. And, finally, I could let myself relax and savour the success of Summit 8000.

*

On the flight home I reflected on the path that had brought me to this point. From that first slide show in the back room of a country pub to now, twenty-four years and countless expeditions later. What a ride. What rewards! I had stood on the summit of every peak higher than 8000 metres on this planet. They hadn't come easily, and nor should they have. I could never have imagined, when I started out, the incredible highs, the lows, the treachery and camaraderie that the journey would bring. Certainly I'd not considered that it would become my one true passion, a need that drove me to a life uncommon. It absorbed me and blessed me with insight into another dimension of existence that only a lucky few will ever experience.

All the hardships, the pain and fear, the costs—to my finances, my career and my relationships—the loneliness, and that bloody bone-penetrating cold … it was all worth it. I was glad that it was over but I knew I'd do it all again in an instant.

Was it worth the cost in human life? Certainly it was worth the risk. I'd like to think that I managed that risk as well as I could, but I know also that I was incredibly lucky when others were not. Of course, I shall always feel great sadness for my friends, so many friends, who were lost to these mountains. I could not have conceived when I started this journey that over twenty of my companions would perish along the way. They paid the ultimate price for their quest to know themselves.

And that, ultimately, is what high altitude is all about. The mountains are a medium through which we can discover who we really are. Altitude exposes our strengths and weaknesses, our true characters. I saw some of the worst but also some of the very best of human nature, and my journey was infinitely richer for having shared it with others.

There was something grounding about not having achieved my goal of climbing Everest without oxygen. It kept my achievements in perspective and reminded me that the mountains are still wonderfully challenging—that adventure is still possible if you seek it. Sure, they can be conquered if you lay a rope from Base Camp to the summit and crank up the gas so much that you barely feel the altitude, but for those who want to test themselves, the big hills can still offer the most extreme challenges. I was living proof of that. Despite all my experience and successes, I'd been comprehensively defeated in my final attempt. That realisation kept my ego in check, and kept the mountains real and wonderful.

Of course, there is more to the Himalaya than just challenge. There is a tangible spirituality, which, if you surrender yourself to it, rewards you with a clarity of vision and an enrichment of the soul that is unmatched by other environments. There is unparalleled beauty. There is camaraderie, humility, wonder and peace. How often have I sat outside my tent on a windless night, peering up at stars that seemed brighter than daylight, or gazed at mighty peaks of extraordinary savagery yet pristine splendour, deep blues of ancient glaciers and unblemished white of virgin snows? How often have I wandered through endless forests of blossoming rhododendron filled with birdsong, and quivered in awe at the sheerness of rock faces that tower to the heavens?

The Himalaya is a place of extremes, a struggle between opposing forces. I have been crushed by the mountains' harshness and nourished by their energy. I have been beaten and humiliated by them. But I have also felt such exhilaration and joy that I've whooped and shouted with carefree abandon. I've shared quiet cups of tea with the most financially impoverished but spiritually rich people on Earth, whose culture is born of, and sustained by, these mystic mountains.

*

I gazed out the window of the plane, catching a last glimpse of the Himalayan chain as it faded into the haze of the approaching monsoon. Summit 8000 had been an incredible experience, but the end of one project is just the starting point for another. Already those adventures were morphing into grand memories. And memories would not sustain me. It was my future adventures that would charge my spirit. I felt a surge of adrenaline just thinking of what they might be.

EPILOGUE

A T HOME, I went back to work and threw myself into my ambassadorial roles. In my spare time I pursued some local adventures and planned expeditions in fields other than mountaineering. At first it felt good not to be distracted by an impending expedition. I enjoyed not having to train relentlessly, or juggle my relationships and work. But life also felt a little empty. My memories of the cold and agony of high altitude diminished, while my desire to rejoin the fray grew ever stronger. The magnetism of high altitude is strong.

In April 2014 I journeyed yet again to Nepal and trekked with friends through quiet valleys and across some high passes, ultimately reaching Everest's base camp. By unfortunate coincidence I arrived there on the day of the worst disaster in the history of that mountain. Thirteen Sherpas and three other Nepalese high altitude porters employed by commercial guiding companies were killed when a serac from the mountain's West Shoulder avalanched into the Khumbu Icefall, crushing them under tonnes of ice. The lifeless bodies of so many young men slung below rescue helicopters were a harsh reminder of the savagery of the mountain environment.

Rather than a pall of despair falling over the mountain, however, there was great anger amongst the Sherpas; demands for compensation were made to the government of Nepal. Threats were levelled by some Sherpas against anyone, including other Sherpas, who attempted to continue their expeditions on the mountain. After some days, government representatives agreed to some of the Sherpas' demands, but most expeditions were cancelled.

While I am not a fan of the increasing commercialisation of these mountains, I was perplexed by the aggression shown by many Sherpas towards foreigners, as if the accident had somehow been their fault. I found that the focus on compensation for future accidents, rather than on identifying ways to prevent, or at least mitigate them, to be particularly worrisome. At the very least, I argued, this incident should serve as a catalyst for change to the mountain guiding system in the Himalaya, which is rife with corruption, incompetence and greed. Compensation is good but prevention is a whole lot better.

In truth, I was not at all surprised that the accident had occurred. With the hundreds of inexperienced foreign clients and hundreds more unqualified Sherpa 'guides' each season, there simply weren't enough skilled or trained decision-makers operating on the flanks of the world's highest mountain. An accident had only been a matter of time. And it could have been much, much worse.

The role of Sherpas on climbing expeditions has evolved significantly. When I'd started climbing in the Himalayas, most Sherpas were employed as high-altitude porters, not guides. Highly experienced foreign climbers led the way up mountains, including Everest. They conducted the risk assessments, found the safest routes, fixed the ropes and led their teams. Sherpas supported that role by carrying the necessary equipment for some teams.

When guided climbing began on the 8000ers in the early 1990s, the Sherpas' role expanded to include more 'guiding'—to the point that many companies began using only Sherpas for all tasks on the mountain: route finding, rope fixing, portering and guiding clients. In fact, most Himalayan 'guiding' companies are now owned and operated by Nepalese, predominately Sherpas. On Everest, the job of finding the route and fixing the rope through the Khumbu Icefall each season has now been officially assigned by the Nepalese government to a team of 'Icefall Doctors', to whom all expeditions must pay a levy.

But only a very small number of Sherpas, perhaps thirty, hold international qualifications as mountain guides. Sherpas are not born with ice axes in their hands. They are like climbers from any other country: they need to learn the ways of mountain climbing, glacier travel, route finding, rope fixing and risk assessment. Indeed, until foreigners came to the Himalaya, Sherpas did not climb at all. With over thirty expeditions just to the Nepali side of Everest in 2014, let alone those to all the other mountains, there are simply too few internationally qualified Sherpa guides to go around. Not even one per expedition. While many Sherpas are now highly skilled and experienced, the majority of Sherpas employed by guiding companies are unqualified, despite both the companies' and the Sherpas' claims that they are 'guides'.

Blaming the clients for this situation is unrealistic, despite the media's mantra that 'Sherpa guides' regularly perish while 'carrying' the rich sahibs to the summit. The Nepalese government welcomes commercial clients without restriction. Guiding companies sign up as many clients as they can get, with the promise of summit glory. And there is no lack of Sherpas willing to work for the guiding companies and take the risks because the money they can get is better than they'll earn doing anything else. Clients just pay the fee asked of them to be shepherded up the mountains, without any real understanding of the underlying guiding system or their Sherpas' experience, which means they, along with their Sherpa 'guides', are often thrust unwittingly into great danger.

None of the current crop of 'Icefall Doctors' has international guiding qualifications. How can unqualified 'government guides' be tasked to find the safest route through one of the most hazardous icefalls in the world? How can they even be *allowed* to take on that role? How can unqualified high-altitude porters (who comprised the majority of the Sherpas killed in this incident) be expected to conduct genuine risk assessments of the route they are following, to determine whether or not they are climbing towards their own doom?

No one could have predicted the precise moment at which the serac avalanche would occur. By all accounts, an even greater tragedy had been narrowly avoided: less than thirty minutes earlier there'd been more than sixty Sherpas in that very spot. But any alpinist with the slightest mountain awareness could have seen that the route was highly exposed to the threat of avalanche from that serac. Any alpinist could have seen that the bottleneck created by poorly placed ladders in the Khumbu Icefall was putting everyone, not just the Sherpas, at perilous risk. But these Sherpas were not all experienced alpinists.

God forbid that my years in the public service have turned me into a bureaucrat, but the government of Nepal must regulate the guided climbing industry in their country. Because an industry is what it has become. Its regulation must consider, amongst many other issues, minimum training and accreditation standards, minimum wage standards, and proper licensing and monitoring of companies that conduct expeditions to the mountains. The appropriate numbers and experience of guided expeditions and their clients should be determined and allowances made for those skilled, unguided alpinists, who still seek genuine challenge without guides or Sherpas but who are being forced off these peaks by their unfettered commercialisation.

Not all Sherpas are unqualified or untrained. Some have considerable alpine experience. And not all companies are unethical; some exceed the obvious ethical standards that are needed. But the industry has become so large and so disparate that only government regulation and monitoring can ensure, or strive for, fairness and safety across the sector. The government of Nepal reaps millions of dollars annually from issuing climbing permits to foreigners. The time has come for it to appropriately regulate the industry, in order to safeguard both its own citizens and those fee-paying foreigners.

Banning all guided climbing expeditions in the Himalaya would safeguard the Sherpas and return the mountains to those who have the skills to climb them. But that is unrealistic, I know, and indeed the Sherpas themselves would protest the loudest. Theirs are the richest valleys in Nepal precisely because of the guiding industry. A balance must be found between guided climbing and private mountaineering. Currently, however, the commercialisation of the mountains is overwhelming all other interests, at the expense of both humanity and the spirit of adventure.

*

Uncomfortable at the tangible tension across base camp, and greatly saddened at the terrible loss of life in this single incident, I walked about fifteen kilometres down a valley to the house of Lama Geshe, one of the most senior and highly qualified Lamas in Nepal, who conducted a *puja* ceremony for me. After the ceremony, and through an interpreter, we chatted about the accident and the impact it would have on Sherpa families throughout the Khumbu region. It seemed that every village in the area had lost a relative in this one incident. It would have been easy to say that the mountain gods had expressed their dissatisfaction with the disrespectful masses polluting their way up Chomolungma's slopes, but I felt that the disaster simply highlighted all that is wrong with unrestricted commercialisation of these sacred summits.

Before I left, Lama Geshe presented me with a blessed prayer string and a Khata scarf for good luck. Returning to base camp several days later, I placed the scarf on a small *chorten*, in offering to the dead men's souls. I vowed to do what I could to bring about necessary changes to the mountain guiding industry in Nepal. (After returning home to Australia, I sent comprehensive letters to Nepal's Prime Minister, the Minister for Tourism and several Nepali newspapers, highlighting what I considered to be the problems and the necessary corrective measures.)

Later, I walked to the edge of the icefall and gazed up at its incredible façade. The ominous threat was not lessened by the earlier avalanche. Everywhere, giant towers of ice teetered precariously, seemingly held aloft by the air itself. But at the same time it was beautiful, inviting. A thousand metres higher than me, the Western Cwm contorted between the sheer walls of Nuptse and Everest's southern flanks, as it led to higher and even more wonderful mountain revelations. Up there the misery and angst of base camp was forgotten. Up there the mountain invited climbers to pit themselves against her, to test themselves, to ask questions and to seek answers.

I found myself trembling—not from cold or fear, but from excitement. I could taste the challenge. I could feel the thin air searing my throat. My heart pounded and, involuntarily, I started to breathe more heavily. To suck in those lungfulls in anticipation of the fight.

How could I possibly want to re-enter that deadly milieu? Particularly after this most recent and harshest reminder of the mountain's mercilessness. But I did want to. That oxygenless ascent of Everest still tempted me.

Should I try again? I thought about why I'd quit high altitude in the first place. *Something about the cold. Or was it the pain?* Already these were just vague recollections. I looked up and imagined myself high on the Lhotse face, its majestic slopes sweeping across and below me for kilometres, a vista of such unparalleled magnificence as to make the Earth seemingly fall away beneath the clouds, leaving me alone and aloft, at the top of world. It was where I wanted to be. Still.

I realised I had not lost my passion at all. Just my confidence. Nearly dying does that to you. But that's the time you have to dig deepest. I had not been defeated on my last attempt; I'd just failed. I recalled my own oft repeated mantra when I'd nearly faltered on so many high summits: *Don't give up. Never give up.* Of course these summits don't come easily; that's what makes them worthwhile. I want to go back up there. I'm not yet done with my journey of self-discovery, and I still have questions to answer. There remains in me a compelling need to revisit 8000 metres. Not just so I can test myself, but to enrich my soul, in the most magnificent environment on Earth. I know that I should stop climbing into such thin air … but I wonder if I can.

ACKNOWLEDGEMENTS

First and foremost, my thanks go to Margaret Gee, my literary agent, without whose passionate championing of my story over several years, to myriad publishers, editors and potential co-authors, this book would never have been published. Margaret pushed me to dig deep and search within and, in the process, I gained more from my expeditions and learned more about myself and my relationship with the high mountains than I'd ever previously understood.

Thanks also to Brent Waters, who provided wise counsel and much-appreciated administrative support behind the scenes.

Thanks to Julian Welch, who provided editorial review and guidance throughout the writing process and without whom the book would not be nearly as coherent, nor the story as fulsome, as I hope it now is.

Thanks to Sir Chris Bonington, Doug Scott CBE and Peter Hillary for their kind words in endorsing the book. Acknowledgement by one's peers is gratifying, but acknowledgement by the greats in one's field of endeavour is the very highest praise.

Finally, thanks to Colette Vella from Melbourne University Press for having the faith to take on the publication of this book and allowing me the latitude to speak the truth where it needed to be told.

GLOSSARY OF MOUNTAINEERING TERMS

AAA – Army Alpine Association, a mountaineering club within the Australian Defence Force

Abseil – to descend a rock face or other near-vertical surface by sliding down a rope

Acclimatisation – the physiological process of the body adjusting to lesser amounts of oxygen

AMS (Acute Mountain Sickness) – brought on by the lower pressure of altitude, it usually occurs above 2400 metres and has symptoms similar to flu, carbon-monoxide poisoning or a hangover. While AMS itself is rarely fatal, it can develop into life-threatening cerebral or pulmonary oedema

Alpine style – climbing light and fast without fixed ropes, load carries or fixed camps

Anchor – a fixed point to which a rope is attached on the mountain to safeguard the climber/s. The anchor usually consists of a piton in a crack, a snow bar, an ice screw or a sling around a pinnacle of rock

Arête – a sharp mountain ridge

Avalanche – a mass of snow, ice and rocks falling rapidly down a mountainside

Base Camp – the camp located close to but below the mountain where the climbing starts

Belay – running a climbing rope through a fixed anchor to safeguard another climber. Usually the climber providing the belay uses a special knot or belay device to brake the rope in the event of the lead climber falling

Bergschrund – a crevasse at the junction of a glacier or snowfield with a steep upper slope

Bivouac – a temporary camp without tents or cover, used especially by soldiers or mountaineers

Buttress – a projecting portion of a hill or mountain

Carabiner – a metal coupling link with a safety closure

Cerebral oedema – excess accumulation of fluid in the intracellular or extracellular spaces of the brain

Chimney – a very narrow gully

Chorten – the Tibetan word for the rock structure built at basecamp for conducting Puja ceremonies

Col – a saddle between two peaks, typically providing a pass from one side of a mountain to another

Couloir – a steep, narrow gully on a mountainside

Cornice – great mushrooms of wind-blown ice that accumulate on exposed ridges and are easily dislodged

Crampons – metal frames with spikes underneath that strap or clip to a boot for walking on steep snow or climbing steep rock and ice

Crevasse – a crack in snow or ice, usually found on a glacier. They can be very wide and deep and are caused by the glacier bending or moving over the uneven surface below. Often they are hidden by windblown snow that covers the opening with a thin veneer that can collapse if a person moves onto it

Death zone – the altitude at which life cannot be sustained indefinitely without auxiliary oxygen. In general terms 8000 metres and above is referred to as the death zone. In reality it is probably lower than 8000 metres

Dexamethasone – a synthetic drug of the corticosteroid type, used especially as an anti-inflammatory agent. It is very helpful in reducing swelling of the brain in cases of cerebral oedema

Diamox – trade name for the drug acetazolomide, which aids acclimatisation by inducing deeper and faster breathing, which in turn increases the amount of oxygen in the blood

Face – a steep mountain slope between ridges

Fixed belay – a situation where one climber anchors him- or herself to a slope and feeds a safety rope to another climber

Fixed rope – rope that has been attached to a mountain slope for the duration of an expedition, allowing climbers to move up and down it independently. Fixed rope is usually used on long, siege-style expeditions or on dangerous or technical ground

Front pointing – using just the two points at the front of the crampons to climb a very steep ice or snow slope

Glacier – a slowly moving mass or river of ice formed by the accumulation and compaction of snow

Glissade – sliding down a steep slope of snow or ice, with the support of an ice axe

High-altitude porters – the Pakistani equivalent of climbing Sherpas

Hypoxia – deficiency in the amount of oxygen reaching the tissues

Ice axe – a mountaineer's best friend. On 8000-metre peaks, my axe is about 70 centimetres long, with a spike at the bottom to use as a walking stick for balance or to probe the snow for suspected crevasses. On steep ground, the head of the axe has a sharpened pick that can be swung into the snow or ice for purchase to assist in climbing. An adze on the backside of the head can be used for cutting footholds

Icefall – where a glacier drops over steep ground and the ice breaks up to form blocks and crevasses. These blocks can be as large as multi-storey buildings but tend to break up the further the icefall drops. Icefalls are extremely dangerous due to the unpredictable collapse of these blocks

Icefall Doctors – a team of Sherpas contracted by the Nepalese government to establish and maintain a route through the Khumbu icefall and the Western Cwm between Base Camp and Camp 2 on Mt Everest, during the climbing season

Ice screw – a metal tube or piton with an external thread and sharp teeth at one end that can be screwed into hard ice as an anchor point. It has a hole at the other end to clip a carabiner into it. The climber's rope can then be passed through that carabiner

Jumar – a clamp that is attached to a fixed rope and automatically tightens when weight is applied and relaxes when it is removed

KKH – Karakorum Highway

Liaison officer – a government representative, often a military officer or official, who is appointed to accompany and oversee foreign expeditions, to ensure that they adhere to the rules of their climbing permit

Moraine – a mass of rocks and sediment carried down and deposited by a glacier, typically as ridges at its edges or extremity

Overboots – insulated gaiters that add a layer of warmth to mountaineering boots

Pitch – a section of climbing between two anchors or belay points

Piton – a metal peg hammered into a crack in the rock to support a belay

Porters – locals employed to carry expedition equipment towards or back from a mountain's base camp. They are not climbers and do not go above base camp

Post holing – making such deep steps in soft snow that they appear to be holes that have been dug for posts to be inserted

Protection – a general term for equipment used as anchors or for setting up belays

Prussik – short lengths of cord to knot onto the main rope in a way that allows a climber to ascend a rope

Puja – traditional Sherpa ceremony of worship that is held close to the mountain to seek safe passage for the expedition

Pulmonary oedema – fluid accumulation in the lungs' air sacs, making it difficult to breathe. It leads to impaired gas exchange and may cause respiratory failure

Rappel – another term for abseil

Rock band – a sheer wall of rock that stretches across a mountain face

Rope up – where climbers tie into opposite ends of a climbing rope, usually around 50 metres in length, to provide safety to each other when climbing on dangerous ground or steep

Running belay – using an intermediate anchor point between the lead and rear climbers. This allows both climbers to move up together until the rear climber reaches that anchor point. The rear climber then removes the running belay to be used further up the mountain

Serac – a pinnacle or ridge of ice, often poorly attached to the mountain

Sherpas – the ethnic group of people, formerly from Tibet, who now live in the high Himalaya of Nepal

Short rope – a length of rope or sling, about 1 metre long, used to tie two climbers to each other where there is a strong chance that one may fall. The short length prevents any buildup of momentum so the second climber can immediately stop the falling climber

Siege style – the traditional style of climbing big mountains, using load carries, fixed ropes and fixed camps

Sledge – the sledge we made for Christian was a sleeping bag tied to a sleeping mat and dragged across the snow with a climbing rope

Sling – sewn-nylon-webbing loops of various lengths used in setting up belays, attaching to anchors and keeping hold of climbing equipment

Snow blindness – burning of the eye's cornea by too much exposure to ultraviolet light. It is common at high altitude due to less protection from the thinner atmosphere. It is extremely painful and causes temporary loss of vision, sometimes for several days

Snow bridge – a bridge of snow that spans a crevasse or other gap in the glacier

Soloing – to climb without being roped to a partner

Technical climbing – climbing that warrants the use of safety ropes and anchors

Traverse – to move diagonally or horizontally across a mountain face. Also to cross from one side of a mountain to the other

Trekking – the term used locally in the Himalaya for undertaking long walks – similar to tramping, hiking, bushwalking, etc.

Whiteout – a weather condition in which the features and horizon of snow-covered country are indistinguishable due to uniform light diffusion. It is very common in blizzards

Wind blast – a strong gust of wind caused by rapid displacement of the air when an avalanche occurs

Wind slab – a hard crust of snow formed by strong wind that sits tenuously on older, weaker snow. A slide can easily be triggered and as it does so, the slab breaks up, usually swallowing any climbers who are standing on it

INDEX

SPONSORS

I HAVE BEEN very fortunate to have been supported in my expeditioning for many years by a range of corporate and private individuals, some on many occasions. I know that this list will not be complete and I apologise to any whom I've left off. I certainly needed and appreciated your support.

I would particularly like to recognise and thank:

Personal sponsors

Geoff and Fiona Chapman
Bob King
Michael and Carmel Christie

Greg and Lorraine Woon
Mar Knox

Corporate

GORE-TEX®
Mountain Equipment, Sydney
Australian Geographic
Sea to Summit
Millet - boots and packs
Spelean Equipment, Sydney
Mont Adventure Equipment, Australia
World Expeditions
Macpac, New Zealand
Pakistan International Airways
Fairydown
Berghaus Equipment
Suunto altitude watches
Dobsons Printing Service
Wild Stuff
Colourchrome
Dick Smith Electronics
Kobold Watches
Larry Adler Ski Shop
Summit Gear

Trek and Travel, Sydney
Mountain Hardwear, USA
Mountain Equipment, UK.
Wilderness Equipment
Fisherman's Friend Cough Lozenges
Petzl Charlet
PMP Digital Printing, Canberra

Thai Airways International
Alitalia Airlines
Sydney Makedonia Soccer Club
Raleigh Bicycles
Garmin GPS
Art to Print Productions
Mountain Designs, Australia
Fuji Film
AGFA Geveart
Gronell boots, Italy
Blue Water ropes
Opentec